Original People
Original Television

THE LAUNCHING OF THE
ABORIGINAL PEOPLES TELEVISION NETWORK

Jennifer David

Copyright © 2024 by Jennifer David

Library and Archives Canada Cataloguing in Publication

Title: Original people, original television : the launching of the Aboriginal Peoples
Television   Network / by Jennifer David.
Names: David, Jennifer, author.
Description: Previously published:
Ottawa, ON : Debwe Communications, 2012.
| Includes bibliographical references and index.
Identifiers: Canadiana 20240431642 | ISBN 9781926886626 (softcover)
Subjects: LCSH: Aboriginal Peoples Television Network—History.
| LCSH: Television Northern Canada—   History. | LCSH: Aboriginal Peoples Television
Network—Biography. | LCSH: Television Northern
Canada—Biography. | LCSH: Television broadcasting—Canada—History.
| CSH: Indigenous television   stations—Canada.
| CSH: Indigenous peoples in television broadcasting—Canada.
Classification: LCC HE8700.9.C3 D38 2024 | DDC 384.55/23092271—dc23

Printed and bound in Canada

All rights reserved. No part of this book may be used or reproduced in any manner
whatsoever without the prior written consent of the author. NO AI TRAINING:
Without in any way limiting the author's exclusive rights under copyright, any use of this
publication to "train" generative artificial intelligence (AI) technologies to generate text
is expressly prohibited.

Photo montages throughout the book: APTN broadcast video images.
Book Design: Ann Doyon

154 Enowkin Trail
Penticton B.C. Canada V2A 0E1

We acknowledge the financial support of The Government of Canada through the Department of
Canadian Heritage for our publishing activities. We acknowledge the support of the Canada Council
for the Arts. We also acknowledge the support of the Province of British Columbia through the
British Columbia Arts Council.

Original People
Original Television

THE LAUNCHING OF THE
ABORIGINAL PEOPLES TELEVISION NETWORK

Dedicated to the memory of Dr. Gail Valaskakis (1939-2007), whose warmth, generosity and passionate support for Aboriginal broadcasting will be long remembered.

And

To my dad, for a life of inspiration.
And if he was still here, he would have been this book's greatest promoter.

CONTENTS

TABLE OF ACRONYMS

Aboriginal Canada is rivalled only by the United Nations for the number and variety of its acronyms, and when you complicate that with government agencies and broadcast industry slang, a guide becomes essential.

ACP	Accelerated Coverage Plan
AFN	Assembly of First Nations
AIM	American Indian Movement
AMMSA	Aboriginal Multimedia Society of Alberta
APTN	Aboriginal Peoples Television Network
CBC	Canadian Broadcasting Corporation
CRTC	Canadian Radio-television and Telecommunications Commission
CCTA	Canadian Cable Television Association
DOC	Department of Communications
DTH	Direct to Home
FCP	Frontier Coverage Package
GNWT	Government of the Northwest Territories
IBC	Inuit Broadcasting Corporation
ICC	Inuit Circumpolar Conference
ICS	Inuvialuit Communications Society
INAC	Indian and Northern Affairs Canada
ITC	Inuit Tapirisat of Canada (now the ITK—Inuit Tapiriit Kanatami)
JBCCS	James Bay Cree Communications Society
KSB	Kativik School Board
MICEC	Manitoba Indian Cultural Education Centre
MBC	Missinipi Broadcasting Corporation
NIB	National Indian Brotherhood
NCI	Native Communications Incorporated
NCP	Native Communications Program
NCSNWT	Native Communications Society of the Western Northwest Territories
NIB	Native Indian Brotherhood
NNBAP	Northern Native Broadcast Access Program
NNBT	Northern Native Broadcasting, Terrace
NNBY	Northern Native Broadcasting – Yukon
NQIA	Northern Quebec Inuit Association
NWT	Northwest Territories OKS OKalaKatiget Society
RCAP	Royal Commission on Aboriginal Peoples
SOCAM	Societé de communication Atikamekw-Montagnais
TNI	Taqramiut Nipingat Incorporated
TVNC	Television Northern Canada

ACKNOWLEDGEMENTS

This book tells the story of a network that would not exist without the dedication and support of a myriad of people. The same is true of the book itself.

First, of course, I thank my family. The hours I devoted to research and writing were hours I took from my husband and young children. Jerico, Grace and Caleb—thank you for giving me time and space to pursue this obsession. There was so much information to integrate, so many stories to tell, and so many times when I was ready to give up; it was their constant support that made this book possible.

I thank my editor, Terry Rudden, for his unfailing optimism and encouragement. Like all good editors, he was able to articulate my thoughts and know what I wanted to say, and sometimes say it better. Thank you, Terry, for sharing that gift with me. And heartfelt gratitude to my friends Dan, Trish and Patty, who reviewed the book and provided more good ideas (and discovered all the copy errors before we went to print)!

In 2010, when I approached Jean LaRose, APTN's then Chief Executive Officer, with the idea for this book, he never hesitated, but provided the network's full support. I thank him for that, and for unfettered access to the basement of APTN's Winnipeg office, where I spent many hours hauling out boxes of meeting minutes and reports, digging through old documents, and happily reliving the past.

I owe a big debt to other writers and researchers who observed, recorded and participated in the critical decades in the evolution of Aboriginal broadcasting. Anyone who wants to understand the early history of TVNC and broadcasting in northern Canada should turn to the same guides I did, and especially *Un/Covering the North: News, Media, and Aboriginal People* by Valerie Alia; *Something New in the Air: The Story of First Peoples Television Broadcasting in Canada* by Lorna Roth, and the writings of Gail Guthrie Valaskakis.

I thank everyone who agreed to be interviewed for this book, sweep the attics of their memories, and share their recollections and perceptions of those extraordinary years. I could have talked to dozens more; but in the interests of time, and my own sanity, I spoke to a small sample of the many voices who shared their time and talents to build this television network.

They are listed at the end of the book.

And finally, a huge chi-miigwech to Theytus Books, a leading organization committed to publishing Indigenous authors. The original edition of this work was very much a labour of love, self-published in 2012 and printed on-demand; I oversaw its marketing, sales, promotion and distribution myself. While the book was well-reviewed, its appeal was largely limited to academics, students of media, and those with a personal connection to this story. But as the 25th anniversary of APTN's launch approached, the time seemed right to tell the story once again to a new generation of readers, and this time with the support of an Indigenous publisher. To my great delight, Theytus Books agreed to re-brand and re-issue this 25th anniversary edition. Thank you for supporting this endeavor, and as always for amplifying the literary voices of Indigenous peoples.

NOTE: Today the word **'Indigenous"** is usually preferred to the word **'Aboriginal'**. However, to honour the spirit of the times, and to reflect the term in common use leading up the launch (as well as the name of the network itself), I will continue to use the word **'Aboriginal'** in this book.

INTRODUCTION

Sometimes a story needs to be told, and it won't let you rest.

I was APTN's Director of Communications on September 1, 1999, the day the network launched —one of a small group of privileged participants in a little piece of Canadian history. In the decade since that day, the "Launch Survivors" have gotten together over dinner, or beer, or in airport departure lounges, and the talk invariably turns to that crazy year of 1999: to the crises averted, politics stick-handled, egos assuaged, and miracles wrought on a shoestring. And the reminiscing would always end with someone sighing: "You know, somebody should really write a book about all this..." I agreed. My own memory of that time was fading. If somebody didn't tell the tale, one of the most unique stories in broadcasting would disappear into the footnotes of academic journals. But no one else picked up the pen; and I finally realized that perhaps this idea kept obsessing me because it was my job to write that book we all wanted to read.

It's a good story, replete with outsize personalities, drama, jealousies and betrayals. But this isn't an exposé of the backroom machinations behind a struggling network (though there certainly were some of those). APTN's mission has been "sharing our peoples' journey, celebrating our cultures, inspiring our children and honouring the wisdom of our Elders." That's what this book is attempting to do as well. Shortly after the creation of Nunavut in 1999, Jose Kusugak, an Inuit leader and ex-broadcaster, was asked to describe the Inuit strategy for Land Claims negotiation. "It's simple," he said. "We knew what we wanted, and we just kept explaining it to the government, and we kept saying no, that's not what we said: THIS is what we said. It was like hunting seal. You just go out there, and you wait. There's no time limit—you simply wait. We're good at waiting. We waited through seven Prime Ministers. Eventually they figured it out."

....

The story of APTN took place during the same decades, and at roughly the same pace. It began with the first satellite experiments in northern Canada in the 1970s, with local societies and short-term projects by filmmakers and producers in tiny communities and on reserves across southern Canada. Supported by initiatives like the National Film Board's Challenge for Change program, a loose network of regional broadcasters across the North lobbied successfully in the early 1980s for the creation of the Northern Native Broadcast Access Program (NNBAP), which established full-fledged broadcast operations in thirteen northern centres, from Terrace in British Columbia to Nain in Labrador. For ten years those organizations trained producers, generated hundreds of hours of native-language programming, and eventually created their own distribution system, Television Northern Canada (TVNC). During the same period, Aboriginal filmmakers and producers in southern Canada began to form networks, looking for ways to get their work seen by broader Canadian audiences. They attracted the attention and support of various political bodies, including the Assembly of First Nations (AFN). It was the meeting and fusion of those two movements—northern native broadcasters and southern independent producers—that finally led to the creation of APTN. That's a dry summary of the political history. But it doesn't capture the personalities and the enthusiasm that drove the movement to its remarkable conclusion. Some of the individual players have become well-known for their leadership and their advocacy. But APTN was really built by a large group of dedicated, unknown, passionate individuals. We were more than a team; we were a family, with some of the tantrums, jealousies, and infighting that implies. But we shared an extraordinary dream; a network that would give new life and new voices to the stories and experiences of First Nations, Inuit and Métis, so that they would never again be marginalized or forgotten. Like any family, we were doing it for the children, for the next seven generations. We convinced others that the dream was worth pursuing, and we achieved it.

Others have written well and in depth of the history and politics of Aboriginal broadcasting. To me, however, APTN is a story about people.

I was part of it, and that is the story I want to tell.
Ottawa, Ontario
January, 2012

PREFACE TO THE 2024 EDITION

I'm sitting here writing this preface to the 2024 edition of "Original People, Original Television". I'm thinking about all the Indigenous media that I support and can access: all-Indigenous developed radio programs on CBC, Indigenous podcasts, award-winning books by Indigenous authors, an Indigenous Screen Office, and Indigenous Theatre at the National Arts Centre. None of these things existed back when we launched APTN in 1999.

It's a different world today— one in which our musicians, writers, filmmakers, and writers have achieved a level of international prominence and accolades inconceivable just three decades ago. Indigenous stories and issues, once almost invisible (sometimes purposefully so), now feature daily in national news. And it's inconceivable that those huge changes would have occurred without the events and the people chronicled in this book.

The rapidly evolving relationship between Canada and Indigenous peoples is perhaps best captured in the term 'Truth and Reconciliation', a household phrase in Canada since the Truth and Reconciliation Commission (TRC) was established in 2009. For six years, three Commissioners travelled throughout Canada, reviewing historical records and listening to the gut-wrenching stories from Indian Residential School survivors. In the Commission's 2015 reports and "Calls to Action", the chair of the Commission, the Honourable Murray Sinclair (retired Senator), set out a vision of reconciliation that called for 'restoring the balance to the relationship between Aboriginal and non-Aboriginal people in this country.'

To me, the creation of APTN represented a major and successful realization of Senator Sinclair's vision of reconciliation. APTN embodied a movement of Indigenous and non-Indigenous peoples, Indigenous and non-Indigenous governments, Indigenous and non-Indigenous communities, coming together for a common cause. We wanted to find a way to restore balance. Our goal was to give voice to peoples that have been historically marginalized, historicized and romanticized in film and television; whose nations were decimated through policies like the Indian Act; whose children were stolen through Indian Residential and Day schools and the Sixties Scoop; whose languages and cultures were systematically eradicated; and who, for Canada, represented nothing more than 'an Indian problem' to be resolved through genocide.

Over the last 25 years, the network has in many ways fulfilled and exceeded the dream of the hard-working and strategic thinking artists, producers, lobbyists, journalists, and performers who first brought APTN to life. The network itself has amassed an impressive range of national and international awards for its programming and, in particular, its journalism. It is an established and honoured player on the national and international media scene.

Yes, much has changed, but as the ongoing struggles for wellness and healing in our communities confirms, much remains to be done. APTN's impressive achievements in its first quarter century have exceeded expectations; however, reconciliation is a lifelong process for all of us.

I believe the need for APTN as an amplifier of Indigenous voices, an incubator for Indigenous talent, and a tireless promoter of our cultures, our communities and our ways of being has never been greater.

Ottawa, Ontario
July, 2024.

CHAPTER I

BACKSTORY

A NEUTRON BOMB—ABORIGINAL
PEOPLE RESPOND TO EARLY FILM
AND TELEVISION

Launch Day: 6 am September 1, 1999

Everyone in Winnipeg knows "The Forks". It's just east of downtown, an open area where the Assiniboine River flows into the Red River—a sacred and ancient gathering place where the Nakoda, Cree, Anishnaabe, Blackfoot and Dakota people would trade, dance, tell stories and meet old friends and family. Over the years a series of major settlements grew and faded here. The confluence of rivers eventually made it a hub of the fur trade, where generations of Métis gathered to sell their furs to the Hudson's Bay and Northwest Companies.

Today The Forks hosts a gathering of a different sort, but with echoes of the past— a new meeting of peoples, a new kind of trade.

The moon is disappearing from the sky, but the sun has not yet risen above the crimson clouds. Elder Tobasonakwat Kinew is kneeling alone at the edge of the Oodena Celebration Circle near the water's edge, preparing sweetgrass. Laid out on a blanket in front of him are his medicine bag, significant feathers, tobacco, containers to hold the sweetgrass, and a ceremonial pipe, a special gift to be presented later on this special day. Beside him is Elder Jules Lavallee, preparing to welcome some new friends to the city he calls home.

As the sun breaks through the fog, people begin to arrive at the Circle, gathering to pray. Others are praying, too—in Yellowknife, in Ottawa, in Iqaluit, in First Nation communities in British Columbia and tiny coastal settlements in Labrador. Today is the culmination of years of prayer—and of dreaming, scheming, sweating, and lobbying. Today—in just twelve hours—a handful of exhausted, exhilarated, apprehensive people will launch the world's first national television network developed by and for Aboriginal people.

Alanis Obomsawin takes her place in the growing circle, face toward the rising sun. One of Canada's leading documentary filmmakers just hours earlier, she had been appointed to the Board of Canada's newest network. Serenity is not a feeling most people experience before a live, three-hour broadcast; but the peacefulness of the setting and the spirituality of the moment touched her. "I wanted everything to go well," she recalled. "And the ceremony gave me the sense of security within myself. I felt ready to try and make this day as wonderful as possible."

Standing at the edge of a growing circle of people is Duane Shuttleworth. Head bowed, he is wearing a red and blue ribbon shirt, and around his waist is a red sash, the symbol of his Métis heritage. Duane is not so calm. He's responsible for organising the day's events, particularly the gala entertainment later that evening. A dozen checklists are competing for attention with two dozen alarm bells in his head. "What are we doing?" he thinks. "People must think we're nuts. We've never done anything like this before!"

Beside Duane is Gil Cardinal, a well-known Aboriginal filmmaker and director. Tonight, for the first time in twenty years, he will be directing a television broadcast. And not just any broadcast—a live, three-hour concert, with a new crew, an untested network and satellite uplink, and a national audience. This sacred ceremony represents the last few moments of peace and focus he'll experience for the rest of the day.

I'm trying to breathe deeply and find some stillness in the moment, in the smoke of sage and sweetgrass and the crisp morning air. Trying to clear my mind of the million details that need to be attended to this day. I'm APTN's Director of Communications, and I will have to convince the media, and a curious country, that we really do know what we're doing. Around the circle are the people I've been working with, laughing with, arguing with—some for years, some for the last few crazy weeks. There's J.C. Catholique from Lutsel K'e in the Northwest Territories, one of the long-time veterans of the Aboriginal broadcasting movement. Peter Crass, who helped build TVNC. Clayton Gordon from Inuvik, looking uncharacteristically solemn. Brenda Chambers, looking characteristically elegant. Cathy Martin. Calvin Helin. Marty Ballentyne, our own burgeoning rock star. Dianne Smith. Dave Tuccaro. And the staff and associates who have worked so hard; Patty Hutton, Jerry Giberson, Patrick Tourigny, Terry Rudden, Joel Fortune. Elder Kinew speaks words of welcome. He reminds us of the importance of the work we are beginning, and offers thanks to the Creator for His gifts. His prayers rise into the lightening sky with the pungent smoke.

Roman Bittman, filmmaker and original member of the APTN Advisory Committee, watches the smoke rise. "Sweat ceremonies and sunrise ceremonies—they're punctuation marks in our lives. But that day was special. We weren't just kicking off another project, or even another TV network. We were giving a voice, a national voice, to our culture. We were making sure our culture would endure."

Abraham Tagalik, APTN's Chief Operating Officer, is standing quietly in the middle of a small group of colleagues and friends, people he's worked with for years, all striving toward the day about to unfold. The last few weeks have been brutal, and the hours ahead will be gruelling. But for the moment there is just the river, the sun, and a surreal sense of calm. He thinks of his mother who had passed away many years before, and feels her standing with him.

"All that work. So many people, so much effort to get us where we are today. You think about where you are and what you're doing, and you just feel lucky and honoured. I was really feeling the support of my family, the support of the Board, everyone's belief for all those years in what we were trying to do, just coming together. That morning and that sunrise ceremony, when I thought of my mom, I felt I had satisfied her and what she saw in me, my potential, that kind of thing. So it was very deep and moving for me."

The prayers finish. There is a moment of silence. Everyone is reluctant to let go of this moment.

Without haste, people begin to walk slowly clockwise around the circle. Most are silent. Some exchange quiet greetings. There are handshakes and hugs and smiles and tears. The fog has lifted and The Forks is warming up. The day has begun.

Imagine turning on your television set. Up comes one of those weird Japanese game shows. People are doing crazy things to each other, speaking in a language you don't know. There's a studio audience that seems to get it, but you don't. You're looking through an electronic window into a culture you can't understand at all. You reach for the remote and click to another channel. Some family is yelling at each other, slamming doors, exhibiting bizarre behavior, all in a foreign language. Again, it's completely incomprehensible. You keep on clicking. But every channel is the same.

If you can imagine that, you can grasp how most television looked to Aboriginal Peoples before APTN.

The "Native as Other" perspective in film is almost as old as the movies themselves.

It began with Robert Flaherty's *Nanook of the North* (1922). Hailed by many as the first modern documentary, it was considered revolutionary for the honesty of its images of Inuit life on the Hudson coast a century ago. As northern broadcast historian Lorna Roth points out, "Despite some simulation, *Nanook* presented a fairly accurate depiction of life in the Arctic and brought to many southern audiences the first glimpse of that remote and enigmatic world."[1] And yet we see the land and its Inuit inhabitants at a distance, albeit through the eyes of a talented and sympathetic documentarian. We are watching an anthropological oddity. Jocular title cards and a faintly patronizing narrative reinforce our separation from the film's subjects.

Nanook set the tone for a generation of future filmmakers. Thirty years later the same amused detachment suffuses The Caribou Hunters, a 1951 National Film Board documentary. Imagine this scene.

Classical music plays in the background. A church bell tolls and clusters of contented Cree families stream out of the church. Now smiling, industrious Indians are making moccasins, and bringing them by dogsled to the Hudson's Bay Company. A narrator speaks for those depicted in the film. 'It is good to get credit at the store, so that when we meet the other Indians coming in from the trapline, we all have a good time', he intones, while a harmonica-playing young man and young woman smile for the camera.

Like *Nanook*, the documentary is "accurate." Yes, Cree hunters did hunt, trap and skin animals. Yes, they did trade at the Hudson's Bay post. But the omniscient narrator is describing the Cree in tones a biologist might use to introduce the inhabitants of a particularly fascinating Petri dish. The "Indians" are unmistakably "Others". They are exotics, creatures to be observed, even admired, by the audience and narrator; but they are not given voice, they do not tell their own story. This is a story about "them", told by one of "us", for an audience of "us".

Aboriginal people are the original inhabitants of the land we now call Canada. How did they become the outsiders?

Daniel Francis, in The *Imaginary Indian,* describes the ways in which the stereotypical, romanticized notion of the Indian served the purposes of law-makers, policy developers and the public's imagination.

> "When two cultures meet, especially cultures as different as those of Western Europe and Indigenous North America, they inevitably interpret each other in terms of stereotypes. At its best, in a situation of equality, this might be seen as a phase in a longer process of familiarisation. But if one side in the encounter enjoys advantages of wealth or power or technology, then it will usually try to impose its stereotypes on the other. This is what occurred in the case of the North American encounter between European and Aboriginal. We have been living with the consequences ever since."[2]

In media, those consequences include decades of Western movies replete with bloodthirsty savages, shifty half-breeds, stoic warriors, and exotic Indian Princesses in buckskin.

The best-known "celluloid Indian" is undoubtedly Harold Smith, better known as Jay Silverheels, a Mohawk actor from Six Nations of the Grand River in southern Ontario. Silverheels, who died in 1980, was a boxer, stuntman, and a gifted actor with more than ninety roles to his credit. But today he's remembered for only one. Throughout the 1950s, he played the Lone Ranger's faithful sidekick, Tonto. It was a stereotypical part—subservient, impassive, and monosyllabic. But it was work, and a rare opportunity for an Aboriginal actor to play a sympathetic Aboriginal character. Silverheels was frequently instructed in his scripts to "say something Indian". To this day, some of the older people in Six Nations will tell you of their favourite scenes where Tonto, laying waste to legions of bad guys, would shout out bloodthirsty war cries in Mohawk like: "Anybody want to go for a burger?" Silverheels' private act of rebellion had Mohawks in stitches whenever they went to the movies, and left non-Aboriginal audiences wondering why those strange Indians were laughing at the mayhem onscreen.

Even the earnest ethnographic films of the 1950s and 1960s, often directed by sympathetic, non-Aboriginal filmmakers, carried their own cultural baggage and dominant societal attitudes. They are suffused with a melancholic, elegiac tone, a sense that Aboriginal stories and ways of life must be recorded and preserved because the cultures were dying, at the brink of absorption into the Great North American Melting Pot.

Many Aboriginal people protested these erroneous and offensive stereotypes. But the message was clear: Indigenous people were vicious, vanquished, or vanishing. And we got the message. When I was growing up in northern Ontario, and the kids would play Cowboys and Indians, nobody wanted to be Indian. Not even us Indians.

»——→ o ←——«

By the late 1960s, television had become Canada's primary source of infor mation and entertainment, a medium that both mirrored and shaped the way that mainstream Canadians saw themselves and their society. Over 90% of Canadian households owned TV sets,[3] including people in First Nation and Métis communities. Some homes on reserves without indoor plumbing or running water had TV sets. TV mattered: it was a window on that bigger, stranger world encroaching more and more on Aboriginal lives. Families whose primary source of information would once have been word of mouth and oral stories—the legendary "moccasin telegraph"—were now watching Detroit's *Eyewitness News* and *Bonanza.*

Whole families watched television when it first arrived, but it was the young people who were mesmerized by the new medium. Second generation Canadian and Aboriginal youth were suddenly drawn into a new world. What seemed strange and incomprehensible to parents for whom English was not a first language was, to the young, a direct connection to the bigger, brighter, English-speaking world "out there". They understood the language, they grasped the context, and a culture that for millennia had emphasized listening to and learning from elders was suddenly turned upside down. Young people were now explaining the world to their elders; and parents with a deep understanding of their own language and culture were perplexed by children who could enter and explore a reality that they themselves could barely grasp.

We all learned about the world through the window of television. And throughout the sixties, the images glowing through that window were those of revolution. It was the decade of American Civil Rights and the women's movement, of student rebellion, anti-Vietnam protests and gay rights; and frustrated Indigenous militants were quick to adopt the playbook. In the United States, it had become clear that decades of polite lobbying within the system were doing nothing to alleviate high unemployment, slum housing, and racist treatment of Native Americans. Aboriginal activists adopted the logic and language of the Civil Rights movements, and created the American Indian Movement (AIM). AIM fought for treaty rights and the reclamation of tribal land, and advocated on behalf of urban Indians living in poverty and despair. Like many of the sixties' liberation movements, AIM's tactics included high profile, symbolic acts of resistance—the occupation of Mount Rushmore, the "capture" of a replica of the Mayflower, and a seventy-one day sit-in at Wounded Knee on the Pine Ridge Reservation, which ended tragically in the death of two occupiers under sniper fire.

In Canada, characteristically, political development played out in a less revolutionary key. In 1967, Treaty and Status groups formed the National Indian Brotherhood (NIB), an umbrella for provincial and territorial First Nation communities and organisations. Their initial goals included recognition of Aboriginal title and acknowledgement of Aboriginal rights. Soon after, in 1969, the NIB was galvanized by the release of the Government's "White Paper". The Honourable Jean Chrétien, then Minister of Indian Affairs, proposed the elimination of the Indian Act of Canada, the rejection of land claims, and the assimilation of First Nations into the Canadian population, with the status of other ethnic minorities. A hard-line NIB rejection of the Government's policy and a series of favourable court decisions led the Trudeau Government to quietly back off from its assimilationist position—at least officially. That was an important victory; and even more important was the fact that the NIB— later to evolve into the Assembly of First Nations (AFN)—had established itself as a new, national voice in Canada's political chorus. Regional voices soon joined the discussions. Groups like the Council for Yukon Indians and the Federation of Saskatchewan Indians also began asserting rights, lobbying, and putting political pressure on governments across Canada.

Meanwhile Inuit took their own path to political development. Since the 1950s, Inuit had had virtually no political relationship with Canada at all— no land claims, no treaties, and no status under Canadian law. But a new generation of bilingual, politicised young Inuit—many educated in residential schools—realised during the late 1960s that Inuit were being sidelined in the political and economic evolution of the North. In 1971, a meeting of delegates at Carleton University in Ottawa established the Inuit Tapirisat (Brotherhood) of Canada (ITC) to represent the Inuit of Labrador, northern Quebec, and the Northwest Territories. The new organisation had to deal with a bewildering range of issues threatening the Inuit way of life— oil and gas development, poverty, lack of health care, low standards of education, the need for land claims. But interestingly, ITC set the protection of Inuit culture and language as one of its highest priority goals.

The reason was simple. English language television was arriving in the North—and it was arriving uninvited.

$$\gg\!\!—\!\!\longrightarrow\!\circ\!\longleftarrow\!\!—\!\!\ll$$

CBC Northern Service radio had been part of Inuit life since 1958. The medium was a natural for the North; Inuit culture is an oral culture, with information exchanged verbally, through gossip and storytelling. And radio programming is relatively inexpensive to produce, easy to distribute by local transmitter, and simple to learn. Inuit took to radio immediately, and the Northern Service quickly assumed a truly northern flavour—chatty, friendly, and participatory, with listeners phoning in constantly to join in the territorial conversation in their own language, Inuktitut. Northern Service radio was an extended community conversation, punctuated by blocks of national news and programming. Inuit naturally assumed that television would follow the same pattern, and adapt itself to the needs and preferences of viewers.

But television is a very different medium. In radio, a single announcer-operator can host and produce a three-hour show from a small, basic studio. But a television production—especially in the late 1960s—required a lengthy setup, many trained technicians, expensive studio space, and a big budget. And most importantly—it required a distribution system to get programming into a viewer's home. In southern Canada, where most households lived in close proximity to each other, local transmitters or cablevision companies allowed people to receive programming through an antenna or a coaxial cable. In the Arctic, however, the population was small and widely dispersed. There were no transmitters, no cable companies, and no direct microwave relay systems linking north and south. There weren't any roads, and no cables could be buried under the North's permafrost or strung across the tundra; there was no cheap way to reach northern residents with TV signals.

Many Inuit caught their first glimpse of television when CBC introduced the Frontier Coverage Package (FCP) in 1967. Television programs were videotaped in the South, then shipped across the North for playback over local transmitters in a few communities. The daily four-hour television package included children's shows like *Sesame Street* and *Bugs Bunny*, Canadian classics such as *Hockey Night in Canada* and *Front Page Challenge*, national news, and American soap operas like *The Edge of Night*. The target audience was RCMP officers, nurses, armed forces personnel, and Hudson's Bay staff—displaced southerners desperate for a taste of home. As for the people who WERE at home—the Inuit – no one thought to ask them what they wanted.

One of those Inuit was Abraham Tagalik, born in Coral Harbour, Nunavut, a tiny settlement on the coast of Southampton Island in Hudson's Bay. His father worked on the DEW Line site in Coral Harbour, one of a network of radar stations set up across the North to detect incoming Soviet bombers during the Cold War. CBC's Inuktitut-language radio programming was a constant presence in his home, and part of the community's culture. But it was television that captured Abe's imagination. "In the summer of 1968, my family moved from Coral Harbour in Nunavut to Churchill, Manitoba. We were only there for about a month. That was the first time I saw a television set. It was black and white, with terrible sound. But the picture was clear as a bell. I thought—now THIS is interesting."

For the most part, FCP's recycled videotapes in the late 1960s didn't affect communities. To most Inuit, radio remained a vibrant community lifeline; television was an interesting oddity for white people.

And then came Anik.

$$\text{»}\longrightarrow\text{o}\longleftarrow\text{«}$$

Experimental satellites had been used to relay television signals as early as 1964, when Syncom-3 transmitted images of the Tokyo Olympics to the United States. In the sixties, as television viewership boomed and more and more channels jostled for space on the TV dial, broadcasters and cable companies realized that the future would demand high-capacity satellites.

On November 9, 1972, Telesat Canada launched the first geostationary satellite serving North America, Anik E-1, followed a year later by Anik E-2. The primary purpose of these and other satellites was to serve the bourgeoning southern commercial market. But once TV signals were up on "the bird", they could be received in any community with a satellite dish, and rebroadcast locally—even in the Arctic. These were no longer old, recycled tapes from the south—this was a real-time flood of information and imagery from southern Canada, pouring into hamlets that had no daily newspapers, movie theatres, or even roads.

The tidal wave of southern programming was both shocking and addictive.

Designed to grab and hold urban viewers long-conditioned to television, the pace and violence of TV was almost surreal to Inuit audiences, a tsunami of images of Vietnam, urban crime, the Holocaust, and people doing incomprehensible things in a foreign language—English.

One elder in northern Quebec summed it up nicely. "People spend a lot of time screaming at each other down there, don't they?"

The National Hockey League became an Arctic obsession. The soap opera *"Edge of Night"* captivated northerners to the point that some hamlet offices changed their hours of operation so that employees could stay home at noon to keep up with the travails of its characters. And the activities that bound northern communities together—socialising, visiting, play—were replaced by the glowing blue box.

"Things changed almost overnight," said Abraham Tagalik. "It was around 1975, and I had been away at school. I came home for one of the school breaks, and one of the first things I noticed was there was no one outside. Before, kids were outside all the time, playing, making our own fun. But no one was playing. No one was visiting. Everyone was in their houses, gathered around the television. That was how TV came north."

John Amagoalik, former President of the Inuit Tapirisat, shares the same memory. "When television first came [to the North], the effect on the community was drastic. People no longer visited their neighbours. Children did not play outside. Interactive activities were broken down."

Rosemarie Kuptana was born in Sachs Harbour, NWT—another Inuk who grew up without television, but was drawn to this new medium. Years later, speaking as an emerging leader of the Aboriginal broadcast movement, she described the introduction of television to Inuit communities as a "neutron bomb—one that leaves the outer shell of the people walking around but kills the soul." She remembered "...fishing and camping for a month in the summer. But when hockey season came around, my father would rush back into town like a maniac on the skidoo so that he could watch TV and my mother went along with him. She'd talk about Andy Moog—the Edmonton goalie—like he was her best friend!"

What was most jarring about the new medium was its complete disconnection from northern reality. Inuit viewers, watching television night after night in their homeland, caught only the rarest glimpses of themselves— and always through southern eyes. In the late 1970s, heading into Cape Dorset to shoot a film on Inuit photographer Peter Pitseolak, NFB producer Wolf Koenig caught a few hours of "northern" television. "In Frobisher Bay, we saw television that was totally irrelevant [to Inuit]. We thought it was insane to see white faces. The Inuit saw none of themselves on TV; what they saw had no relation to their world."[4]

The face of North American television in the 1960s remained overwhelmingly white. The portrayal of blacks in mainstream media had at least progressed from *Amos and Andy* to *The Cosby Show* and *The Jeffersons*. But Aboriginal people were still either invisible, or confined to one of their traditional roles—victims, villains, or sidekicks.

Many of the Aboriginal people drawn to media at that time were determined to change the colour of television with programs and performance that would counter the stereotypes. Some succeeded; but most discovered that network television is formulaic in its structure, conservative in content, and more interested in winning and selling to audiences than in challenging their preconceptions. Young Aboriginal filmmakers like Willie Dunn and Gil Cardinal weren't interested in producing 27.5 minute, packaged episodes with commercial breaks, titles, credits, stock characters and stock situations; they wanted to tell their own stories, in their own words. And as it happened, others in Canada were adapting the medium to do just that.

The invention of portable, low-cost video production equipment and access to community cable television systems encouraged people to use television as a tool to tell community stories. Conventional formats were irrelevant; the tools and the product were less important than the process of community animation. This approach was piloted by the National Film Board's *Challenge for Change,* launched in 1966. It was a ground-breaking program that used film and video to explore social concerns and promote social development. *Challenge for Change* rejected the notion that media production was the exclusive domain of a professional elite; it put community members in charge of the production process, encouraging them to shoot, edit, and tell their own stories onscreen. It threw out the notion that the final, packaged program was the end result; the program was just a step in the process. Videos and films were often sent to government officials, whose responses were then incorporated into the production. The goal, as the program's name implied, was social change, not slickly packaged conventional documentaries.

NFB filmmakers worked with and trained crews in marginalised communities, including unemployed fishermen on Fogo Island in Newfoundland and urban poor in the St. Jacques district of Montreal. As part of the program, the NFB also established "The Indian Crew". Up to this point, the Board's films had been "about" Indians, from a white perspective: *Challenge for Change* handed the camera over to the other side.

Noel Starblanket, Willie Dunn, Mike Mitchell and several other trainees spent five months learning the fundamentals of production, then began to produce a remarkable series of films that combined filmmaking and community development. *These are my People,* produced in 1969, was the first filmed history of the Mohawk community of Akwesasne to include the Longhouse traditions. *The Ballad of Crowfoot* was a haunting, bitter meditation on the expansion of the Canadian west from the viewpoint of the famous Blackfoot Confederacy Chief, built around a ballad by director Willie Dunn. Dunn also directed *The Other Side of the Ledger,* a sardonic counterpoint to the Hudson's Bay Company's self-satisfied celebration of its 300th birthday in 1972, focusing on the exploitation of the First Nation and Métis trappers who built the Bay's fortunes.

The work of the Indian Crew was a far cry from *Nanook,* and marked a historic break with the "native as anthropological curio" school of documentary. Gil Cardinal, Métis filmmaker, noted that the Indian Crew signalled "... the beginning of Aboriginal films being made by Aboriginal people at the NFB (and most likely in the rest of Canada)."

Other pockets of Indigenous production began forming across Canada. Wolf Koenig, appalled at the irrelevance of the programming he had seen in Frobisher Bay, organised the *Sikusilarmiut* animation workshops for a small group of young Inuit in Cape Dorset, a community renowned for its carvers and printmakers. The workshop was a huge success, yielding a series of innovative, unique pieces that won international attention and awards. A second workshop in Frobisher Bay provided documentary training, and led to the creation of the Nunatsiakmiut Native Communications Society in 1975. Nunatsiakmiut began producing short films for CBC television—local vignettes, cultural profiles, and eventually weird and wonderful dramas, including a memorable Inuktitut horror-science fiction thriller featuring a tinfoil-wrapped alien.

In 1970, the "Man in the North Conference on Community Development", sponsored by the Arctic Institute of North America, was held in Inuvik. The Conference focused on the importance of respecting northern aspirations, especially the need for more Aboriginal communications and broadcasting. As noted in the conference report, "It is felt that locally-run radio stations would be more important than the satellite communications program, which is felt to be a gadget conceived for southern purposes, and not for northern residents. It is felt to be yet another method to feed more southern culture into the North without making any provision for an exchange."[5] The Conference recommended that each northern community be provided with its own community radio station and video-taping equipment.

The federal Department of Communications responded one year later with the Northern Pilot Project (NPP). The Project was designed to "explore the use of intermediate communications technology for community development"[6]. Two-way radio-telephone networks, community radio stations and videotape machines were provided to several Cree communities in northern Ontario and Inuit communities in the N.W.T. Local residents were encouraged to experiment with new technologies, looking for new approaches that could best meet their social, cultural and communications needs.

Expanding on the success of the NPP, the Department of the Secretary of State launched the Native Communications Program (NCP) in 1973 to fund Aboriginal media projects. These included trail radio services and local newspapers, some of which evolved over the years into independent, profitable national publications. Media was the height of cool; young, politicised Aboriginal people were attracted to the new organisations, and began building an informal national network for sharing information.

It was clear by the mid 1970s that the stars were lining up. Satellite technology had made television available to virtually any community in Canada. Low-cost, portable video production gear was replacing bulky, expensive film equipment as the production format of choice. And a growing body of creative, bilingual and politicised Aboriginal youth were growing interested in media as a career, taking advantage of burgeoning training and employment opportunities.

The stage was set for something. The catalyst, not for the first time, was a government misstep—an apparently innocuous decision to extend CBC service to small, remote communities.

In 1973, CBC proposed a new Northern Broadcasting Plan to increase the amount of southern programming in northern communities and expand local coverage and production. The Plan would have opened the door to enhanced community-based and native language programming: but it came with a high price tag, and was ultimately rejected. Instead, the North got the Accelerated Coverage Plan (ACP), which increased the volume of southern programming flooding into northern communities—including those that had not yet received any satellite television at all.

Just a few years earlier, the ACP would have moved forward without comment or protest. But the North in 1975 was not the North in 1967.

The Northern Quebec Inuit Association (NQIA), in the final stages of negotiating a multimillion dollar land claims agreement for the region was vehemently opposed to the introduction of television into Arctic Quebec. Their position was simple. Many communities in the region still lacked basic radio or telephone service; so why would the government subsidize the intrusion of southern television, without even consulting Inuit? Why weren't Inuit producing their own programming? Josepi Padlayat, communications officer for NQIA, put it bluntly. "We don't have to let them use us through TV. Let's have our own rights concerning TV. We want it our way, not the white man's way."

In fact, the proposed extension of service was offensive to many northerners. The community of Igloolik, noted for the strength of its culture and language, simply refused to accept the new service. The hamlet council declined additional southern programming until Inuit were given more control over content. One young observer of the debate in Igloolik was Zacharias Kunuk, a budding director who would become the first Inuk to win an international film award at Cannes.

The lines were drawn. Inuit would no longer accept the wholesale importation of southern programming into their homeland.

The launch of Anik E1 and E2 put Canada at the forefront of global telecommunications. The Canadian aerospace industry had world-class expertise and products to sell on the international market, and the government was determined to let the world know about it. And what better place to demonstrate made-in-Canada technology than the Arctic? The isolation, the extreme climate and terrain, and the lack of technical infrastructure made the North a perfect laboratory for testing the new toys, and the special appeal of Inuit culture and language could be counted on to capture international interest.

With those goals in mind, the Department of Communication funded Naalakvik I, a 1976 pilot project in northern Quebec. Working in collaboration with the NQIA, an Inuit organisation called Taqramiut Nipingat Inc. (TNI) used the Anik A Hermes satellite to link eight radio stations across the territory.

Encouraged by the technical success and Inuit response to Naalakvik, the Department of Communications announced the experimental Anik-B Communications Program. TNI in northern Quebec launched NAALAKVIK II, an ambitious plan to establish an interactive television mini-network in five Nunavik communities.

The second project, developed by the Inuit Tapirisat of Canada (ITC), was called "Inukshuk", named for the iconic stone cairns used for millennia by Inuit as navigation aids and food caches. This modest three-year, two million dollar project transformed the way Inuit would see and use television technology, and set in motion a movement that led a quarter century later to a national Aboriginal television network.

Lyndsay Green was a sociology graduate hired by the federal Department of Communications in 1973, to work on the Northern Pilot Project. In 1975, she was surprised by a phone call from James Arvaluk, president of ITC. James had met Lyndsay in Nunavut through the project two years earlier. Now he was calling to invite her to head up the Inukshuk team. "I said, 'well, what kind of budget do you have to run this program?' And they said, 'we don't have any. Oh, and, by the way, we don't have any money to pay you either.'"

So she accepted.

"Of course I did. It was just so exciting. What impressed me was that communications was ITC's highest priority. They were totally behind Inukshuk —and when you're working on a project like that, support is a lot more valuable than money. Money you can always find."

The concept was innovative, but simple. Small television "studios" would be established in five Arctic communities, with staff trained to record videotapes locally. These would be shipped to a network hub in Frobisher Bay. The feeds from those five Inukshuk centres would be combined and uplinked from the Frobisher centre, then picked up in all communities across Nunavut.

The basic idea sounds straightforward; implementing it would be anything but. ITC was proposing to train local producers in television sound, lighting, camerawork, directing, editing, research, writing , and set design—as well as community animation, promotion, transmitter operations, scheduling, and the hundreds of tasks involved in running a small network. All this was to be achieved in a territory one third the size of Canada, with no universities and the lowest rates of education and literacy in the country, in a climate so cold that camera cables routinely froze and shattered like glass. The network concept was untested. No one had ever attempted this volume of television production this far north—and certainly not with brand new, untried crews, in Inuktitut.

But as Rosemarie Kuptana once said, "Sometimes it helps not to understand that a project is impossible. Knowing that might slow you down." And she was right. Miraculously, within a year, the Inukshuk infrastructure was in place.

Communities contributed space where they could find it. The network headquarters, studio and uplink centre in Frobisher Bay were crammed into a couple of unused classrooms in a ramshackle adult education centre. Baker Lake's production facility was a plywood shack. Small engineering miracles were performed in the various Inukshuk communities, and young Inuit, intrigued by the opportunity to learn something about this new medium, signed up for training.

In southern Canada, a career in television usually begins with a two-year college program, followed by a couple of years as a production assistant or cable puller. Most of the Inukshuk trainees had never completed high school—some had never been at all—and English, for most, was a second language. Trainees included a full time hunter, a printmaker, a furnace repair man, and a veteran of the Cape Dorset animation workshops—a cross section of contemporary Inuit, linked only by their curiosity about television.

The trainers were an assortment of independent filmmakers, community animators, and community television producers from different parts of Canada. Many had either worked on or studied the *Challenge for Change* movement. Their role was not to train southern-style "producers": Inukshuk trainees were taught to find ways to make new tools meet real local needs.

As Program Director of Ottawa Cablevision, Patrick Tourigny was used to working with local organisations. A former technical producer at CJOH and Skyline Cable, Patrick had become bored with commercial TV, and had found his niche helping groups to access the free channel that cable licensees were obliged to provide to the community. Keith McNeill, one of Pat's on-air operators, told him that a northern group with offices in Ottawa was looking for advice on low budget, community-based television production, and on training community volunteers. Pat was intrigued. He set up a meeting with Lyndsay Green, and brought along Terry Rudden, one of his community animators. Both Pat and Terry were delighted at the prospect of seeing the medium put to real use at the local level, even if "local" meant two thousand kilometres north. They agreed to put the Ottawa Cable studios at the disposal of Inuit trainees and provide them with some practical experience, and Terry was granted time off to run production workshops in Frobisher Bay.

"My usual training sessions at Ottawa Cable would be a three-hour workshop showing volunteers how to light fake plants for an interview set," said Terry. "Then a week later I was sitting out on the ice in Frobisher Bay, figuring out with the Inukshuk trainees how to film a snowmobile blowing up for a segment on safety. That was a lot more fun." For both Patrick and Terry, the Inukshuk experience marked the beginning of a lifelong involvement in Aboriginal broadcasting.

Inukshuk trainers quickly discovered that Inuit were incredible adaptors. The culture that adopted and absorbed rifles, trade, snowmobiles, and Christianity, and emerged with its values intact, took to video production immediately.

Rudimentary production instruction led quickly to Inukshuk's first broadcasts. The resulting programming looked nothing like the slick southern product Inuit viewers had been used to: but they were riveted to their television sets. For the first time they were seeing their communities, their people and their reality on that little blue screen. Instead of kitchen renovation programs, they watched hunters demonstrate kayak building and Inuit seamstresses teaching traditional sewing and beading. Interactive community forums and meetings on a possible Inuit land claim replaced news coverage of American politics. There was throat singing, storytelling, birthday greetings, cooking shows—and laughing.

"There was always lots of laughter," said Lyndsay. "Inuit are great storytellers. Listening, hearing and watching people tell stories—that was just sheer joy. People were thrilled to see themselves on television in their own living rooms."

Inukshuk was a ground-breaking success in every way. The programs were raw, real, and relevant, and Inuit were enthralled. ITC had proved that Canadian satellite technology and production equipment worked just fine in the Arctic, that Inuit could master the technology and adapt it to their own ends, and that Inuit audiences were starving for television that reflected their own culture.

From the government's perspective, Inukshuk was primarily an experiment in satellite technology, with an eye on the international market for Canadian telecommunications products and expertise. Inuit, not surprisingly, saw the project differently.

"The satellite project was an important component of Inukshuk, yes—but it wasn't everything," said Lyndsay Green. "What we were really doing was establishing production capacity. The ITC Board was thinking big right from the beginning. They never saw this as a cute little community video circulation project, or a few hours of transmission on an experimental satellite. They knew exactly where they were going. Inukshuk was always intended to turn into an Inuit broadcasting system."

The success of Inukshuk, Naalakvik II, Ironstar Radio in northern Ontario, and other regional projects drove the message home to national policymakers and regulators. Native audiences needed native programming, not southern leftovers; and native producers were more than capable of meeting that need.

The message was received—sort of. In 1981 the Canadian Radio Television and Telecommunications Commission (CRTC) licensed Canadian Satellite Communications Inc. (Cancom) to distribute four television signals and seven radio signals to remote and underserved areas of Canada, including the North. But for the first time, the CRTC urged Cancom to accommodate Aboriginal programming in its service packages, noting that "...the extension of southern-originated broadcasting services to the North and to native communities in particular carries with it a concomitant responsibility to facilitate the development of native-originated broadcasting services." It was little more than a suggestion, not a condition of license; but the Cancom package did subsequently include two native-language radio signals.

A more significant CRTC initiative began in 1979. Pay television (a generic term for subscription-based TV services), was just emerging as a market force in the mid-seventies. The Department of Communications saw the pay TV industry as a potential stimulant for satellite usage and high-tech development, and urged the CRTC to review the regulatory issues raised by the new services, including their potential impact on northern Canada.

The CRTC agreed, and appointed Commissioner Réal Therrien to head up the Committee on Extension of Service to Northern and Remote

Communities. Therrien was an anomaly on the Commission, one of the only members with actual experience in radio, television and telecommunications. He took the unprecedented step of actually holding Committee hearings in the North, travelling with committee member John Amagoalik, an Inuit leader who had worked on the Inukshuk Project. The Committee heard residents' concerns in settlements across the North, and received nearly 400 letters and briefs, most calling for more relevant northern television programming.

The Committee took over a year to collect and analyse the input from northerners. But from ITC's perspective it was worth the wait. The final report—*The 1980s: A Decade of Diversity—Broadcasting, Satellites and Pay-TV*—was an unequivocal message to Canada. The wave of southern broadcasting was threatening Canada's most unique cultures; but the medium itself could help preserve them.

The "Therrien Report" stated explicitly that: "Canada must fulfil its obligations to provide opportunity for its native peoples to preserve the use of their languages and foster the maintenance and development of their own particular cultures through broadcasting and other communications." [7]

To make that happen, the Committee proposed that federal funding be provided to native communications societies to train staff and produce programs.

That was the policy endorsement ITC had been waiting for. They immediately applied for, and received, a network license, and in 1981 incorporated the Inuit Broadcasting Corporation (IBC), a new and independent organisation. The personnel, facilities and equipment were those of the Inukshuk project. But ITC recognised that no credible media outlet could operate under the wing of a political organisation; IBC was conceived as a permanent and completely independent Inuit broadcast operation.

Other northern broadcasters were quick to seize the opportunity. Northern Native Broadcasting, Yukon (NNBY) and the Native Communications Society of the Northwest Territories (NCS) were also granted broadcast licenses, and began producing Aboriginal language programming. Both started in radio, but quickly branched out into television.
One of the people attracted to this new medium was George Henry, a

young Tlingit from the Yukon and a recent journalism graduate. George came from a traditional family, and was raised in Teslin, a small commuity on the Alaska Highway north of Whitehorse. He had studied at Ryerson (now called Toronto Metropolitan University) in Toronto with fellow northerner Catherine MacQuarrie, a Métis woman from the NWT. Upon completing his journalism training, George moved back to the Yukon. Both George and Catherine were captivated by television, and both would play a seminal role in the emerging Aboriginal broadcast movement.

In January 1982, barely a year and a half after the final Inukshuk project broadcast, Canada's first all-Aboriginal television broadcaster launched its service with a ninety minute special. IBC's inaugural broadcast aired at midnight on the CBC Northern Service channel, a scheduling arrangement northerners would soon become resigned to. Despite its timeslot, IBC quickly became became very popular across the eastern Arctic and northern Quebec.

"IBC always went on late, usually after 11 o'clock," said Abraham Tagalik, who had moved to Iqaluit and joined CBC Radio, producing Inuktitut language programming. "It didn't matter: they always had a big audience. Everybody gathered around the TV to watch Inuktitut programming, and everyone was talking about the shows. That really sparked my interest. But I realised it was political as well. I had heard that Igloolik wasn't going to allow television into their community until they got the kind of TV they wanted. That was a real eye-opener for me. I thought, that's right—we don't have to settle for what they're willing to give us."

The Therrien Report was just one of several studies to examine Canadian broadcasting and cultural policy in the 1970s and 80s that concluded Aboriginal voices were missing. Experimental satellite projects, occasional documentary films and broadcast licenses were all very well: but none addressed the fundamental gap in Canada's public broadcasting system.

≫——→ o ⟵——≪

Public broadcasting is an essential facet of Canada's media environment, and the element that distinguishes it most clearly from the American system.

In the US, public media are funded primarily by corporate and individual donors; in Canada (and throughout the world), public programming is supported by policy and legislation.

In the days before cable and satellites, most "Canadian" television was, in fact, American, flooding into Canada from transmitters south of the border.

Television in the U.S. had evolved rapidly, following the path laid down decades earlier by radio. The American system was characterised by private ownership, minimal regulation, and content driven by advertising revenues and sponsorships.

With one tenth of America's population, Canada could simply not afford a purely market-driven, commercial broadcasting system. Parliament recognised that when it first established the Canadian Radio Broadcasting Commission in 1936. Their goal was to establish a broadcast system that would reflect Canada to Canadians, unite the country, and provide a window for Canadian talent and content. That required public funding to support a national broadcasting service, and a regulatory framework to ensure that broadcasting in Canada would serve the goals of the country as a whole.

The same considerations applied in 1952 when CBC television was estabished. There was little direct economic incentive for private Canadian broadcasters to invest in new Canadian product: it was easier and cheaper to buy and recycle American television programming. But by funding institutions like the CBC and the National Film Board, and passing broadcast regulations requiring specific levels of Canadian content as a condition of license, the government managed to create a demand for Canadian talent that would not otherwise exist in an unregulated market flooded by cheap, popular American products.

The strategy worked. By 1958, CBC could be seen 'coast to coast' (with the North still conspicuously left out). Along with the National Film Board, it was producing world class programming, training and employing the founding generation of Canadian broadcasters, and providing a cultural counterpoint to the invasive and persuasive flood of American signals into Canadian homes.

The creation of the CBC, and federal regulatory and financial support for broadcasting and film, had proven that policy and funding could create a national system to promote Canadian culture and stave off a wave of sophisticated programming from a rich southern neighbour. It was a lesson the Inuit broadcasters took to heart.

The federal response to the recommendations of the Therrien Committee Report was announced two years after its release. In 1983 Minister of Communications Francis Fox travelled to Frobisher Bay, visited a pirate radio station, had his photo taken in an elegant parka, and announced Canada's new Northern Broadcast Policy.

The Policy vindicated years of political lobbying by Aboriginal groups, community consultation, innumerable studies, and tireless internal advocacy by bureaucrats from DOC, the Secretary of State, INAC and other departments. It addressed many of the areas of concern raised by northerners, recognising the need to provide northern Aboriginal people with programing choices and opportunities to develop their own programming, with access to distribution systems, and with the opportunity to participate in formulating future policies that could impact on their communities.

And there was more. Minister of Communications Francis Fox also announced the Northern Native Broadcast Access Program (NNBAP), committing more than $33 million over four years to assist 13 regionally-based northern native communications societies to produce television and/ or radio. IBC, NNBY, TNI and NCS-NWT were already up and running: the NNBAP funded the creation or expansion of Missinipi Broadcasting Corporation (MBC) in Saskatchewan, Northern Native Broadcasting, Terrace (NNBT) in BC, Native Communications Inc. (NCI) in Manitoba, the Aboriginal Multimedia Society of Alberta (AMMSA), the Wawatay Native Communications Society in Ontario, Societé de communication Atikamekw-Montagnais (SOCAM) in Quebec, the OKalaKatiget Society (OKS) in Labrador, the Inuvialuit Communications Society (ICS) in the NWT, and the James Bay Cree Communications Society (JBCCS) in Quebec.

The NNBAP wasn't just a production fund, providing limited money for a specific documentary or a series. It was a long-term program designed specifically to create an Aboriginal public broadcasting system to do the job that the CBC couldn't.

The announcement was met with jubilation in the North. The NNBAP and the Northern Broadcast Policy seemed initially to be the culmination of everything northern broadcasters had worked for—an incredible success story.

Upon closer examination, however, the Program's limitations became clear. To northern broadcasters used to making programs on a shoestring, the annual funding of $13M seemed like a fortune. They quickly discovered it was not. The annual contribution was calculated using a formula that had no actual basis in reality—an assumption that an hour of television cost $5,000 to produce. At the time, more experienced broadcasters set production costs at $12,000 to $14,000 per hour [8] for production, even in the South. Aboriginal broadcasters, however, were working in some of the most remote and inaccessible regions of the country, with higher operating costs that reflected their isolation. And while networks like the CBC could hire trained and experienced staff anywhere in the country, the NNBAP groups would be training their own journalists, technical producers, directors and managers from scratch.

Many of the newer groups decided to start with just one medium, either radio or television, assuming that the Program's relatively long duration would give them time to expand into both. One was NCS-NWT, a Yellowknife-based communications society which had published *The Native Press*, a successful and well-known newspaper, since 1972. Catherine MacQuarrie was working for the paper as an editorial assistant. On the basis of her Ryerson degree, she was promoted to the position of Broadcast Manager, and assigned to establish radio and television services. Like Abraham, Rosemarie, and other northern founders of the Aboriginal broadcasting movement, Catherine, who spent her early years in Baker Lake, had grown up in isolation, with no media— no television, no telephone, no radio. She remembers the introduction of the Frontier Package, with its outdated hockey games on tape; and even then she was struck by the lack of northern images on television. But television intrigued her. She moved to

Toronto to study journalism, then returned North with her newfound skills and went to work for NCS-NWT. The opportunity to lead the organisation into video programming was tempting, but she understood the real cost of television production. After a long, hard look at the resources and expertise available in Yellowknife, she recommended to the organisation that they begin in radio.

"TV was sexy and all that. But in terms of preserving Aboriginal languages and cultures, and really becoming a daily presence in peoples' lives—I thought radio was a better choice."

It was a judgement call made by several Aboriginal broadcasters, all confident that the NNBAP would continue to grow as promised. Unfortunately that did not happen.

»————→ o ←———— «

Just one year after its launch, projected increases to the NNBAP were frozen; and in subsequent years the broadcasters experienced cut after   cut to their budgets—an experience common to public broadcasters everywhere. The funds promised for new services were not going to be there; organisations like NCS-NWT would have to cut back on their radio operations, or seek funding from elsewhere, if they wanted to expand into television.

The resources the NNBAP provided to northern broadcasters may not have been adequate, and the Program may not have lived up to everyone's expectations. But from the perspective of southern Aboriginal producers, it seemed the northern broadcasters had just hit the jackpot. Producers in Vancouver, Edmonton, Montreal and Winnipeg demanded to know why the NNBAP was providing $13M to the sparsely populated north, while leaving ninety percent of Aboriginal people out in the cold. The answer was simple—money.

The federal bureaucrats who designed the NNBAP in 1982 were faced with tough political and budgetary choices. A national Aboriginal broadcasting program was seen as too expensive. Northerners already had a track record of success, infrastructure in place, and a strong, united lobby; and northern Canada was a smaller place—at least, in terms of population. So the

Program was limited to communities north of the "Hamelin Line", an arbitrary geographical division based on criteria for "northerness" developed by geographer Louis-Edmond Hamelin. There was no particular reason to use the Hamelin line as a criterion for eligibility. In fact, the boundary was quietly modified by federal officials to ensure that two politically important groups (Ontario and French-speaking broadcasters in Quebec) could be funded. Its only real use was that it allowed the Government to refuse funding to the huge Aboriginal majority in southern Canada.

The split between north and south, between Government-funded, non-profit northern media and independent, struggling southern producers created a cultural division between have and have-not Aboriginal broadcasters that persists to this day. Elaine Bomberry, a producer and arts activist from Six Nations in southern Ontario, recalled her community's response to the NNBAP ten years later during the Royal Commission on Aboriginal Peoples.

> "[W]hen the government drew that invisible line across the country and said that these communities north of this line need communication societies to preserve their languages, to preserve their songs, they gave them money for satellite networks, radio, printers for the newspapers and in the South we didn't get that. So when we started our radio station at Six Nations, we used that against the CRTC and told them that it was a form of genocide because they didn't give us the opportunity in the South to access those kinds of money so we could preserve our languages as well." [9]

Whatever its shortcomings, the Northern Broadcast Policy and the NNBAP ushered in a new stage in the evolution of Aboriginal media. Canada had recognised that native people were entitled to public broadcast services that met their needs, and had funded over a dozen Aboriginal organisations to train staff and produce relevant cultural and linguistic programming. More Aboriginal producers were creating better programming every month.

But there was one critical element missing. More and more shows were being produced, all right; but no one had quite figured out how to get that programming to its intended audiences.

CHAPTER II

THE CONCEPT

THE DEATH OF A THOUSAND CUTS AND THE LAUNCH OF TELEVISION NORTHERN CANADA

9 am September 1, 1999

Jim Compton, APTN's Director of Programming, lopes into the lobby of the Fort Garry Hotel. You can hear him coming up to the second floor mezzanine long before he arrives, shouting out greetings in his 'radio' voice to well-wishers in the lobby as he flies up the stairs, trademark braids bouncing behind him.

He's late. He and Abraham had taxied from the sunrise ceremony to a breakfast show interview—with no breakfast—at a local television station on the other side of Winnipeg. Abe had left to join the Board, and Jim is now racing to a meeting with staff and contractors at the Fort Garry hotel, an elegant old CN châteauesque style, built by the Grand Trunk Railway in 1913. Just across the railway tracks from The Forks, and Mission Control for APTN launch day. He is meeting with Randall (Randy) McKenzie and Tookie Mercredi, the executive producers of tonight's broadcast, and touching base with Jordan Wheeler, who is writing the script for the broadcast hosts. He had contemplated joining the newly-elected Board members on their breakfast boat cruise, but had realised there just wasn't enough time. He has interviews lined up, a press conference to attend, a script to rehearse, and a staff meeting at lunch to prepare for. He also has to make sure that a week's worth of videotapes scheduled for broadcast on the new network have actually arrived in Yellowknife from Ottawa, and are ready to go. "I was totally overwhelmed with stress. But it was one of the happiest days of my life. I'm not sure I showed it."

Down at the river's edge, east of downtown, APTN's Board of Directors are being ushered by Captain Liwicki and his wife Leo onto the Wendebee, an elegant private yacht that had once hosted Prince Charles. The name of the yacht sounded impressively Aboriginal: in fact, it was named after the owner's two daughters, Wendy and Debbie.

The cruise is a blue-ribbon affair. Standing by the bow is the mayor of Winnipeg, Glen Murray, chatting with newly-appointed Board member Dave Tuccaro. Aboriginal cabinet minister Eric Robinson is laughing with board member Brenda Chambers and a corporate representative from Telesat. The banks of the Red River glide by as waiters serve breakfast on silver trays.

"Yeah, it was a little over the top", says Abraham. "But we thought we should

have something special to thank the Board, the government, the broadcasters that backed us up over the years—everyone who supported us. I could feel the seconds ticking before the broadcast and I knew the day was going to be crazy. But you know what? Sometimes you just have to relax and enjoy the moment."

Abraham, a lifelong hunter, had grown up in and around boats; he loves this. Every few minutes, though, he glances at the sky. It's still gray.

Jeremie Torrie is hunting, too—for shots. With camera in hand, the Ojibwe film- maker is clambering onto every available surface and projection of the yacht, trying to capture the people and the mood of the cruise. As an Aboriginal producer from Winnipeg, Jeremy was one of a hardworking team of lobbyists who had convinced APTN to move its headquarters and production centre to the city. So today's celebration is his celebration too. He approaches Elder Jules Lavallee and his wife Margaret, and convinces them to lean out over the taffrail of the boat and shout, "We love APTN!" They oblige him. "It felt a little silly at the time," Jules recalls. "But it was fun."

While the dignitaries and executives are cruising the Red River, Jordan Wheeler is holed up in a tiny, airless room in the Fort Garry hotel, ankle-deep in crumpled paper, pounding out pages. He's been up most of the night writing the script for the inaugural broadcast. There's a small monitor and video playback unit beside him, and a stack of videotapes—8 to 10 minute clips prepared by producers across Canada to be fed into the live launch broadcast. The printer is grinding out draft after draft after draft, and Jordan is struggling to stay on top of it all. He's a seasoned screen- writer, and knows all about pressure and deadlines; but nothing could have pre- pared him for the intensity of this gig.

"It was easy at the beginning. I had written some general things about Aboriginal history and TVNC and that kind of thing. But then I realised I really couldn't do the bulk of the writing because I was waiting for the segments. And the segments came in at the last minute. So it was down to the wire, writing this thing."

Peering anxiously over his shoulder, numb with fatigue, is Executive Producer Randall McKenzie. "I missed the sunrise ceremony and slept in that morning, we were so tired. When I woke up my first thought was, 'OK, this is it. This is the day.' I was pretty scared. Tookie and I knew that right up until the broadcast started we had some control over everything; but after that, we'd have to let it go.

It was going to be on its own." This final draft of the show's script is the last chance Randall will have to shape the evening. He glances out the window. It's cloudy. Oh, God. What if it rains?

Laura Milliken, who had flown into Winnipeg only a couple of days before, is still getting herself oriented. She is standing in a big field at the Forks, watching the crew erect the outdoor stage, setting up the scaffolding and lighting that in just ten hours will illuminate dozens of Canada's most distinguished Aboriginal performers. She is the stage manager for tonight's live show; it will be her job to make sure that every single singer, dancer, host, speaker and musician is prepared, equipped, rehearsed, made-up, ready for their cue—and happy. She had just finished a gig as stage man- ager for the National Aboriginal Achievement Awards, a huge production, and until today she hadn't really worried about this event—it was, after all, a much smaller show. But as she watches the set-up crews assembling the stage, and as the first young dancers begin to gather around the front of the stage, she realises that this is going to be different; it's going to be both a live show and a live broadcast. No asking the audience to wait patiently while the next act assembles on stage. No editing. No second chances.

The biggest part of any television system is the part that doesn't show. As viewers, we think of television in terms of production—studios and field cameras—and our home receiver. But the heart of broadcasting is distribution—the process of getting sound and pictures into your home.

In southern Canada, that's never been a challenge. In the 1970s and 80s, most Canadians lived within a narrow band of cities north of the US border. Television signals were transmitted between cities and regions by microwave, satellite or cable. Within settled areas, programming was then broadcast over the air to TV sets with antennas within range of a transmitter, or sent by copper wire or optical cable from a cable company. Personal satellite dishes were years away.

But there were no cables, phone lines or microwave links—or even highways—connecting the Arctic to southern Canada. All television signals in the North, and on many remote reserves, arrived by satellite. And satellite time was still a rare and very expensive commodity. Inukshuk and the other groundbreaking experiments had been granted free access to Anik for the duration of the projects, but those days were gone.

The issue was summed up succinctly in the findings of the 1986 Task Force on Broadcasting Policy, dubbed the Caplan-Sauvageau Report, which stated:

> "Although these societies receive funding for production, little thought was given to guaranteeing ways of distributing such programming. It was assumed in the original NNBAP that access to existing distribution systems, such as CBC, would be adequate to enable native broadcasters to reach their intended audiences."[10]

It was becoming painfully obvious that assumption had been mistaken.

CBC's northern television service was one of several regional services augmenting the CBC national network. CBC's mandate is to provide broadcast programming that "reflects Canada and its regions...and reflects the multicultural and multiracial nature of Canada", to ensure all voices were represented on Canadian television. But fiscal, geographic and other constraints made this difficult; the network's limited resources forced it to aim most of its programming at the mainstream, urban, southern, non-Aboriginal viewers who made up the majority of its audience.

CBC operated on a system of tiers, based on the priority of the programming. All viewers in Canada received CBC programming like *The Journal,* deemed by the network to be of national importance. Then each of the regional services was allowed a limited number of hours for news and featured programs within their zone. Aboriginal broadcasters got the leftovers—the post-midnight and pre-dawn timeslots that neither the network nor the regions wanted. In a submission to the CRTC, Rosemarie Kuptana put it succinctly: "God made our land the land of the Midnight Sun. It took CBC to make it the land of midnight television."[11]

Even these late night slots could be, and often were, preempted. Stanley Cup finals, election coverage, breaking news—national CBC programming took precedence over the Northern Service, and the Northern Service took precedence over Aboriginal broadcasting. Many senior CBC officials—most notably Doug Ward, then Vice-President of Regional Programming— were sympathetic to and supportive of the Aboriginal broadcasters; but satellite time was a rare and expensive resource, and there just wasn't enough to go around.

Even so, the Inuit broadcasters were lucky. Some northern regions had virtually no distribution options at all. Producers at the newly established Wawatay broadcast unit prepared a satirical plan to ship videotapes to their potential audiences in northern Ontario using specially trained carrier pigeons.

The solution, however improbable, was obvious. Aboriginal broadcasters needed their own satellite transponder.

»———→ ○ ←———«

Rosemarie Kuptana first joined CBC in Inuvik as an announcer/operator, before moving to Ottawa. Initially hired as assistant to Josepi Padlayat, then President of IBC, she was quickly promoted to Production Coordinator, then

Executive Director, then elected President in 1984. It was clear to Rosemarie that the problem of distribution was likely to remain the major barrier facing the emerging Aboriginal broadcast movement.

Debbie Brisebois, IBC's new Executive Director, agreed. A former journalism student, Debbie had been working as a media liaison officer with ITC when IBC was created. She was fascinated with the North; and when a contract position with IBC became available, she jumped, and shortly afterward came on staff. She and Rosemarie both saw that IBC's survival would depend on access to guaranteed distribution. And the best possible option—however unimaginable—was obviously a northern television network.

The idea had first been proposed in a 1982 discussion paper drafted by IBC, a planning document which had also grandly proposed to take over the entire operation of the CBC Northern Service. That plan was quickly dropped, but the concept of a northern channel was not.

One of the unintended consequences of the NNBAP was the emergence of a new, informal network of like-minded young Aboriginal broadcasters. The Program provided a forum in which these new media activists could meet, brainstorm, develop ideas and learn from each other. "We were all pretty much working on our own in the early days, but we were all talking to each other about the same problems," said Debbie Brisebois. "And the biggest problem was distribution." As cancellations and late night timeslots among the groups increased, the notion of a northern channel began to look more and more attractive.

IBC revisited its 1982 discussion paper. "We took the original plan for a northern network, tightened it up, and submitted it to the government, with copies to some of the other groups," said Debbie. "It was a trial balloon. We wanted to see who would jump in and who would back away."

The first response came quickly. "It was late on a Friday night, just a few weeks after we had submitted our position paper," Debbie recalls, "And Rosemarie and I were the only ones left in the office. And these two guys came in, waving a copy of our paper around. They said, "What are you doing? Why didn't you talk to us?""

The two guys were George Henry and Ken Kane from Whitehorse. After journalism school, George worked at CBC radio in Whitehorse as a producer and announcer before moving to NNBY. Alog with Ken Kane, he had been instrumental in persuading NNBY to jump with both feet into radio and television production. They now found themselves struggling with exactly the same distribution challenge as IBC, and had reached the same conclusion; the North needed its own transponder—its own channel on the satellite. The discussion that night moved from the IBC office to a downtown restaurant and continued late into the night, as the four broadcasters compared notes and brainstormed approaches.

That evening marked the beginning of a strategic partnership that would quickly expand from NNBY, IBC and TNI to include the whole Aboriginal broadcasting community across the North. But while the initial discussion paper proved a catalyst for drawing the broadcasters together, the federal reaction was initially disappointing.

"We got no formal response from the Government on the position paper, even though we flogged it everywhere we could," said Rosemarie. "We pitched the dedicated northern transponder idea at every possible CRTC hearing, at every meeting with every Deputy Minister, at every AGM we attended. It was a lot of work. But for the longest time we didn't seem to be getting any response. And the distribution issue was getting worse and worse. CBC had no time left to give us."

"We had been working for two years on a new children's show called *Takuginai*" recalls Debbie Brisebois. "It was going to be the first Aboriginal-language children's show on TV. We did two years of research, audience testing, consultation with teachers and elders—we built a special studio and trained a special crew. An unbelievable amount of work had gone into getting it just right. We promoted the first show for months. Everyone knew about it, everyone was excited, and everyone was watching. The day it was supposed to premiere, Ronald Reagan was visiting Ottawa, and everything else got bumped off the air. So people tuned in to see Inuktitut-language puppets—and got Ronald Reagan."

With the tacit agreement of the other NNBAP broadcasters, and some quiet backstage support from sympathetic bureaucrats, Rosemarie, George and others stepped up the lobbying.

"We met with anybody that would talk to us," said Rosemarie. "David Suzuki, Jean Chrétien, any federal politician who was interested in broadcasting or native issues. We weren't going to take no for an answer. If we couldn't get in one door, we'd try another."

Their persistence began to bear fruit. References to native broadcasting began to appear in federal reports and academic papers. The 1986 Caplan-Sauvageau report dedicated an entire chapter to Aboriginal broadcasting, including recommendations to affirm "the right of native peoples to broadcasting services in Aboriginal languages" that research and consultation should be carried out among Aboriginal people in the South to identify regional needs, and that Native language broadcasting should be provided with "sufficient funds to cover the cost of...training." Perhaps the most important recommendation was: "as production levels warrant and as public funds become available, a separate satellite distribution system should be established to carry native-language programming produced by independent native communications societies and the CBC." [12]

The movement got another boost in early 1987 when Ross Harvey, a Deputy Minister with the Government of the Northwest Territories, organised a formal meeting of stakeholders in Yellowknife to talk about how a dedicated northern channel might work. Greg Smith, a founder of the Inuvialuit Communications Society and its Executive Director in the early 1980s, helped coordinate and chair the meeting. The participants were a diverse group with diverse goals—civil servants, northern broadcasters, educators and consultants, and during the opening statements there didn't seem to be much agreement; each speaker was firm about what they wanted to see in any service. But over the course of two days of discussion and debate, a consensus began to take shape. "Reaching agreement wasn't actually that difficult," Greg recalled. "Everyone knew each other, everyone was running on NNBAP funding, and everyone was used to meetings." By the end of the two days participants had agreed, in broad strokes, on their vision: a new organisation, Television Northern Canada (TVNC), which would share a satellite channel, managed by the members and dedicated to northern programming. The goals of the new network would be the promotion and protection of cultures and languages of Canada's northern peoples.

The report emerging from the meeting provided the first glimpse of what

TVNC might actually look like, with a description of how such a network could be governed, funded, managed, and structured technically. It gave shape and substance to what had been a broad, amorphous concept. From this point forward, broadcasters, funders and bureaucrats could work toward a tangible concept that looked, for the first time, like an achievable reality.

The meeting and subsequent report caught the attention of communications policy shops within the federal, territorial and provincial governments. The 1983 NNBAP had been touted as a "Liberal" party achievement, a nod to an Aboriginal electorate that traditionally voted Liberal. But a surprising axis of political support was emerging within the new Progressive Conservative government. The Premier of the Northwest Territories, Dennis Patterson, was a Frobisher Bay lawyer and a strong supporter of IBC. He was also a prominent Conservative with the ear of the federal cabinet, many of whom were genuinely progressive, with a real interest in Aboriginal Affairs. Flora MacDonald, the Conservative Minister of Communications, was particularly intrigued by the TVNC concept, and saw it as a realistic response to the Caplan-Sauvageau report. And when the Minister comes onside, things happen.

In June, 1988—just six years after the initial IBC position paper, four years after the fateful Elgin St. summit between IBC and NNBY, and one year after the Yellowknife planning meeting—the Department of Communications announced $10 million for four years to establish Television Northern Canada. The funding would cover a three-year planning stage, the lease of a satellite transponder, and the establishment of uplinks and local transmitters in communities across the North from Labrador to the Yukon. The new network was scheduled to begin broadcasting in 1991 following the launch of the new Anik E-1 satellite.

The missing piece of the puzzle had finally fallen into place: Aboriginal broadcasters across the North would produce the programming, and TVNC would handle distribution.

Jerry Giberson, IBC's Director of Operations, was assigned the daunting task of pulling together the hundreds of technical and organisational threads. The three-year planning window had initially seemed generous—until Jerry worked out what actually had to be done.

The first step was incorporating an organisation based on the loose, collegial group of associates that had been involved to date. The founding members of the new not-for-profit network would be IBC, NNBY, TNI, the OKalaKatiget Society in Labrador, Native Communications Society-NWT, the Inuvialuit Communications Society (ICS), as well as Yukon College and the Government of the Northwest Territories (GNWT). The final member was the National Aboriginal Communications Society (NACS), an advocacy group funded by the federal Department of the Secretary of State, representing all NNBAP-funded organisations.

The membership was virtually the same collection of broadcasters and educators who had met in Yellowknife—northern groups with programming to distribute to northern audiences. Each of the territorial governments hoped to use the new network to broadcast coverage of their legislative proceedings, and northern school boards were already working on educational programming. Non-native broadcasters like the CBC and NNBAP-funded Aboriginal radio networks became associate members. The associates had no voting status on the TVNC Board, but did provide programming to the new network. Associate members included CBC Northern Service, Kativik School Board in northern Quebec, Labrador Community College, Northern Native Broadcasting-Terrace, Telesat Canada and Wawatay Native Communications Society.

TVNC's mission statement summarised the goal of the new organisation.

> Television Northern Canada shall be a dedicated northern satellite distribution system for the primary benefit of Aboriginal people in the North, by which residents of communities across northern Canada may distribute television programming of cultural, social, political and educational importance to each other, increasing communications access and promoting dialogue in their remote and underserved homelands."

The technical side of the organisation was relatively straightforward.

Programming would be uplinked from three sites co-located with the TVNC members in Whitehorse, Yellowknife and Iqaluit. Those three sites could broadcast live from their studios, or play back videotapes from the other TVNC members. The programming would be fed to the satellite, bounced back down to TVRO (Television Receive Only) dishes in 96 northern communities, then relayed to a transmitter for local broadcast.

The real challenges were management and administrative, the biggest of which was scheduling. TVNC's coverage area stretched across five different time zones; a live suppertime newscast from the Yukon would be seen at 11 pm in Labrador. Certain shows—children's programming, for example— needed to be aired within a specific time block. And, of course, each of the member organisations wanted to ensure that they received a fair share of prime time slots. But through endless meetings, considerable goodwill, and the spirit of northern consensus, a schedule took shape.

The last hurdle was a formality—the preparation of an application to the CRTC for a network license.

As the network took shape, the programming produced by TVNC members was hitting new heights of both quality and popularity. Despite late-night timeslots, recurring cancellations and absurdly low production budgets, Aboriginal programming remained a huge hit with northerners. Audience surveys from this time showed that 90% of Inuit in Labrador watched regional Inuktitut-language programs regularly, 94% of First Nation viewers in the Yukon watched Nedaa (NNBY's flagship program), and 92% of Inuit in Nunavut said they were satisfied or very satisfied with IBC programs.[13] Young children were learning language skills, adults were learning traditional crafts, and northerners were beginning to turn to their regional Aboriginal broadcaster as an important source of news and entertainment.

Talented, creative young artists were drawn to the new medium, and began to develop production techniques to overcome the low-budget limitations. A group of trainees in Baker Lake discovered a special effect that appeared to make their station manager, Peter Tapatai, fly. When they persuaded him to don red long johns, wellington boots and a blue cape, a northern legend was born. *Super Shamou*, a paunchy, balding, amiable superhero, starred in several vignettes, a comic book, a poster campaign, and became an improbable hit on the southern art-video circuit. *Nedaa*, the flagship news program of the Yukon, attracted corporate sponsorship and achieved a level of polish comparable to that of any slick southern newsmagazine show. And in Igloolik, Zak Kunuk and Paul Apak, two IBC employees, began to perfect a low-key, intensely personal documentary style that would eventually lead to an astonishing international film award at the Cannes Festival.

All this success, of course, meant it was time for the axe to fall.

$$\gg\!\!\longrightarrow\circ\longleftarrow\!\!\ll$$

Like most non-profit organisations in Canada, Aboriginal broadcasters listened carefully to each new federal budget, usually tabled in February. Some referred to it as "reading the tea leaves"; cultural groups who depend on government programs learn quickly to track the political winds. But there was no reason for concern in February 1990; while the federal government had made noises about the national debt and deficit, the guarantee of funding for TVNC seemed to confirm their commitment to Aboriginal broadcasting.

Catherine MacQuarrie was in Yellowknife on Budget Day 1990. "I had just found out I was pregnant, and I had quit smoking that very day. Then I got the call from Ottawa. We were going to lose seventy percent of our funding by the end of the fiscal year, which was six weeks away. We were running the newspaper and a full radio service, and getting ready to expand into television. And suddenly we had six weeks to figure out how we were going to survive with almost three quarters of our funding gone. I called in the editor and the broadcast manager to tell them the bad news. And then I went out and bought a pack of cigarettes."

The news was shocking. Without consultation and without warning, the $3.45 million NCP, which funded Native publications and radio stations in both southern and northern Canada, was eliminated completely and immediately. The NNBAP was being slashed by 16%, approximately $2.2 million. No rationale was given; the cuts were not based on the value or success of the Programs, but on the likelihood of political repercussions.

Similar cuts were made to women's programs, but a national outcry reminded policy makers that women represented 50% of the electorate, and the funding was hastily restored. As one cynical observer put it at the time: "Natives don't control that many ridings, and they all vote Liberal anyway. This is a cut the government thought they could get away with."

And they did. Public reaction in the North was swift and furious: there were demonstrations in several communities, and Secretary of State Gerry Weiner was burned in effigy—a first for Frobisher Bay. But women's, arts, and cultural groups in the South were also protesting, and the anger in the North drew little media or political attention.

The cuts had an immediate and profound effect on all the NNBAP-funded societies. Several long-standing newspapers shut down immediately, or limped along for a year before closing. IBC shut down its entire Kitikmeot operation: among the layoffs was Inuit elder James Kavanna, an audience favourite who had decided five years earlier to enter the television industry at the tender age of sixty-five.

Some organisations, like the tiny OKalaKatiget Society of Labrador, vowed to continue to do the same with less. In most cases, the result of that decision was simply a more prolonged cycle of exhaustion, cuts, and layoffs. But many northern producers could not accept the notion of shutting down what they had worked so hard to build.

The cuts would have been catastrophic at any time; but the impending launch of TVNC made the decision almost surreal. The federal government was creating a whole new Aboriginal channel, while decimating the producers who were supposed to program it. Some broadcasters felt the decision was too damaging to have been an accident, but not everyone agreed. "Everyone tended to see deliberate assimilation conspiracies in those funding cuts", said Terry Rudden. "But not this time. This was just pure, ham-fisted incompetence." Hooked on the North, Terry had moved on from training workshops with the Inukshuk Project, and joined IBC for ten years as their training director. Late in 1989 he decided it was time to make room for new skills in the organisation, and accepted a job with the NNBAP. The day after he tendered his resignation at IBC, the NNBAP funding cuts were announced. His last act at IBC was writing strongly worded letters protesting the cuts; his first act as a bureaucrat was responding to them.

"It wasn't just that the right hand didn't know what the left hand was doing," he said. "The hands were attached to two different bodies on two different planets."

The cuts forced a reconsideration of TVNC's strategy. Many of the radio only NNBAP groups had been ramping up their production capacity, seeking alternative sources of funding so that they could contribute programming to TVNC. Those plans were now out the window; everyone was going to have to scramble just to sustain their existing programming. New services were out of the question.

The TVNC Board wrestled with new approaches to generate revenue to replace the lost funding, and to fill potential gaps in their schedule. Advertising, the sale of unused transponder space, infomercials, corporate sponsorships, and many other options were discussed. One option, however, was not.

The members agreed that the cuts could not be allowed to kill TVNC. The network would proceed with the requirements for a broadcast license, and stick with its original launch schedule.

The need for an Aboriginal voice at the national level was brought home to Canadians that summer when a handful of Mohawk warriors took action to defend their territory from the encroachment of a golf course onto their traditional lands outside Oka, Quebec. The legal dispute erupted into a blockade, and then escalated into an armed standoff, with sympathetic demonstrators erecting highway and bridge blockades across the country. Dazed Canadian viewers were confronted nightly with images of violence, some of which have become iconic—smoke and burning barricades, steely-eyed confrontation, men masked with bandannas and brandishing warrior flags and rifles. The perspective of the mainstream media was, once again, that of non-native onlookers watching violent demonstrators setting fires, threatening the peace, and confronting "our" soldiers and "our" police. During the occupation there was little or no serious media analysis of the legal foundation of the Mohawk claim to their land, or recognition of the ignorance, racism and frustration that had brought about the crisis. Media stereotypes prevailed—stereotypes not that far removed from the Wild Indian clichés of the forties and fifties.

The Mohawk side of the Oka story would eventually be told by documentary filmmakers like Alanis Obomsawin. Alanis is Abenaki, from the Odanak First Nation in Quebec. Initially a singer, writer and artist, she became a filmmaker in the late 1960s, winning a reputation and many awards for her uncompromising documentaries on issues important to Aboriginal people. Alanis spent 78 days behind the barricades, recording shocking, heartwrenching footage that would eventually form the basis of four powerful films on Kanesatake. But her award-winning documentaries of the stories and people of this time and place would only be broadcast in 1993. In the meantime, the story was told almost exclusively by non-native journalists, with the Aboriginal story largely limited to fuzzy silhouettes among the pines, filmed over the shoulders of soldiers and police.

History was being made, and there was no doubt whose perspective was going to dominate the record. The Oka crisis was a constant shadow in the background as the TVNC board prepared its broadcast license application through the summer of 1990, a sobering reminder of why TVNC was needed.

The Canadian Radio-Television and Telecommunication Commission (CRTC) regulates Canada's broadcasting industry. In order to broadcast radio or television signals or to own and operate satellite networks, a license is required. The CRTC acts within the policy framework of the Broadcasting Act and the Telecommunications Act; it ensures that Canadian content is fairly represented in the mix of services available to viewers, and creates policies to regulate the broadcasting and telecommunications industry.

The case of TVNC was unusual, since the network's funding had been announced before TVNC could even apply for a broadcast license. Nevertheless, a license would still be required. Jerry Giberson and Ross Harvey, recently seconded from the GNWT to support the network, began working on the application.

Advising them was Patrick Tourigny, who had left the cable industry and joined the CRTC as Policy Advisor on Pay and Specialty Services. Pat had followed the development of northern broadcasting closely ever since his early support for training in the Ottawa Cablevision days. As a policy advisor, he was delighted at the chance to support the movement once again, and determined to see the TVNC application go through.

"There was never any doubt that TVNC was going to be approved for a license," he says."But we had to make sure they had a solid plan, and that the federal government was serious about the funding. So I helped stickhandle it through the CRTC."

One result of Patrick's "stick handling" was a subtle shift of focus in the wording of the application. While the Aboriginal broadcasters had provided the impetus for TVNC, the original proposal described the network as a "northern broadcast undertaking" because it included the GNWT and Yukon College; both public, non-native institutions with plans to provide educational programming. Patrick urged the TVNC Board to describe TVNC as both a northern network and a native undertaking. This slight change had enormous implications eight years later: as a network with members in three territories and three provinces, TVNC would be able to present itself as a de-facto national Aboriginal service, a major selling point in its transition to APTN.

After months of research and drafting, all the "i"s were dotted and all the "t"s were crossed. George Henry, Jerry Giberson, Ross Harvey, and Alex MacGregor (an engineer and technical advisor) presented TVNC's application for a license at a public hearing in the summer of 1991. TVNC had done its homework, and the presentation was brief and upbeat. George Henry, in particular, spoke passionately about the need for a dedicated satellite. The last statement of the submission was a simple, powerful summary of the case for TVNC. "Information is power. To own and control the vehicle of one's own information and cultural dissemination places responsibility directly in the hands of those most concerned; the Aboriginal people of northern Canada."

In a decision delivered in October, 1991, the CRTC agreed. "TVNC represents the culmination of several years of planning and negotiations on the part of the consortium members. As a direct result of their considerable efforts, northern Aboriginal peoples will finally have access to a native-controlled broadcasting service dedicated to meeting their specific linguistic and cultural needs."

CRTC Chairman Keith Spicer was ebullient, telling the *Ottawa Citizen:* "TVNC's diverse programming is a wonderful example of how the broadcast industry can help Canadians forge new links with one another across our vast country." [14]

And there was even more good news in the summer of 1991. The federal government—the same government which, one year earlier, had slashed NNBAP funding—announced significant changes to the Broadcasting Act, the first since 1976. Among its other provisions, the new Act stated that the Canadian broadcasting system would have to "serve the needs and interests, and reflect the circumstances and aspirations, of Canadian men, women and children, including equal rights, the linguistic duality and multicultural and multiracial nature of Canadian society and the special place of Aboriginal peoples within that society." It was a powerful statutory acknowledgement that Aboriginal peoples had the right to a broadcasting service that met their needs.

The last hurdle had been cleared, and TVNC was a licensed television network. Now the real work of implementing the vision and the plan started in earnest—technical installations in all the communities to be completed and tested, offices to be established, corporate policies and procedures to be hammered out, and new staff to be hired and trained.

One of the first people to come on board at TVNC was Scheduling Officer Linda O'Shaughnessy. Linda was a young Inuit woman born in Baker Lake, Nunavut. Her family moved to Ottawa for a few years in the 1980s, and she attended high school there. "It was a co-op high school program, and I got to do my co-op at IBC. That got me interested in TV." So she continued her studies at Algonquin College, specialising in radio and television arts. The creation of TVNC provided her with the rare opportunity to work in her field within an Aboriginal organisation. "I was living in Ottawa, but I knew there was going to be a job in Iqaluit. That was fine: I thought perhaps I might try it for a year." Soft spoken, well-organised and unflappable, Linda proved to be the perfect scheduling officer, soothing ruffled feathers, calming anxious producers and dealing with the dozens of daily crises inherent in management of program traffic. As of this writing, nearly twenty years after she joined TVNC, Linda is still with APTN.

With staffing and technical design well in hand, TVNC turned its attention to the upcoming launch. A Planning Committee was struck to develop the concept for the inaugural broadcast. One of its members was Abraham Tagalik, who by this time had moved from CBC over to IBC, and was working as Programming Director in Iqaluit. Some member of the Committee wanted a low-key, cautious first broadcast to shake the bugs out of the system: but Abe wasn't interested in playing it safe.

He said, "Let's do something spectacular. Let's link Iqaluit, let's link Yellowknife, let's link Whitehorse. Let's do a big bang here to start the network. We needed something to bring all the players together. We knew the whole northern audience was going to be watching: it was our first and best chance to show people what the network could really do, and give them a taste of what it would be providing."

TV audiences in the South are used to daily national news programs that seamlessly integrate hundreds of segments, live and taped, from around the world. But nothing on that scale had ever been attempted in the North. If it worked, Abe argued, TVNC's launch would showcase both the capacity and the spirit of the new network—a live, three-hour show from the three uplink centres in Whitehorse, Yellowknife and Iqaluit, incorporating community celebrations, live performances, and taped documentary material on the network's history and members.

The Committee agreed. The broadcast was scheduled for January 21, 1992.

》———→ ∘ ←———《

The announcement of a new network didn't attract much media attention in the South. Few national reporters—and few Canadians—understood the Arctic, the history of northern broadcasting, or the significance of TVNC. There was mild curiosity about TVNC's exotic locale, as when the Toronto Star quoted Pat Tourigny shortly before the launch: "Even TVNC's weather reports will be different. When it's 25 degrees below zero in Yellowknife, the southern stations just say it's cold. An Aboriginal broadcaster will say, 'it's a beautiful sunny day and a good day to go ice fishing." But for most journalists, the story was too complicated; and for most Canadians, TVNC was a remote cultural curio they would never see.

CBC management, however, was watching with great interest. Relations between CBC regional offices and Aboriginal broadcasters in the North were characterised by mutual support and respect, tempered with a little friendly rivalry. As launch day grew closer CBC staff lent support, equipment and encouragement to their new "competitor". In Iqaluit, the local station manager quietly set up a spare transmitter at the local high school, where the live launch event was taking place, to feed the signal to TVNC's head end. "I'm sure that was illegal," Abraham said. "We probably should have gotten a broadcast license and all kinds of permissions. But we were all on the same wavelength. Everyone wanted this to work, and we just kind of made the necessary happen."

Just days before the launch, CBC Newsworld, intrigued, agreed to carry a portion of the three-hour launch broadcast on the national network. A northern party had just gone Canada-wide. For anxious producers across the North, the ante had just been upped.

The launch broadcast was built around nine segments, switching at twenty minute intervals from Iqaluit to Yellowknife to Whitehorse, then back again for a new cycle. The Whitehorse segments, produced by broadcaster Joanne Henry, would be hosted out of NNBY's studios, featuring music, and interviews with Board members, staff, elders and supporters of NNBY.

Yellowknife decided to host their launch segments right out in the community. "We wanted a real celebration, an old-fashioned party with bannock, tea and dry meat, and people from all the neighbouring communities," said Catherine MacQuarrie. "So we rented the Yellowknife Elks Hall, the real heart of town, where all the parties happened, where people had been to weddings and played bingo. And I got my mom and her friends, we hauled out the lard and the flour, and for two days, we just made as much bannock as we could make."

Abraham decided that Iqaluit's segments would be staged in an area nick-named "The Pit" at the local high school, a community gathering place overlooking the town. As the site most accessible from the South, Iqaluit got to host the Governor General of Canada, Ray Hnatyshyn. Their line-up also featured a young singer whose first album, not yet released, would make her a household name across Canada—Susan Aglukark.

Terry Rudden was seconded from the NNBAP to coordinate the overall production. "I was never a great producer", he recalls. "But I was a great planner, and that's all TVNC needed. All the great producers were already working flat out on their regional segments. Plus, they got me for free."

The program quickly took shape, and as launch day approached, producers in the three locations rehearsed their talent, readied their segments, and promoted their respective events. On the afternoon prior to the launch the producers held a final conference call to review the line-up, agree on changes, and confirm contingency plans for any of the hundreds of potential disasters inherent in a live broadcast. The call concluded with a round of cheerful, nervous good wishes.

The warm fuzzies melted later that evening when George Henry, a former NNBY Board member, phoned the Iqaluit production team. George had arrived back in Whitehorse to participate in the launch broadcast, and was calling to let Iqaluit know that the Yukon was pulling out of the joint broadcast, and would air their own launch special independently following the main network launch. Following an hour of panic, the issue was resolved by a call to Joanne Henry, producer of the Yukon segments, who happened to be George's sister. Everything was settled, Yukon was back in, and no bill was ever submitted to TVNC for the large hole that one team member punched in the drywall beside the phone in Iqaluit during the conversation with George.

Launch day dawned clear and very, very cold, right across the Arctic. For Linda O'Shaughnessy, now the network scheduling director in Iqaluit, the day was about tapes, dozens of them—intros, program previews, pre-taped greetings from politicians and celebrities, backgrounders on the TVNC member organisations, mini-documentary segments about the network, and a special audio cassette, solemnly hand-delivered by an RCMP officer, containing the official Vice-Regal March that had to accompany the Governor General's entrance. Every tape to be checked, re-timed, cued up, labelled, and loaded for playback.

As the sign-on approached, Terry Rudden, an obsessive worrier, ducked into an empty edit suite for a few moments of silence before the madness of a live, three-hour broadcast. His peaceful meditation ended when the door swung open, the light clicked on, and Abe Tagalik ushered in the Governor General and his wife. "This is the edit room. And this," said Abraham, without missing a beat, "is our launch coordinator. We keep him in here until we need him."

Ten minutes before launch, and a final sound and video check of the network switching system. In Yellowknife, George Tuccaro paced the stage at the Elks Hall, joking, singing, and warming up the audience. George was the consummate northern media host—MC of Yellowknife's famous True North concerts, a popular figure at community events, and a well-known CBC radio and television commentator. His eagerness to host the TVNC launch was typical of the cooperation between northern public broadcasters. On launch day, there was no rivalry.

In Iqaluit, one minute before broadcast, a nervous sound man cued the audio tape with the Governor General's march, unaware that the sound was feeding into The Pit. The Governor General and his RCMP bodyguard, both waiting backstage, heard the cue, looked at each other, shrugged, and moved through the curtain onto the stage. There was a weak ripple of confused applause. The floor director lunged forward, and, in a heroic act of potential treason, shoved the startled representative of the Queen back behind the curtain just as the cameras came up.

And then TVNC was on the air, and suddenly no one was nervous anymore. Now it was just a television show, and everyone knew what to do.

The first words heard on the world's first Aboriginal TV network were a prayer from elder Akeeshoo Joamie, asking the Lord to guide TVNC to success. Abraham Tagalik, huddled in a hooded parka, greeted viewers from the driveway just outside the studio, windblown in midwinter Arctic darkness, his voice almost inaudible under a howling wind. Cut to Yellowknife for greetings from Catherine MacQuarrie, George Tuccaro, and an Elks' Hall jammed with cheering Yellowknifers warmed up by Catherine's mother's bannock. Then to the Yukon, where beaming broadcast veterans Joanne Henry and Bob Charlie welcomed Canada to its newest network.

Back to Iqaluit, where Governor General Ray Hnatyshyn reminded the audience at Inukshuk High School, and the thousands watching, that TVNC was the embodiment of the most memorable phrase in Canada's national anthem, the 'true North strong and free'. Down in Ottawa, a group of employees, fans and friends of native broadcasting, gathered on Parliament Hill to watch the launch, burst into applause.

The emotion in all three locations was almost overpowering. Abraham, backstage, scanned the audience in Iqaluit. "They were all there. Inuit broadcasters from Northern Quebec, from Labrador, from Ottawa, from Montreal. Bureaucrats who had fought on our side. Family members. Friends. All the people who had built the network. It was very moving."

No one was particularly moved in the control room, where the gremlins that infest every live broadcast had just materialized. Terry Rudden was on the phone to Yellowknife, ten minutes into the first Iqaluit segment. "I was counting them down to their first feed. And I heard a very quiet "pop"; our Yellowknife monitor went black, and someone at the other end of the phone said, very softly: "Oh, shit."

The TV lights had blown a fuse in the Elks Hall. And not a common household fuse, but a massive industrial fuse. An audience of hundreds, including the crew and performers, were sitting in the dark, with three minutes to their first segment.

"Joanne Henry in the NNBY Whitehorse studio told us Yukon could be ready in two minutes. We told Yellowknife they had twenty minutes to fix whatever was wrong, and revised the program line-up on the fly."

Iqaluit counted down to Whitehorse, and Whitehorse was ready. A beaming Joanne Henry lit up the studio with her smile and her greeting, "Welcome to a new day in Aboriginal broadcasting!" Jerry Alfred, a Keeper of the Songs for the Northern Tutchone, tore into a song. Yukoners reminisced about the road to TVNC and marvelled at the achievement. "Not too many people get to realize their dreams or see their visions become a reality. I've been fortunate; this is going to be one of those days," said Ken Kane. "It will stay with me forever. This is a great day to celebrate." Yukon Premier Tony Penikett congratulated the new network.

Meanwhile in Yellowknife, some unsung broadcast hero raced out of the Elk's Hall, down the street to a nearby hotel, and "borrowed" the necessary fuse. Somehow within twenty minutes the crew got power up, everything rebalanced and remixed, restored the connection, and Yellowknife was ready for the next switchover. To host George Tuccaro, this was all business as usual. "The power was always going out in Yellowknife back in those days. I just kept talking in the dark, and the lights eventually came back on."

George laughed and joked with NWT Premier Nellie Cournoyea, then introduced a line-up that included everything from the NWT's finest traditional throat singers to contemporary rock bands. At the back of the hall, an exhausted Catherine MacQuarrie watched the culmination of the last years unfold. "I get teary-eyed thinking about the launch," said Catherine MacQuarrie. "The place was packed, about 300 or 400 people. I remember a lot of laughter and the look on people's faces. It was an amazing feeling. This group of people—they had started in a world where there was no media, and they had created their own television network. It really happened." There wasn't time for too much tearful introspection, though—as George introduced the Métis Dancers, she hurried to the serving table to check on the bannock supply.

Backstage, Wayne McKenzie, on loan from CBC, was monitoring the feed and lining up videotapes to feed into the show. Wayne was a young Gitxsan from B.C., intensely interested in television, and a technical producer with CBC—the only game in town. But as he cued and rolled segments in to the launch broadcast, he realized he was seeing a whole new world opening up. "That was a really big night for me," he said. "I just soaked it all in. I remember thinking, 'This is going to mean big things for Aboriginal broadcasting.'"

In the audience and enjoying the party was J.C. Catholique, a Dene from Lutsel'Ke on the shores of Great Slave Lake. He had joined NCS in its early days as a photographer and columnist; within months he would become president of the organisation and join the Board of TVNC. Like everyone else in the room, he was caught up in the spirit of celebration. But that night, for the first time, he caught a glimpse of what might be possible. "We could see what was going on, up on these big TV screens. It would go from Iqaluit then to Whitehorse, then to us in Yellowknife. And I thought, what if this kept going, and it went around the world? What if it was for all

Aboriginal people? That thought stayed with me for years."

Back to Iqaluit, and the jubilant audience grew quiet as a slim, shy Inuit singer in jeans stepped onstage. Susan Aglukark was at the very beginning of her performing career; but her sweet, clear voice singing "Song of the Land" offered a hint of the superstar she would become.

But the evening belonged to another Inuit star. Joanassie Salomonie, the Iqaluit host, announced one last, special guest. "He just flew in all the way from Baker Lake. Ladies and gentlemen—Super Shamou!" The North's own superhero strode onstage in his trademark red underwear and Wellington boots, and the crowd erupted in laughter and applause. He was immediately surrounded by a swarm of awed children, and led them offstage to the celebratory cake.

Yellowknife ended its segment on a high note with music, applause, and a promise from George Tuccaro. "We'll see you on the airwaves when we come back with Television Northern Canada!"

The last word of the night was left to Joanne Henry in Whitehorse. "Glad you could join us for this first broadcast of TVNC", she said. "A new window on the world has just opened. And everything you've seen tonight is just the beginning." It may have been the most prophetic statement of the whole evening.

"In Iqaluit, we watched the credits roll," said Terry Rudden. "And then the screen faded to black, and we just stared at each other. Some folks in the control room were crying, some of us were hugging. Mostly we were just dazed and exhausted. Then Jerry said: 'Anybody want to watch it again'? And we did. All three hours. And then we all went home and went to bed."

CHAPTER III

THE AUDIENCE

THE NEED TO EXPAND SOUTH

Noon, September 1, 1999.

Empty donut boxes and crushed cups litter the backstage. The setup crew down at the Forks is running on the broadcaster's Breakfast of Champions—pure Timmy's coffee and carbs. They've been working since dawn, assembling the stage, the lights, and the sound system for the three-hour extravaganza, the live concert and broadcast that will feature dozens of entertainers, with Susan Aglukark as the headliner. No sunrise ceremony, no boat cruise for the techs— these guys are putting together the nuts and bolts of tonight's launch, and there's no time for reflection about the meaning of it all. This is TV, and there's a show happening tonight.

The hired production team from CKND, the local Canwest Global station, pulls in backstage. Global has been contracted by APTN to provide a mobile truck, cameras, technical crew and a dish to uplink the signal to the satellite for relay into homes across Canada. Compared to the APTN staff and volunteers, the hired Canwest-Global crew is remarkably calm. The same team had just completed live coverage of a week of the Pan-American Games. This little one-nighter is no biggie. Just another contract.

Their matter-of-fact attitude puts Randall McKenzie at ease. "They knew what they were doing, and they had everything we needed. All I really wanted one of those cool cameras with the jib, so it could manoeuvre and get good shots of the entertainers, and they had one. I was glad about that."

Laura Milliken is pacing back and forth on the stage, going over the final list of performers just faxed to her. She's realizing that this is, in fact, nothing like the National Aboriginal Achievement Awards. She stops pacing, and does a quick calculation in her head. There are thirteen artists on the list. Duane Shuttleworth, the event organizer, had told each performer they could sing up to four songs. Duane is a fundraising and organizational genius, but he's never worked in live television. Laura has.

Thirteen performers, four songs each, average of four minutes per song. That ate up the entire three hour window. But there are speeches to fit in there, and introductions, and set changes. "They have got to be joking," she thinks. What is she going to say to the performers?

Bruce Spence is breathing a sigh of relief. He has just submitted the final script he wrote for the on-stage hosts. Bruce is an Ojibway writer, born and raised in Winnipeg and contracted by APTN to write intros and stage chat. That was no big deal for Bruce – until he learned that he was going to be scripting for Alanis Obomsawin and Marty Ballentyne. "Yeah, I was nervous having to write for those two. Especially for Alanis. I wrote something in the script with the word 'warrior' in it, but we had a different opinion of what that word meant. So I had to make some adjustments to the script. That gave me just enough time to make copies and get them over to them, and rehearse." Then his job was done. Now he could have lunch and wait until the show started at 7 pm.

Gil Cardinal is sitting in front of the stage, stopwatch in one hand and clipboard in the other. Crews are setting up microphones, running cables and hanging backdrops while musicians try to get the mix on the monitors, dancers rehearse their steps, and the kids of the crew members and performers chase each other between the mic stands.

In just five short hours he is going to have to sort this chaos into a coherent broadcast for a national audience of—well, no one is quite sure. Everyone in Canada? Maybe just our immediate families?

It's been more than twenty years since Gil directed a live TV show. His last few years have been spent directing films. Exhausting, exhilarating, painstaking work, yes. But on a film set, the director is in control. Live TV, on the other hand, is a high-wire act without a net. There's no tape-delay, no second chances. Every glitch is seen immediately. Gil sits in front of the stage, trying to visualize every moment, every angle, every camera position.

"I was sitting there, making notes and sketches, and I was getting lost. Totally lost. I mean, you could sit there all day, playing with a pen and paper, trying to figure out this shot, this shot, that shot. I was falling way behind. And the clock kept ticking…"

The TVNC Board quickly discovered a sobering reality long understood by couples everywhere. Weddings are fun: marriages are hard work.

But in between, there's usually a honeymoon, and for a few weeks the northern broadcasters basked in the glow of their new network. The launch had proved that they could handle a challenging broadcast; and the national media and northern audiences were surprised and impressed with the new service.

TVNC was the North—raw, real, and unlike anything Canada had ever seen on television. Instead of how-to programs on home renovation, TVNC featured a detailed, close-up guide to making rope out of a freshly extracted caribou intestine. Tamapta from the Inuvialuit Communications Society and Nedaa from NNBY were magazine-style shows in a familiar format, but there were no serial killers, wars, or celebrity sexual misconduct in the programs. Headline news was more likely the death of an elder or a community meeting on an impending self-government community consultation.

One of the most popular news segments ever aired on TVNC was the story of an eight-legged caribou foetus, discovered by a hunter in Baker Lake, Nunavut. The grisly footage of the bloody foetus was replayed for several days, by request, as northern audiences passionately debated what exactly this strange portent meant. The footage was included in TVNC's promotional reel and, to the secret delight of northern broadcasters, inevitably made government officials blanch at screenings.

Many non-native viewers in Yellowknife and the South were shocked at the prominence of hunting programs, with graphic footage of seal, caribou and muskox being shot and dressed. In some non-native circles, the new channel earned the sobriquet the "Killing Channel". But most TVNC viewers lived in communities where hunting provided a significant portion of the household's groceries, and such fastidious critiques were incomprehensible and irrelevant. Elders were fascinated by hunting techniques from other regions, and younger hunters eagerly absorbed the older hunters' tricks.

And so TVNC found its groove, and Linda O'Shaughnessy settled into the task of programming the network for the long-term.

TVNC was different from other Canadian networks. It was strictly a distributor, not a producer of programming—no network news, no network specials. Everything shown on TVNC was either produced by its members, or acquired. The TVNC members were adamant about this; TVNC exercised no editorial or technical control over their programs.

That created a problem, summed up by Peter Crass, TVNC's Board representative from the GNWT. "Suddenly we had a network that could go on air twenty-four hours a day, seven days a week. But because of the NNBAP cuts just a couple of months before, we didn't have enough funding to produce nearly enough programming to fill those timeslots." The network had to shop for series in the South, seeking out programs that might interest northerners; NFB films, literacy programs, or shows like Dotto's Data Café, a series about using computer technology.

Some of the choices were a bit dubious, including a family counselling program produced in California that featured a very blonde host, offering New-Age advice from a sunny set overlooking the Pacific. That series was not renewed for a second season.

TVNC, with all its quirks, captivated many people, and not just northerners. The network began to receive fan mail from odd corners of the world, including an embassy in South America whose staff had accidentally found this new channel on their satellite feed, and were hooked.

Audiences were happy with the new service. The only common complaint was the lack of original dramatic programming on the network. But the real drama was shaping up behind the scenes.

Private broadcasters are governed by boards and shareholders, with a relatively simple mandate—earn a profit, and meet the terms of your CRTC license. Public broadcasters like the CBC draw direction from a broader but still focused mandate. But as a coalition of public broadcasters, TVNC had to synthesize and reflect several different mandates. Some members were primarily educational broadcasters, while others emphasized cultural or news programming. Some produced 100% of their programming in the Aboriginal language of their region, while others, serving regions with very few native-language speakers, opted for English.

This diversity of mandates was complicated by a two-tiered governance structure. TVNC's full members were the northern, Aboriginal broadcasters funded by the NNBAP, as well as the GNWT and Yukon College. Other educational broadcasters, Telesat Canada, CBC North and southern Aboriginal broadcasters were associate members, without voting privileges. For years the NNBAP groups had been forced to lobby CBC and the governments for airtime or funding; and now, despite the spirit of collaboration that brought TVNC into existence, members were reluctant to admit the CBC as an equal player.

The issue was most often scheduling, and access to preferred timeslots. Since the full members approved the schedule, associate members often found themselves stuck with late night or unpopular timeslots—an ironic echo of the situation the full members had faced themselves just a year earlier.

Associate members felt the network should prepare its schedule based on programming content, quality and audience need, not the status of the producing organization. The educational broadcasters (GNWT, Yukon College and Kativik School Board) wanted clarification as well; was TVNC committed to educational broadcasting, or only to language and cultural programming?

TVNC had established a Programming Committee to handle the issue of content; but these were fundamental questions about the network, and the Committee asked the Board for a policy decision. The Board (whose directors were appointed exclusively by the full members) decided to give first priority in scheduling to full members, and to defer enhancing the status of associate members for two years. That deferral only exacerbated the problem: there seemed to be confrontations at most meetings. "People were drawing their marks in the sand," said Abraham Tagalik. "You could understand why. The Aboriginal broadcasters were claiming their territory. Their funding was getting cut, they were fighting back, and they didn't want to give up an inch. There were a lot of battles. I could understand it, but it was really hard to work like that." He remembers one stormy set of discussions that ended with Marie Wilson, head of CBC Northern Service, asking him privately: "What's the matter? Have we got leprosy or something?"

All in all, managing the prize was tougher than winning it had been—sometimes because of substantive issues, but just as often because of different cultural approaches. Many Canadians don't understand how profoundly First Nations differ from each other, and from Inuit cultures. Inuit do not consider themselves to be First Nations, but a distinct people with a very different culture. And those differences led to some tough meetings. "I had always worked in Nunavut," Abe recalls. "I was used to working with people that I had known most of my life. We have our own way of dealing with conflict—a lot of joking, a lot of talking. But this was the first time I was introduced to real quarrelling at the Board level. Some people had a confrontational way of doing things—I mean full frontal assault—and I thought, 'that's not a good way to do it. It's not my way, and it shouldn't be our way.'"

Further exacerbating these cultural differences were personality issues. George Henry, whose drive and vision had helped create both NNBY and TVNC, was on the Board; and while his tenacity and aggressiveness were exactly what the broadcasters needed at the negotiation table, his abrasive, caustic approach was an anomaly in an organization trying to operate on consensus. His attitude shocked, and occasionally alienated, those who worked with him. Even Catherine MacQuarrie, who went to journalism school with George, found him hard to take. "He was dogged and he was persistent. He was very articulate and a great spokesperson for the network. When he was good, he was amazing," she recalls. "But there were some brutal board meetings because of his manner. He had this bullying nature and a strong personality; and frankly, those meetings weren't very pleasant."

Emotions ran high, and boardroom discussions were intense and sometimes acrimonious. But this was all backstage, and members accepted it as the growing pains of a new organization. What mattered was that northern audiences, for the first time, were finally enjoying a full service TV network infused with their language and culture, and reflecting their reality.

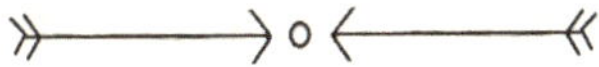

The idea of extending TVNC's service into the South had been part of the vision since the first discussions of a northern network. "In some people's minds", said Catherine MacQuarrie, "TVNC had always been a stepping stone to something bigger."

There were many reasons to seek southern distribution. In the early 1990s southern Canadians, for the most part, knew less about the North than they did about Mexico or central Europe. Northern issues like self-government, land claims, resource development or environmental degradation were not part of the national political dialogue, even though they impacted half of Canada's land mass.

In southern media, the North was an invisible giant, represented by occasional news stories on oil and gas, and old NFB vignettes. A network like TVNC would highlight northern people, cultures and issues to which most Canadians were oblivious.

Northern producers, like producers anywhere, also wanted a bigger audience for their work. With a decade of experience under their belts, Aboriginal filmmakers were emerging as confident, skilled pioneers, with an original and distinctive approach to narration and production. This growth was best exemplified by Igloolik filmmakers Paul Apak and Zak Kunuk, originally IBC employees who left to create their own production company, Igloolik Isuma. Isuma first attracted southern attention with Nunavut, a unique series of historical dramas from an Inuit perspective, produced for TVOntario. Their innovative approach would eventually result in a feature film, Atanarjuat the Fast Runner, which would win worldwide audiences, praise, and eventually a Golden Camera Award at the Cannes Film Festival.

Audiences, exposure, greater political influence, a desire to inform Canadians and share the unique cultures of the North—all good reasons to ponder southern distribution. And then, of course, there was money.

The burden of programming the new network with original material was taking its toll on the NNBAP groups. Underfunded to begin with, and now coping with funding cuts and the pressure of increased broadcast commitments, many exhausted staff members were leaving their organizations.

"I was totally burned out", said Catherine MacQuarrie. "We were stretched way too thin and we were juggling a lot of balls, and I just wasn't able to keep them all in the air."

From Labrador to Whitehorse, staff turnover crept up. By the early 1990s, those who remained found themselves working longer hours in aging facilities with failing equipment. The Inuvialuit Communications Society was so chronically understaffed that manager Debbie Gordon-Ruben found herself doing multiple jobs: overseeing the entire operation while generating story ideas, booking travel, lighting and shooting segments, conducting interviews, and editing entire programs herself. Television may seem like an exotic industry to some, but to Debbie, it all came down to pockets. "I was alone on a lot of shoots where you'd usually have a three-person crew. I always had to make sure I was wearing a jacket that had enough pockets to carry all the cables, microphones and tapes, everything. You just had to get used to it. We all did it. We had no choice."

There was no doubt that southern distribution for TVNC would mean revenue. Larger audiences would justify higher advertising rates; and greater exposure to southern and international markets for members' programming would open up the possibility of sales to other broadcasters. George Henry, now Vice-Chair of TVNC, saw southern distribution as the only answer to the slow erosion of funding for TVNC and its members. "The time has now come for TVNC to market itself and improve the look of the network," he told the Board bluntly. "We need to specifically market the lower half of Canada. The money is there."

The idea was appealing. But most people, including some TVNC members, were skeptical. There was something a bit presumptuous about a year-old regional television service, serving a population somewhat smaller than that of a single southern city, offering to become a national network. And apart from the general hubris of it all, there were some practical obstacles.

In the 1990s, before the proliferation of satellite and digital signals, networks relied on cable companies to distribute their signals. Those cable companies had a limited number of channels they could offer to customers. Convincing a cable company to give up one of their profitable services to carry a brand new, unproven network with uncertain commercial potential was sure to be a huge challenge.

Advertising rates are based on the number of people a broadcaster can reach. A move into the densely cabled south would increase advertising revenues; but it would also drive up programming costs. Networks buy the rights to television programs for a specific region and a specific time period. TVNC was able to buy programs cheaply because they were only being aired in the North; but acquiring programs for a national audience would be significantly more expensive.

Some also wondered how southern audiences would respond to TVNC. Would viewers in Toronto warm to a detailed, close-up, step-by-step "how-to" show on killing, gutting and skinning a seal? Would they accept the slower pace and low-budget look of northern programming? TVNC's schedule was perfectly tailored for northern audiences, but large chunks of it—coverage of the NWT legislative assembly, or Inuktitut regional news without subtitles—would be of dubious interest to a Haida audience in BC, let alone a non-Aboriginal viewer in Québec City or Saskatoon.

And, with barely enough funds to keep the existing network going, how would TVNC afford the massive planning and lobbying effort necessary to convince the CRTC to promote southern carriage of TVNC, to persuade a distributor to pick it up, and to encourage southern viewers to actually watch?

George Henry was never one to worry too much about potential problems. He was fond of pointing out to the skeptics that they were raising exactly the same kind of objections that had been raised to TVNC in the eighties. And TVNC was working, wasn't it?

In the fall of 1992 the CRTC announced a series of structural hearings into satellite and digital technology, and issued a call for comments. The CRTC wanted to know what policy changes would be needed to accommodate Canadian specialty services in areas like distribution, technology, packaging and carriage. It all sounded like very dry stuff. But George Henry, trained as a lawyer, saw the hearings as an opportunity to get TVNC's position on Aboriginal broadcasting within the Canadian broadcasting system on the public record. In 1993 he appeared before the Commission, insisting that TVNC must be included in any discussions about increasing Canadian content and developing new technologies to reach more Canadians.

As a first step towards southern distribution, TVNC began to test the waters with some potential allies. Since its 1981 licence to provide TV and radio signals to the Arctic, Cancom had proven itself supportive of northern broadcasters. So in 1993 TVNC approached Cancom with a proposal: would Cancom work with TVNC to make the northern network available to cable companies in southern Canada?

Cancom's response was positive, but cautious. There were difficulties. TVNC would have to convert some of its uplinks, purchase decoders, and meet standards set by Cancom. There would be an increase in the cost of program acquisition; and TVNC would have to resolve conflicts with members like GNWT who had acquired license rights to programs for northern-only distribution. And once those technical and administrative challenges were overcome, TVNC would still have to compete for a spot on the dial, with a wave of new specialty channels being considered for licence.

Nevertheless, Cancom agreed to endorse the project. In December 1993 the Board approved George Henry's motion "to direct management to begin developing a work plan for the extension of carriage of TVNC's signal into southern Canada, through the Cancom service."

George was elected TVNC Chairman in 1994, and the campaign for southern distribution swung into high gear. The TVNC Board and senior staff began an endless round of meetings with anyone who seemed to offer policy, financial, or technical support—government officials from Heritage Canada, Industry Canada, and Indian and Northern Affairs, cable companies, regulators, other broadcasters. And of course, the network never missed an opportunity to appear before the CRTC. Between 1994 and early 1997, TVNC made nearly a dozen different presentations to the Commission, at hearings on the Cable Production Fund, Cancom's license renewal, and the Information Highway. "They would appear at just about every policy hearing," said Pat Tourigny. "They were knocking on every door, trying to find some answer to their distribution problem." At every presentation, George Henry would urge the Commission to acknowledge and support Aboriginal broadcasters, and to help TVNC find southern distribution and much-needed revenues.

The Commission was sympathetic; but the problem, as always, was money. Pat Tourigny promoted the idea of southern distribution for TVNC within the CRTC; but even Pat had his doubts. "Southern distribution was a great idea. But the CRTC wasn't a funding agency. The money was going to have to come from somewhere."

One positive step was the Commission's inclusion of TVNC on the list of satellite services eligible for carriage in southern Canada. That didn't guarantee any cable operator would include them, since nearly all Canadian-owned services could be added to the list; but it was a first step.

»———→ ο ←———«

At TVNC's Annual General Meeting in the spring of 1995, George Henry repeated the familiar messages—the need to increase members' revenues through access to southern markets, and the critical role of Aboriginal television in the Canadian broadcasting system. But then he introduced a surprising new wrinkle. "A First Nations first level of service must become part of a national basic service on Canadian cable," he told the Board. "And a portion of the cable revenues should flow back to Aboriginal broadcasters."

This was considerably more ambitious than the idea of "TVNC South". For the first time, George was proposing a new national Aboriginal network that all cable subscribers would receive as part of their basic service, just like the CBC.

The notion seemed impossible. TVNC hadn't been able to find a single southern distributor, and now George was proposing a whole national service, with mandatory carriage? Most members were incredulous. Furthermore, his description of a "First Nations channel" rankled the Inuit members, who didn't consider themselves "First Nations".

But George was persuasive, and the members were pragmatic. If George wanted to shoot for the stars instead of the moon, so be it. Most assumed that, whatever George wanted to call it, the southern service was still going to be basically TVNC, with a new name and perhaps some new programming.

With the Board's blessing, Jerry Giberson informed the CRTC that the network was planning to file a new license application "to enable TVNC to become a national Aboriginal channel, distributed across southern Canada." This letter circulated through the Commission, eliciting internal reactions that ranged from enthusiasm to disbelief. But the first formal notice of TVNC's new vision was now on record.

Now on the list of Eligible Satellite Services, TVNC approached several southern distributors to lobby for inclusion in their packages. There wasn't much interest. Shaw agreed to include TVNC in a new direct-to-home (DTH) satellite network package; and Homestar, as part of its promise of performance to the CRTC, committed a portion of its revenue to TVNC member producers. But apart from that, no bites. The fact that cable companies could carry TVNC did not mean that they would. It became clear that voluntary carriage wasn't going to generate the revenues that members needed to deal with diminishing funding and rising costs: TVNC would have to make a strategic choice among its distribution options.

The preferred choice, of course, was George's dream; designation as a mandatory service, meaning all Canadians would receive the TVNC signal, just like CBC and CTV. But TVNC's legal counsel advised against seeking that. One year earlier, the CRTC had conducted a comprehensive review of how and under what rules all current television networks would be broadcast. Since TVNC hadn't been on the list of Eligible Services at the time, the network hadn't filed a submission, and TVNC's lawyers felt it would be "inappropriate for TVNC to request that it receive guaranteed access to cable capacity in the context of the Commission's current proceeding." So it seemed that mandatory carriage was out.

Another option was to seek "dual status", a term used to describe the distribution of certain specialty services. Networks with dual status, such as Vision TV, were intended, but not required, to be distributed as a part of the basic tier, for a very small per-subscriber fee set by the CRTC or, if the network consented, on a high penetration tier for a negotiated fee. Some, like MuchMusic, chose the higher penetration tier and negotiated a higher fee while others, like Vision, opted for wider exposure on basic for the lower fee. These networks were on a short list of services that cable companies could pick and choose from to assemble basic cable packages for subscribers.

Given those options, TVNC could apply to amend its existing licence to qualify as a network with priority cable and DTH carriage on the basic tier. This would mean no subscriber fees, but a chance to earn copyright payments and advertising revenues. Or TVNC could apply for a specialty service licence, which could generate subscriber fees and advertising revenue; but the option of carrying the network would still be left up to the cable companies.

In either scenario TVNC would still be at the mercy of cable companies, which could choose to ignore the network, place it on a discretionary tier, or bundle it as part of an expensive package with other specialty channels. The end result would be a patchwork of inconsistent agreements and a grab-bag of carriage models across southern Canada. That was unacceptable to George Henry, who insisted that TVNC should settle for nothing less than a national, mandatory service. TVNC's lawyers argued that this was unrealistic: their view was, "…the mandatory to basic alternative asks for too much, too soon after TVNC was authorised for national distribution, and it would invite significant negative reaction from the cable industry." George wouldn't budge.

All the additional lobbying, research and preparation of CRTC submissions was costing TVNC money it didn't have. In December 1995, TVNC's finance coordinator warned the Board that TVNC was "treading a fine line" and could "easily run an operational deficit" if spending was not brought under control. The network's financial position was becoming precarious, the status quo wasn't working, and TVNC was facing some tough decisions.

Its members were suffering as well. Brenda Chambers, NNBY's representative on the Board, put it bluntly. "How can TVNC provide an opportunity for our members to make money, to stay alive? In our meetings with the Department of Canadian Heritage, they keep telling us we need 'sustainability'. Increasingly, it seems that the only way to achieve that will be to create a whole Aboriginal network for all of Canada."

A report published in 1996 by the Department of Canadian Heritage confirmed support among the broadcasters for national expansion. "Most groups supported carriage of TVNC signals on southern cable systems, in order to broaden the audience and to reach Aboriginal peoples in southern and urban areas. This measure would generate revenue both through cable subscription charges, and by raising the number of viewers reached by advertising and sponsored programming."

But cable companies still had little or no interest in TVNC, largely because the network remained virtually unknown south of the 60th parallel. It had become part of day-to-day life across the North, like The Bay and CBC Radio; in southern Canada, however, only a handful of broadcasters and regulators had ever heard of it. If TVNC was going to generate any interest, it was going to have to make a grand entry. And in Canadian broadcasting, there's only one place for that.

The Banff International Television Festival is a tiny and demure sliver of Los Angeles glitz held in a resort town famous for its national park, hot springs, fudge shops and overpriced hotels. It's a yearly feeding frenzy of producers, investors, distributers, executives, writers, actors and celebrities, all pitching ideas, signing deals, and trying to fill timeslots for upcoming television seasons. If TVNC was going to step out onto the national stage, Banff was the place to do it.

I had been hired by TVNC in 1995, just months out of journalism school, to help the network with communications, and it was my job to promote TVNC at every opportunity. The Board chose the 1996 Banff Festival for our coming-out party; and like any debutante, we were determined to do it right.

To increase the network's visibility we decided—two months before the event—to hold TVNC's Annual General and Board meetings in Banff, to coincide with the Festival. Booking fifteen rooms during Canada's largest media blowout in a tiny resort town was just about as hard as getting a network licence. But staff finally found rooms at the King Edward Hotel. The Hotel describes itself as "historic", and that it was, evocative of a decaying, late 19th century inn. It was at the noisiest intersection in town, squatting above a saloon—in this case, the Hard Rock Cafe. Fortunately, nobody was in Banff to sleep.

TVNC was everywhere that week. We booked what is grandly termed a "Hospitality Suite"—actually just a glorified hotel room—at the luxurious Banff Springs Hotel, right across from the Festival site. Delegates arriving at the Festival found the lid of a thermal cup in their "swag bags", with a note inviting them up to the TVNC suite to pick up the cup itself—and of course, to meet some TVNC people, screen some unusual programming, and participate in a draw for a beautiful Inuit carving.

George Henry and Abraham Tagalik were taking part in several panel discussions during the Festival, and TVNC producers and members attended every workshop and every screening possible, pumping hands and talking up the network.

It worked. Like the thermal cup lids in the swag bag, TVNC may initially have seemed an amusing novelty to many. But over the course of the Festival dozens of media and industry representatives watched the programming, chatted with the producers, and heard George and Abe share their passion for the network. Exposure at Banff failed to trigger an immediate wave of lucrative distribution deals; but the Canadian media establishment left the Festival knowing that there was a feisty new kid in town.

The real action in Banff, however, happened at the Annual General Meeting.

Previous AGMs had been small, low-key affairs of TVNC members. As part of its profile-raising, TVNC opened its Banff meeting to other Aboriginal organisations, government departments, and television executives. It was the first time many Aboriginal communicators in southern Canada had the opportunity to connect with the northerners.

"Our own board was meeting in Calgary at the time," recalled Dave McLeod, producer and radio host from Native Communications Inc. in Manitoba. "We said, 'let's take some time out to drive to Banff to listen to what TVNC has to say.' We were all pretty excited about it, and we wanted to be there."

What Dave and the other attendees heard at the meeting was a strong, passionate pitch from George Henry on the need for a new, national Aboriginal network. Armed with maps, documents and reports, George Henry outlined TVNC's efforts to secure southern distribution. He explained for the benefit of the new arrivals the importance of the existing network in the North's media landscape, and its critical role as distributor for the NNBAP-funded groups. The network had originally hoped to persuade cable companies to carry TVNC just as it was seen in the north—hunting, native languages, and all. But TVNC now had a bigger vision.

"Through national cable and satellite connections, the North, Aboriginal communities and major centres across Canada will be linked to TVNC", George told the AGM. "That's the first step in creating a national Aboriginal channel." TVNC would continue to seek cable distribution in the South for the existing network, but work towards a broader network, aimed directly at a national—and international—audience. No one knew what that network might look like, in its structure or in its programming; but that was the dream.

Several TVNC members were surprised, and a bit uneasy. To talk about a new national Aboriginal network in-house, or in a policy document, was one thing. To announce your intention to the world at a high profile meeting, with government, media and southern producers hanging on every word, was quite another.

But Dave McLeod and others at the meeting were electrified. "George was full of passion about the possibility of a national Aboriginal television network", he recalled. "It was all very exciting. Of course there were naysayers, people who just didn't think it was possible. I understood that Aboriginal people had been kicked around for so long that some people were cautious. Dreaming about an Aboriginal network was almost too radical. But at that meeting George convinced a lot of people. He stood on top of the mountain and preached. Yes, an Aboriginal television network could work! Yes, Canada had a responsibility to do it! And yes, Aboriginal people have the talent to make it happen! All these years later, that is the message that I remember."

Many southern groups reacted with the same excitement to George's call for a national network. And no wonder. While northern broadcasters had fought for and achieved successes like the NNBAP and TVNC, southern Aboriginal producers had struggled for decades in a funding and policy void.

The Northern Native Broadcast Access Program had been created to produce programming for northern Canada, and TVNC served communities in the Territories and northern edges of the provinces. There was no comparable system of support for the creators and artists in southern First Nation and Métis communities, or in Canadian cities. Support for their work was adhoc, and limited to specific projects. The National Film Board and CBC funded a limited number of Aboriginal productions, most of which were showcased reverently at film festivals, exhibited in small galleries, or aired once and archived. But in southern Canada there was no support for broadcast organisations comparable to the NNBAP.

In the early 1990s, Aboriginal artists created the Aboriginal Film and Video Art Alliance in partnership with the Banff Centre for the Arts, to promote and preserve First Nation culture through the production and distribution of film and video. The partnership collaborated on a number of projects, but the Alliance dissolved in 1998. Some southern Aboriginal producers established artist-run film and video production and distribution centres such as Tribe in Saskatchewan and the Urban Shaman Gallery in Winnipeg. Others partnered with existing film and video centres, like V Tape in Toronto. These centres provided training and opportunities for Aboriginal people to develop skills and share stories. But the works produced through these facilities—often short subjects, experimental works, or personal documentaries—seldom found an audience outside the limited alternative video or indie film festival networks.

Many southern Aboriginal producers looked to the emerging Internet as a tool for broadcasting programs and linking communities. The world of online media obviously held tremendous promise as a forum for cultures and languages; and in 1994 Loretta Todd, Alanis Obomsawin, Buffy Ste. Marie and other influential, forward-looking producers met at the Banff Centre for the Arts to establish a nation-wide computer-based, multi-media telecommunications network. The resulting organisation, drumbytes. org, coordinated various online exhibitions, and created an open-source web site for artists; a precursor to Wikipedia. But in the primitive days before YouTube and high-speed wireless, the Internet was not a practical alternative to conventional broadcasting systems. The project ended when one of its strongest and most creative advocates and contributors, Ahasiw Maskegon-Iskwew, died in 2006.

Twenty-five years after *Challenge for Change* and the NFB's ground-breaking First Nations film-makers, Aboriginal media in Canada was still a nearly invisible niche. Many artists like Tantoo Cardinal and Graham Greene had moved to the United States to work on American programs. Those who remained in Canada, if they were lucky, occasionally got to work on programs designed, managed and produced by mainstream networks like CBC or Vision. At *North of 60*, a CBC hit series that showcased many of Canada's best known Aboriginal actors, writers and directors, all final creative and programming decisions were made by non-Aboriginal corporate executives. The best known Canadian "Aboriginal" film of 1994, *Dance Me Outside*, was a box office hit for First Nations actor, writer and director Jennifer Podemski. But Jennifer neither wrote nor directed; the film was based on short stories by a non-Aboriginal author, scripted by non-Aboriginal writers, shot by a non-Aboriginal cinematographer, and directed by a non-Aboriginal director.

Dance Me Outside was a fine film, and inspired a follow-up TV series on CBC. Its director took pains to include Aboriginal production trainees on the crew, and its writers were commendably open to advice on the cultural setting they were trying to recreate. But *Dance Me Outside* underscored the lack of progress over the years by southern Aboriginal artists in media. Most of the brown faces were still in front of the camera.

In November 1996 the federal government released the long-awaited Report on the Royal Commission on Aboriginal Peoples (RCAP). Launched by the Mulroney Government in the wake of the Oka Crisis and the failed Meech Lake Accord, the Commission had worked for five years on a broad and ambitious mandate—to study and report on the evolution of the relationship between various Aboriginal peoples, the federal government and Canada as a whole. Under the chairmanship of George Erasmus, public hearings were held in nearly a hundred communities across the country, hundreds of thousands of pages of testimony and presentations were collected, and 350 studies were conducted on matters ranging from the state of land claims to the forced relocation of Inuit.

The five-volume, four-thousand page report was heralded as the most important Aboriginal policy document since the 1969 White Paper—an encyclopaedic assessment of the state of Aboriginal culture and society in Canada, and a wake-up call to many Canadians from the invisible nations whose land they share.

The Report dealt in depth with many key cultural issues—the preservation of languages, intergenerational loss of knowledge, opportunities for Aboriginal artists. It affirmed the importance of Aboriginal media, and specifically television, in creating a new relationship between traditional and emerging cultures, and between Aboriginal people and Canada. It called for higher visibility for Aboriginal productions and performers on mainstream television networks, and it urged the government to commit enhanced and ongoing core funding to support the Aboriginal media and production industry.

The Report quoted the Caplan-Sauvageau recommendation for the creation of "...a third national broadcasting network, an autonomous Aboriginal-language service similar to the CBC and Radio-Canada networks." However, the Commission stopped short of endorsing the concept, noting that "... given the cost and the current economic environment, this does not seem realistic." Instead, the Report recommended that southern communities carry TVNC as a way to ensure broader access to Aboriginal television programming. "For the relatively modest price of a satellite downlink, cable systems could carry TVNC and independent Aboriginal programming."

The Commission's failure to endorse the creation of a national Aboriginal network was a disappointment. But the support for TVNC's original position on southern distribution—carriage in the South by cable operators— was encouraging.

The government, however, was not bound to accept any of the Report's recommendations, or implement any of its policy suggestions—and by and large, it didn't. The federal response to the Report, issued after more than a year, was primarily a self-congratulatory litany of federal good deeds since 1993, coupled with a list of short-term program measures. The Commission's calls for a fundamental redefinition of the constitutional relationship between Aboriginal peoples and Canada were ignored. The RCAP laid the groundwork for future initiatives, including the movement for Residential School compensation and recognition. But most analysts agree today that the findings and recommendations of Canada's most expensive, longest- running Royal Commission were essentially ignored. 1996 ended on a series of low notes.

Earlier in the year, the GNWT issued a Request for Proposals to provide the government with a high-speed telecommunications network. It would be a lucrative contract, and the profits could help TVNC pursue a network licence and supplement the dwindling funding for TVNC member producers.

TVNC was a not-for-profit organisation, but there was nothing in its charter that prevented it from incorporating for-profit subsidiaries. Working in partnership with its ally Cancom, TVNC incorporated DrumCo (Drum Communications), a new telecommunications company offering "information highway" services to northern and Aboriginal communities. TVNC invested considerable time and money in the design and incorporation of DrumCo, and in the development of a proposal to the GNWT. But DrumCo lost the bid, and TVNC lost its investment in corporate development.

There had been no surge of interest among southern cable operators in adding TVNC to their service; there would be no southern cable revenues to supplement members' production funding. The vision of a national Aboriginal network had attracted some interest among southern producers, but no substantive support: the CRTC was polite, but unable to provide funding or political endorsement.

And then in early 1997, a power struggle in another corner of Canada's tangled media community opened a surprising door.

CHAPTER IV

FIRST DRAFT

TVNC AS CANADA'S THIRD
NATIONAL NETWORK

3 pm —September 1, 1999

The temporary media room at the Fort Garry hotel is buzzing with journalists, gathered for the last pre-launch press conference. As the Director of Communications, I'm in my element. I'm pumping as much positive energy as I can into every greeting, every handshake. My biggest fear was that no one would show up, but I am relieved to see that both the national press and the Winnipeg journalists have decided that this is going to be a feature story.

It's been a rough ride, and even on launch day APTN is still viewed in some media quarters with hostility or condescension. But the reporters here are mostly supportive, caught up in the moment, willing to suspend their reflexive scepticism—for today.

Abraham and Jim field most of the questions. One journalist asks pointedly if we were ready to broadcast tonight. I feel my smile lock. We go to air in four hours. Live. First show and we're going live. Nobody goes live anymore. Especially not for three hours. Especially not with dozens of musicians and speakers and an untested, patched together distribution system, fed all the way from the Northwest Territories and...

"Yes," Abe responds. "Everything is ready, and we're all very excited." Jim nods. Good. Thank God reporters can't read minds.

The press conference ends and Jim dashes back down the stairs, through the lobby and out to the street, already late for a check-in at The Forks. He's going to be even later—his car is gone, towed away from the no-stopping zone where he parked it for the press conference. "Good," he thinks. "That's my bad luck for the day used up."

I check in on Randall and Tookie, closeted in the makeshift edit suite down the hall from the writers and the launch organizers, and find Tookie, looking grim, slashing the shooting script with a red marker. It seems several of the backgrounder segments that have just arrived are too long: they don't fit within the split-second schedule that network programming requires. Randall is on the phone arguing with one of the producers to cut some visuals so he can make the segments fit the standard length. The producer is reluctant. It is not a pretty scene.

I leave them to their crisis and rush over to my makeshift media room, a ramshackle bright red trailer tucked in behind the stage at the Forks. I'm dragging an old-style cell phone with a flip-top lid, big as my hand and heavy as a brick, fielding calls as I walk. This one's from a journalist from Australia, wanting to know whether we're ready to launch. "Absolutely. Everything's all set, and everyone's very excited…"

And I realize it's true—a prickle of excitement is starting to replace the numb, exhausted feeling I've been fighting all day. Three and a half hours to go.

In the field in front of the main stage, a group of 70 children are gathering. They were recruited through Ma Mawi Wi Ichita, a local Aboriginal child and family service organization. It's still overcast, but it's nice enough for the children to sit on the grass. Volunteers armed with red, blue and yellow paint are drawing the APTN logo on everyone's face. Each child is given a piece of heavy construction paper in each of APTN's colours. They're practicing where to sit, where to stand and when to hold up their colours. They will be one of the first acts on the stage when the show begins at 7 pm.

Laura Milliken is on stage, walking the performers through their technical rehearsal, and breaking the bad news. She tells each act as they walk up the stairs, "OK, I know you have three or four songs prepared, but you're only going to get to do one of them. Okay, maybe two short ones. Yes, I know Duane said you could do three or four but we have to keep on a tight schedule here. One song. Or two." She's not sure the message is getting through. These are Canada's best Aboriginal musicians, she thinks to herself. A three-hour show is not long enough.

Everything is running behind. Marty Ballentyne and Alanis Obomsawin are realizing that they're probably not going to get to rehearse their script—the script Bruce Spence had sweated to get to them on time. But they're not worried. Marty's a rocker who fronts his own band, and Alanis has been singing and performing for years. "Bruce is a very good writer," recalled Marty Ballentyne, "And he gave us some great stuff to work with. We got a short run-through, and then we just had to jump out and do it." No problem.

Izzy Asper wanted a network. The CEO of CanWest Global owned a number of licences in various parts of the country, and reached a substantial percentage of the Canadian audience. But Global was considered a "station group", not a national "network". Only CBC and CTV were licenced as conventional television networks by the CRTC; Asper wanted the opportunity to comment from a lofty "network" perspective on Canadian broadcast legislation, regulation and policy.

Having lost his bid for a conventional TV station in Alberta, Asper quietly lobbied some of his associates in the federal government for an opportunity to make a pitch for network status. Shortly afterward, an Order in Council from then Department of Canadian Heritage Minister Sheila Copps instructed the CRTC to issue a call for comments on the concept of a third national network; and in April 1997, the CRTC requested submissions on whether the establishment of "one or more additional Canadian national English-language, French-language or bilingual television networks would serve the objectives of the broadcasting policy for Canada set out in the Broadcasting Act."

But before hearings were held, Global acquired several television stations from Western International Communications in BC and Alberta. Izzy now owned a de-facto network with holdings in nearly every region of Canada. The CRTC had called for hearings on a single issue at the request of a single broadcaster, and now that broadcaster no longer cared. "They almost considered cancelling," said Patrick Tourigny. "There was no need; Global bought all those stations, and Izzy got his national system anyway."

At a TVNC scheduling committee meeting in May, Jerry Giberson mentioned that the CRTC was calling for comments on new national networks. While it was clear that the Commission's interest had nothing specific to do with Aboriginal programming, TVNC's unofficial strategy had for years been to intervene at any opportunity, often at the surreptitious prompting of Pat Tourigny. So Jerry proposed yet another letter of intervention, to yet another hearing. It couldn't hurt; maybe something would come of this one.

Determined to maintain a national profile, the Board once again decided to hold its 1997 meetings in Banff in June, just before the television festival.

There was a special reason to attend that year. Telefilm Canada, successor to the Canadian Film Development Corporation, was the federal cultural agency charged with promoting the development and promotion of the Canadian audiovisual industry. At the Banff Television Festival the previous year, George Henry had approached the Chair of Telefilm, Francois Macerola, with a novel proposal—why not add a national Aboriginal production award to their English and French language awards? Macerola agreed to co-sponsor two awards honouring the best Canadian Aboriginal-language production and the best English or French-language Aboriginal production. Winners would receive $10,000 in pre-approved Telefilm funding, free registration to the Banff Television Festival, and access to post-production facilities at the Banff Centre for the Arts. It wasn't an Oscar or a Nobel Prize, but for a struggling Canadian film-maker—especially an Aboriginal one—the awards would mean a lot. The first winners would be announced in Banff.

In the summer of 1997, however, there was literally no room available in town—not even at the memorable King Edward Hotel. After some frantic scouting we opted to hold the meetings at nearby Nakoda Lodge, on the Stoney Nakoda Reserve. Tucked away on tiny Lake Chief Hector, nestled in the Rocky Mountains, halfway between Calgary and Banff, the lodge had an elegant dining room, walking trails and cabins for guests. It was quiet, remote, and beautiful. TVNC's meeting room featured wraparound windows overlooking the private lake.

The pastoral setting was somewhat at odds with what followed.

Perhaps attracted by the venue, there were an unusually large number of participants and observers at the AGM, including nearly every member (except Kativik School Board), two associate members, a dozen observers from the Department of Canadian Heritage, and staff from member organisations and TVNC.

The meeting began sombrely with an unusually downbeat Chairman's Report. The previous fiscal year had been "challenging", George told the members, and the current fiscal outlook was bleak. TVNC would need an additional $248,000 to cover equipment and infrastructure costs. The Department of Canadian Heritage had agreed to provide the additional funding, but only as an advance on existing funds, not as new money.

TVNC's one attempt at business development had failed. Drumco had not won the single RFP it bid on, and did not pursue any other significant opportunities. The CRTC had approved the distribution of Homestar, one of Canada's few direct-to-home satellite networks, and with it the distribution of TVNC into southern satellite subscriber's homes; but they had rejected the proposal that Homestar dedicate a portion of its production fund to TVNC, ruling that "TVNC does not qualify as an existing, independently-administered Canadian production fund." Homestar would commit its funding elsewhere.

TVNC had appealed to virtually every potential carrier imaginable, without success, Financially, the network was on its last legs, and further federal cuts to the NNBAP were rumoured.

Without the support of the CRTC or other Government intervention, Canada's most unique television service would fail. There was , "only one way forward for TVNC," said George. If the network was going to survive, and if its members were ever going to supplement their funding, TVNC would have to move into the South—and quickly.

He summarised the draft CRTC submission for the third national network proceedings. The argument was simple. With a national licence and a national mandate, TVNC was already Canada's de facto third national network. All that was lacking was national distribution, and the authority to ensure southern cable and DTH providers would carry their service. "Without a requirement for either priority carriage or favourable tierage and linkage arrangements, TVNC will continue to face severe impediments in attempting to negotiate and secure national carriage with cable operators." The solution would be "some mechanisms or regulatory incentives for cable operators to carry the Aboriginal network."

Marie Wilson, Director of CBC North, was dubious about the potential for revenue generation. She pointed out that CBC was considered a public broadcaster with a nationally licenced network on basic cable, but didn't collect subscriber fees. "How can TVNC become a public, national network," she asked, "and at the same time ask for subscriber fees"? George shrugged. "TVNC will set a precedent," he replied, "We'll do both." Other people's assessment of what was possible never really mattered much to George.

Many northern members were still uneasy about a move into the South. TVNC was a truly northern service, uniquely attuned to the needs and preferences of northerners. That was what they had fought for. What if southern audiences didn't "get it"? What if competition for southern audiences forced the network to change its programming, its languages, its corporate structure?

George downplayed their concerns. There was a huge Aboriginal audience in southern Canada, he said, both on reserve and in the cities surely they'd be attracted to TVNC. He reminded the Board that the letter wasn't proposing any change to TVNC's vision; it was simply a request for support in seeking national distribution.

The matter was unresolved. After a short break, the meeting moved on to its next item—the selection of a Chair for the upcoming year.

Abraham Tagalik, the current Vice-Chair, was nominated first; then Nap Gardiner, representing the National Aboriginal Communications Society, stood up and nominated George Henry, the incumbent. Abe was a popular and easygoing broadcaster, a friend of everyone in the room. George, however, was a three-year veteran; most participants expected him to win a fourth term.

Before anyone could second Nap's nomination motion, George rose to his feet and declined the nomination. Then he sat back down.

The entire room was silent with shock. George had been a founder of NNBY, a driving force in the creation of TVNC, and the standard bearer for southern distribution. No one had seen this coming, and George offered no reason.

The explanation emerged later in the meeting, with the financial reports. Notes with the financial statements highlighted some irregularities regarding George's use of the TVNC corporate credit card. George heatedly denied any wrongdoing. But he declined to run again.

The only remaining nominee for Chair was Abraham, and he was selected by acclamation. "I was probably just as surprised as everyone else in the room," says Abe. "I didn't set out to become the Chairman. I was just interested in making sure the organisation ran smoothly. It was just another one of those times at TVNC when the stars lined up."

Immediately following Abraham's acclamation, an impromptu item was added to the agenda. The Board reviewed and approved the contentious letter of intervention to the CRTC regarding third national networks. The approval came with only one comment: to change the name and signature at the bottom of the page from George Henry to Abraham Tagalik, as Chairman.

That simple change of signature signalled a major shift in TVNC's approach and corporate culture. George Henry's strength and stubborn refusal to compromise his vision for Aboriginal broadcasting had brought TVNC an impressive distance. His contribution to the recognition of Aboriginal programming, and to the eventual creation of APTN, had been immense. But his abrasive personality and confrontational style had alienated many potential allies in government and industry, and had created suspicion and discomfort within TVNC itself. The meeting at Nakoda Lodge marked the end of his work promoting a national Aboriginal television network on behalf of TVNC.

The next day, after the AGM, TVNC's Board of Directors passed its first official resolution authorising TVNC to proceed with southern distribution:

> WHEREAS TVNC has identified revenue-generating opportunities by expanding into southern markets; and
>
> WHEREAS TVNC feels that it would be beneficial to promote an Aboriginal channel among Aboriginal and non-Aboriginal people across Canada,
>
> THEREFORE BE IT RESOLVED that the members of TVNC agree to proceed with these initiatives that would lead to the creation of a national Aboriginal channel, as funds become available.

This motion set out a more cautious approach than George's vision. It did not call for the creation of an entirely new channel with an expanded mandate, southern programming, or structural changes. Rather, it reflected the vision of the majority of northern TVNC members—a "TVNC South", an expansion of the existing northern service, providing southern Canadians with a glimpse of northern Aboriginal life, stories and perspectives. It emphasised that the Aboriginal network would be established to ensure revenues for northern TVNC members.

With George's departure, Abraham's election and a formal commitment to southern expansion, the 1997 meeting marked a sea-change for TVNC on a number of fronts. And the political climate was changing as well. Fernand Belisle, Vice-Chair of Broadcasting, had left the CRTC. Belisle had not been a supporter of TVNC or Aboriginal broadcasting, and was unimpressed by the network's efforts to secure southern distribution. Moreover, he had been offended by George Henry's aggressive style. His replacement, Charles Belanger, had been a senior manager at CANCOM, and was a familiar with and sympathetic to TVNC's goals.

The simultaneous change in leadership at both TVNC and the Commission ushered in a welcome new spirit of cooperation, and TVNC moved swiftly. Staff quickly set up a series of meetings with key CRTC decision-makers, this time with Abraham as spokesperson. The message was the same: TVNC needed the Commission's support to find southern distribution. But the messenger was different, the meetings were positive, and several spokespersons for the Commission began to hint at a new willingness to help out. There was a definite sense that the tide, for a change, was turning in TVNC's favour.

The Board decided to seek support in other quarters as well. Abraham and TVNC Vice-Chair J.C. Catholique attended an AFN Chiefs meeting that summer to gauge their interest in a national network, and to look for potential allies. The meeting went well, and on their return, Abraham and J.C. proposed a resolution be brought forward to the Chiefs at their annual assembly that November, requesting endorsement of TVNC's efforts to find southern distribution.

The realisation that a national network was becoming a serious possibility prompted new discussions within TVNC. "In the summer of 1997 we all felt a bit like a dog chasing a car," Abraham remembers. "At some point the dog has to be asking itself—wait a minute. What am I going to do if I actually catch this thing?"

»——→ o ←——«

The biggest question was exactly how southern distribution could increase revenues to the network and its contributors. It was assumed that cable companies would pay a fee to TVNC to carry the service—but how would money flow to the members? Initially the concept seemed simple. TVNC members were funded by the federal government to produce native- language content, and raised some additional revenue by selling commercial slots in their programs; but they got no payment from TVNC for their programming, because they owned the network. Legal advisors pointed out that, as non-profit organisations providing programming to another non-profit organisation under their control, members could not simply divide the hypothetical cable revenues amongst themselves. Any payment would have to be in the form of a contract for services rendered or programs acquired. This seemed a minor distinction at the time, but for the first time it underlined a major difference between TVNC and its successor, APTN. TVNC was essentially a cooperative, whose members managed its scheduling and provided its programming. A viable national network, however, would need to have a structure like other conventional broadcasters, with fixed licence fees paid to producers.

The concept of a national network was catching on—and not just within TVNC. In an article in Nunatsiaq News in October 1997, Zak Kunuk, President of Igloolik Isuma Productions, complained that IBC was paying too much to its 'Ottawa-based managers' and not enough to northern producers. Isuma submitted a proposal to the Department of Canadian Heritage to create a new network, SILA Specialty Channel Ltd., which would take over TVNC and NNBAP funding and operate out of Igloolik. TVNC and IBC were furious; Zak and Paul Apak, the creative force at Isuma, had both been employed by and trained at IBC. The proposal was quietly dismissed by Canadian Heritage, but the resentment lingered for years.

And yet another vision was emerging in Manitoba.

Jim Compton was a well-known Salteaux television producer and journalist from Winnipeg, host of CBC's award-winning documentary Drums and the popular Sharing Circle, an Aboriginal newsmagazine show. Like most Aboriginal producers, he had been frustrated for years by the lack of access to audiences. In 1994, the Women's Television Network (WTN) launched in Winnipeg. Jim studied their licence application and began assembling notes for his own policy paper, setting out the need for an Aboriginal network.

Jim's first exposure to TVNC occurred during the Royal Commission on Aborigial People (RCAP) consultations, when he accompanied the Commissioners on their five-year round of community visits and videotaped the proceedings. The Commission visited TVNC's studios in Yellowknife, and Jim saw firsthand what the northerners had done. "I thought about that a lot," he said. "And when I read the final RCAP report and saw the reference to a national Aboriginal television network, it all came together, and I thought—that's something worth doing."

Convinced that an Aboriginal network was inevitable, Jim began to work with Ron Missyabit and Tobasonakwat Kinew at the Manitoba Indian Cultural Education Centre (MICEC) to establish the Aboriginal Broadcast Training Initiative (ABTI), a program for Aboriginal television producers, directors and writers. TVNC was still very much on Jim's mind; but it seemed to him a very northern organisation, not yet representative of Aboriginal people in southern Canada.

In October, 1997, ABTI invited TVNC to take part in "Dreams to Airwaves", a conference scheduled for February 1998, to discuss the creation of a "Native Broadcasting Network". The organisers had invited George Henry to be their keynote speaker, and asked TVNC to participate in a panel discussion on the pros and cons of a native broadcasting network. But the real world had outstripped the conference planners; TVNC wasn't very interested in discussing the need for a native network, since they were building one. George was working as a legal consultant in Vancouver, and his relationship with TVNC had soured. Abraham contacted Jim and Ron, and explained TVNC's status and plans. Surprised and impressed, MICEC post-poned the conference, and asked if TVNC would organise such a conference for the summer of 1998. Abraham agreed to discuss the idea with his Board.

As things turned out, however, TVNC would be too busy applying for an Aboriginal television network licence in the summer of 1998 to organise a conference on how to apply for an Aboriginal television network licence. And Jim Compton would be part of the team.

Momentum was building on several fronts in the fall of 1997. The network launched a letter-writing campaign to all cable companies and First Nations (many of whom operated their own cable or broadcast systems on reserve), encouraging them to include TVNC in their package of services. The industry was changing, and more and more Canadians were subscribing to direct broadcast satellite (DBS) distributors; so TVNC began to woo providers like LookTV, StarChoice, and ExpressVu, arguing that carriage of TVNC would strengthen both their service and their licensing applications to the CRTC. Political support would be essential. The network hired a lobbyist to help frame TVNC's case for presentation to Members of Parliament and government officials. New Commissioners were being appointed to the CRTC, and TVNC prepared a briefing package for them on Aboriginal broadcasting and the network's plans.

To support the lobbying effort and raise the network's profile in the south, TVNC also decided to establish a committee of prominent Aboriginal people. Their role, defined in a formal terms of reference document, would be twofold to promote the network and its plans for extension of service, and to advise on the form and nature of the service itself. The Terms of Reference called for "...a group of dedicated Aboriginal people who will lead the process and provide valuable input. This group must be comprised of people with strong ties to Aboriginal communities and organisations to ensure proper consultations with Aboriginal producers, communities, Band Councils, organisations and cable companies." TVNC was looking for guidance, recognition, and a bit of Star Power to generate buzz in the Aboriginal community.

The Board prepared an initial list, and Abraham, somewhat nervously, began making phone calls to Canada's Aboriginal cultural elite. Buffy Ste. Marie wasn't available, but John Kim Bell, founder of the National Aboriginal Achievement Foundation, and a distinguished Mohawk composer and conductor, agreed immediately. So did film-maker Alanis Obomsawin, whose series on the Oka Crisis was winning international acclaim.

Roman Bittman joined as well. A Métis producer and director associated for years with The Nature of Things, Roman was working with the Nova Scotia Film Development Corporation to help Aboriginal producers finance their projects, and knew first-hand the challenges they faced. So did Gemini award-winning director Gil Cardinal, who was preparing to shoot his mini-series Big Bear for CBC.

The highest profile advisor to come on board was Gary Farmer. Best known as an actor for his performances in the film Powwow Highway and The Rez, Gary was also a director, musician, publisher of Aboriginal Voices magazine, and a tireless promoter of Aboriginal culture, film and broadcasting. "Gary was my first call," says Abe."And of course I was nervous. Here's a guy who has worked with Marlon Brando, and I'm calling him and asking him to be on our Advisory Committee." Gary was delighted, and quickly became one of the network's most enthusiastic advocates. He immediately began pouring his own resources, contacts and efforts into the project.

The timing was perfect. TVNC had just received an invitation to appear before the CRTC to make a submission regarding third national networks. And their submission was going to get a dry run: just days before the hearing, TVNC would also be presenting its case and asking for a resolution from the Chiefs at the AFN Special Assembly in Québec City in November, 1997. As Abraham was committed to another event, TVNC sent Jerry Giberson and Gary Farmer to gather support at the AFN Assembly.

》————》○《————《

AFN meetings are a mini-United Nations—a frantic round of dealmaking, policy development, politicking, schmoozing, and networking. The Québec City meeting already had a full agenda—First Nations veterans, land claims, residential school survivors—a wide range of pressing social issues affecting communities across Canada. And for the first time, they were going to be pitched to support the establishment of a national Aboriginal network— and not just one pitch, but two.

Jim Compton, Ron Missyabit and Tobasonakwat Kinew had been quietly lobbying chiefs since the summer. "We really didn't know where TVNC was at," said Jim."But we knew this whole idea was going to need political support. And the AFN is the place to get it."

Jim had drafted a resolution endorsing the creation of a "national native broadcasting network". It proposed a private-sector, specialty network, similar to the WTN licence Jim had studied years earlier. Jim and crew arrived at the AFN meeting; as their cameras followed new Grand Chief Phil Fontaine through the meeting, Jim talked up his network concept among the delegates. The idea stirred some interest among several regional vice-chiefs, including Bill Erasmus from the NWT.

It was a very different resolution from the one that Gary Farmer and Jerry Giberson were circulating among the Chiefs, which endorsed southern distribution of the TVNC network. AFN wouldn't entertain two resolutions on the same issue from two different groups. As soon as he realised there were resolutions circulating, Jim agreed to pull his resolution off the table. But it wasn't that simple.

"By the time I got back to my room, Gary was on the phone. The Chiefs wanted to meet with all of us. They said we couldn't just withdraw a resolution. We needed to come to some kind of agreement." Jim headed down for a long, frank talk with Gary and Jerry. He was apprehensive. TVNC was already up and running—but how could a purely northern network improve things for southern Aboriginal producers?

"I knew Gary, and I trusted him. I was willing to support a fair and equitable network that let the South in too." After several drafts, they hammered out a new resolution and submitted it to the Chiefs. The resolution was straightforward:

> WHEREAS the Assembly of First Nations is committed to supporting initiatives that encourage Aboriginal self- sufficiency; and
>
> WHEREAS Television Northern Canada is a national Aboriginal television network that broadcasts nearly 100 hours per week of original Aboriginal programming in English, French and more than 10 Aboriginal languages and expanding its northern network into southern Canada to establish a national Aboriginal television network; and
>
> WHEREAS all regions of Canada need to be represented on an Aboriginal television network, TVNC will ensure that process is established to include proper representation for communities in southern Canada;

THEREFORE BE IT RESOLVED THAT the Assembly of First Nations supports TVNC in its efforts to establish a national Aboriginal channel that will enhance understanding among Aboriginal and non-Aboriginal people; and

FURTHER BE IT RESOLVED THAT the Assembly of First Nations mandate the Executive of the Assembly of First Nations to add the development of a Native broadcasting network to the portfolio of one of the Vice-Chiefs; and

FINALLY BE IT RESOLVED THAT the Assembly of First Nations will work in conjunction with TVNC to gain support from Aboriginal communities and political organisations to realise the goal of a national Aboriginal channel.

The text was simple, but its implications were huge. Written just days before TVNC's presentation to the CRTC, the resolution committed TVNC to a vision remarkably like the one articulated by George Henry, a national Aboriginal channel, mandated to reach both Aboriginal and non-Aboriginal audiences, and representing all Aboriginal regions of Canada.

The motion passed unanimously. To some chiefs at the meeting, it was just another agenda item, a ritual endorsement of an implausible, feel-good idea. But Jean LaRose, a member of Grand Chief Fontaine's communications team, was intrigued, and impressed at the strength of the support. Jean, an Abenaki from the Odanak First Nation, had studied communications and public administration, and had worked at AFN as Director of Communications for several years under a number of different Grand Chiefs. This kind of unanimity was unusual clearly this was an initiative worth keeping an eye on.

Gary and Jerry were delighted with the meeting, and so was Abraham when they briefed him. TVNC had established its first formal strategic alliance with a major southern Aboriginal group, and all had agreed that collaboration between North and South was the way forward.

The endorsement from AFN was important in other ways. Contrary to popular misconception, AFN is not an "Aboriginal Government" but an organisation of First Nation government leaders. Nevertheless, it is the country's largest and most influential body representing First Nations; and its support sent a strong signal to the rest of Canada.

"That resolution was a big step for us," said Abraham. "It convinced a lot of people that the time had come. From that point on, the snowball really started to roll."

AFN assigned Ghislain Picard, Regional Vice-Chief from Québec and an experienced broadcaster, to work with TVNC. With the ink still wet on the AFN resolution of support, Abraham and Gary moved quickly on to the next venue, the CRTC hearings into a third national network.

$$\gg\!\!\longrightarrow\!\!\!\succ \circ \prec\!\!\longleftarrow\!\!\!\ll$$

It was no big deal. TVNC's presentations to the Commission were becoming regular events. The submission by Abraham and Gary was smooth and assured, and made a strong case for TVNC as Canada's third national network. They pointed out that TVNC was already an established public network with a track record of success. Its programming was utterly unique, and perhaps the most distinctly Canadian service on air.

Abraham pressed the point that the Broadcasting Act explicitly called for a broadcast system that would recognise "the special place of Aboriginal people within Canadian society." American channels were flooding the cable systems, and every conceivable specialty channel was being licenced. Why were Aboriginal peoples once again fighting for something most Canadians took for granted; a channel that reflected their reality? He pointed out that the cost would be insignificant, as little as 8 or 9 cents per subscriber, per month.

"Is a few cents too much to ask to maintain Aboriginal language and culture and to ensure a voice for Aboriginal people in the media?" asked Abraham. "We don't think so."

Abraham and Garry responded to a few questions, thanked the Commissioners; and that was that. Another presentation at another CRTC hearing. Abe flew back to Iqaluit, Gary returned to Toronto. No one sensed that this hearing had been any different.

The thick, grey veil of bureaucracy settled over the Commission's post–hearing deliberations, and TVNC staff turned to the more mundane task of trying to run one of the world's most dispersed networks on a budget more suited to a small Ontario cable station. Not surprisingly, distribution problems were cropping up again.

All TVNC members shot and edited their programs on videotape, then shipped the tapes to the nearest of three satellite uplinks used by the network. TVNC maintained the system of local transmitters in ninety- six communities across the North, but each of the three uplinks was managed by the TVNC member organisation in the community. NNBY had the contract to uplink programs shipped to Whitehorse, NCS managed the Yellowknife operation, and IBC handled Iqaluit. This uplink function was critical, requiring split-second timing and careful adjustment and monitoring of the complex satellite equipment. When something went wrong at an uplink site, the entire audience knew it. In the winter of 1997, it was clear that things were going wrong in Yellowknife.

Increasingly, master control operators were failing to show up for their shifts. Sometimes the wrong program was uplinked; sometimes audiences saw nothing at all, or sound and pictures were so distorted as to be unwatchable. The situation was aggravating for TVNC's audiences, but even more for the producers who watched aghast as their shows were missed or mangled. It reflected badly on the network as a whole: TVNC was pitching itself as a third national television network, but failing to serve its own viewers.

The issue came to a head when Yellowknife failed to broadcast a series of programs from ICS that included paid advertising—ads that never made it to air. That was the last straw. ICS demanded permission to bypass Yellowknife and ship their programming an extra thousand kilometres to Whitehorse. The Board met, and after much debate, made a difficult decision. TVNC had to maintain technical standards and guarantee a professional level of service to its members and its audience. The network would therefore take over its own distribution, consolidating operations in Yellowknife and ending its contracts with IBC and NNBY. Linda O'Shaughnessy moved from Iqaluit to Yellowknife, and began the complex task of establishing a single, centralised scheduling, uplink and logging system for the network. Her consummate diplomacy and obsession with detail proved to be exactly the combination that was needed, and to everyone's relief the network quickly stabilised. In the long run, the consolidation of a single uplink and scheduling unit in Yellowknife helped to set the stage for APTN.

The Board met with its Advisory Committee for the first time by teleconference in late 1997, nearly six months after the group was formed. By this time the Committee had already been on the job for half a year, working with Abraham and TVNC staff to lobby and spread the word, and providing southern input as the new network took shape.

The Committee's role was a delicate one. They brought valuable experience, perspective, and links to Government and the private sector to the table. They were professionals, at the peak of their profession. But they were also a committee of the Board, and their mandate was purely advisory. Over the course of that first meeting, it became clear that some Board members were growing concerned about the role and influence of the Committee.

Discussion at the meeting focused on the scope and scale of the change facing TVNC. There would have to be a name change, new scheduling criteria, a new Board structure, new distribution initiatives and a review of membership criteria. And of course, the new network would have to consider its programming offerings in light of a whole new, national audience.

For members who still envisioned the new network as TVNC-South, the meeting was a sobering wake-up call. Leanne Brassard, NNBY's representative, insisted on the importance of TVNC's original mandate, reminding the Committee that "we want to ensure that northerners can still speak to each other on a new network." Sammy Duncan of TNI emphasised that "TNI wants to continue to have a say on the Board." Jim DeLaurier of Kativik School Board expressed the Board's concern about scheduling, control and structure of the new network, and asked bluntly, "Will a new network assist TVNC members in their original goals?"

The meeting ended with positive reassurances all around, but with no real resolution. Over the next turbulent year, that fundamental clash of visions would threaten to tear the new network apart.

»————⟶ ∘ ⟵————«

While the CRTC pondered its decision on the third national network hearings, TVNC reviewed its options for national carriage. A consultant's report analysed three possible models. "Basic carriage" meant that cable and satellite operators would be required to carry TVNC, like CBC, as part of the core bundle of channels received by every subscriber; "dual status" carriage gave operators the opportunity to negotiate another arrangement. Most new services were being called "specialty channels," and allocated to the rapidly growing range of digital channels.

Each option had its pros and cons. Basic carriage would guarantee TVNC the largest number of potential viewers, but no one really knew at that point how much interest there would be. It also seemed unlikely that the Commission would grant that kind of status to a new and untried network, or allow adequate subscriber fees.

Dual status seemed the more promising option, except that the CRTC hadn't issued that kind of licence in nearly a decade. The digital specialty alternative was rejected out of hand; it would mean TVNC would have to join dozens of obscure services competing for viewers at the far end of the dial. The network decided to pursue dual status, and continue with an analog signal instead of a digital signal.

AFN's motion of endorsement had triggered expressions of support from virtually every other national Aboriginal organisation, including the Métis National Council, the Congress of Aboriginal People, Inuit Tapiriit Kanatami, Pauktuutit Inuit Women's Association, the Native Women's Association of Canada, and the National Association of Friendship Centres. Suddenly the idea of a national network was on everyone's agenda. Bolstered by the rising wave of support, TVNC began to step up pressure on government, pressing their case with key officials within the Department of Canadian Heritage, Indian and Northern Affairs, Industry Canada, and in meeting with Members of Parliament from all political parties.

From the outside, TVNC was looking good—the network's profile had never been higher, political support was rising, programming was improving, and southern distribution looked like a real possibility.

Very few people realised that the network was on the verge of going broke.

TVNC was caught in a bind. Funding had been barely adequate to support its operation as a simple distribution system. The network's only chance for long-term survival was to extend the network south, an effort that had required years of lobbying, travel costs, legal costs and consultants' fees. There were no palatial offices, padded expense accounts or exorbitant salaries being paid; the simple truth was that TVNC had to spend money in order to achieve southern distribution, and the money was running out. The network already owed a huge debt to Telesat, the company that provided TVNC's satellite services. Telesat was supportive, but Telesat was also a business; they wanted to be paid.

At the end of 1997 the Board was faced with a stark choice; cut back on the effort to achieve southern distribution and consolidate as a northern network, or roll the dice, keep on lobbying, and hope for a breakthrough.

In the end, said Abe, there really was no choice. "We had come too far to turn back. It was a huge gamble, but everybody agreed—we had to move ahead. If the idea of southern distribution didn't work out, we'd be rethinking the network anyway. We knew we'd be okay till March, till the end of the fiscal year. After that…"

The CRTC had been mulling over the submissions on a Third National Network for three months. Abraham wasn't too anxious about it, TVNC's expectations weren't high. It would be nice to get one more acknowledgement of TVNC's good work, one more motherhood statement on the value of Aboriginal programming, one more positive quote to include in the next round of hearings. Beyond that, the Board was focusing on developing political support.

But the stars, it seemed, were continuing to align themselves on TVNC's behalf. Pat Tourigny had been prepared to go to bat for TVNC when the Commissioners finished the hearings and began their deliberations in December. "There were a number of ways the Commission could have responded to TVNC's request," he said. "I told them they could grant TVNC a mandatory licence, and then I suggested an option that would have gotten about 80% cable penetration. I didn't know how much support there would be for mandatory, and I didn't push it. And then Commissioner David Colville said, 'Well, these people have been trying for ten years to get justice. Why not make them mandatory?'"

Commissioner Andrew Cardozo agreed. Andrew was an expert in labour market issues, cultural policy and employment diversity. He had founded the Pearson Shoyama Institute, and served as executive director of the Canadian Ethnocultural Council. He had just been appointed to the Commission, and had not been part of the Third Network Hearings. But he had a long history of support for multiculturalism and employment equity; and while he initially knew very little about TVNC or northern Aboriginal broadcasters, he believed in a broadcast system and environment that would reflect the real diversity of Canada. As a new Commissioner, he had been briefed on the hearings, and participated in the Commission's decision. Like Patrick, he was surprised at the level of support among his fellow Commissioners. "I spent years fighting for employment equity where you often have to work against the system, beating down walls. And suddenly I was in the system, in a decision making position, assuming I was going to be the only minority voice in the wilderness. But some of the Commissioners were very positive. And we came out with a very positive response."

That response was released on February 6th, 1998, in a tenpage decision regarding the Third National Network hearings. One paragraph, buried near the end of the document, responded to TVNC.

> "The Commission recognises that TVNC is a unique and significant undertaking serving the public interest and the objectives of the Broadcasting Act, especially those objectives that relate to the special place of Aboriginal peoples within Canadian society. Such a service should be widely available throughout Canada in order to serve the diverse needs of the various Aboriginal communities, as well as other Canadians. The Commission will consider any application by TVNC designed to achieve these objectives. The Commission expects any application by TVNC to demonstrate how it will adapt its programming service to reflect the diversity of the needs and interests of Aboriginal peoples throughout Canada."

It took a few readings before the meaning of that brief paragraph sunk in. The CRTC was explicitly inviting TVNC to transform from a northern network into a national network.

The door was open.

CHAPTER V

THE STORYBOARD

CRAFTING APTN

5 pm September 1, 1999

I'm watching the sky. Everybody is watching the sky. For the first time we're seeing glimmers of sun through the overcast, but the clouds are thick in the air and there's a damp feeling to the breeze.

It's warm at The Forks, and a crowd is beginning to build. A huge outdoor hospitality tent stands next to one of the three tipis erected by the Winnipeg Native Alliance, signaling that this is a major Aboriginal event. The APTN Board is here, mingling with launch day sponsors and local dignitaries. Some of the performers have finished their rehearsal and are milling about, getting something to eat and waiting for their cue to get ready backstage.

It's even hotter inside the hospitality tent. Music is playing, and white-clad servers with silver trays are squeezing through the invitation-only crowd, passing out hors d'oeuvres from the posh Fort Garry hotel. Abraham is wearing a beautiful sealskin vest as he moves through the tent, greeting well-wishers, shaking the hands of funders, hugging old friends. The vest is a great fashion statement, but a bad choice for comfort—he's roasting.

J.C. Catholique, Chair of the APTN board, signals to Abraham. It's time for the speeches.

Jose Kusugak, President of ITK and a former broadcaster himself, speaks movingly of the impact television had on him, his family and his community. AFN Grand Chief Phil Fontaine expresses the pride of all Aboriginal people in this achievement, and the great promise that APTN represents. Then it's Abraham's turn. Looking past the crowd in the tent to the stage swarming with APTN staff and volunteers, Abraham reminds the guests.

"…this network would not have been possible without the work of the staff and the Board, and the years of dedication that people put in to see this through. It took a lot of players to make this network a reality; and I want to thank you all, each and every one, in a big way, for everything you've done."

Then Tobasonakwat stands and presents the network with a very special gift. He had worked all night to create a ceremonial pipe for APTN in the traditional style, with a T-shaped stone bowl and a wooden stem. He invites all the Board members to stand in a circle. "This pipe will help APTN in its journey into the communication field from this day forward," he says.

To many present, it's an attractive gift, nothing more. But those familiar with First Nations understand that something unusual had just happened. The pipe is one of the most sacred objects in the culture. In ceremonial usage, it is filled with tobacco and passed around a circle as a form of prayer and solidarity. Its smoke is believed to carry prayers to the Creator.

"When Tobasonakwat passed around the pipe that day, it was very significant, and I was personally moved," recalls Jules Lavallee, who would become one of APTN's elders, and would continue to use that pipe at APTN gatherings.

Roman Bittman is also moved, "I had already had some cultural dealings with Tobasonakwat. I knew just how important, how powerful that gift was." In the years to come the pipe would be taken out at special Board meetings or other important gatherings as a reminder of the importance of culture to this new network.

Across the field in the stage area, last-minute preparations are still underway. While the VIPs enjoy their catered Fort Garry reception, the technical crew and staff make do with take out from the food court nearby. Those that can eat, that is—most people are too busy, or too nervous.

Jordan Wheeler is staring numbly at his heroic little printer, finally cranking out the last version of George Tuccaro and Evie Mark's script for the broadcast. The formatting is all over the place, and as he reads the pages he spots minor errors. But at this point, he's right down to the wire. It's time to get the script to the hosts and let it go. He's half dead from lack of sleep; this has been the toughest challenge of his writing career. But now, he realises with a shock, he's done. He can head over to the stage and enjoy the spectacle of everyone else scrambling.

Dawn Olivence and Mark Nabess are scrambling. They're two students with the Aboriginal Broadcast Training Initiative, run by Ron Missyabit. Ron had arranged for the students to volunteer at the launch, and Dawn had been looking forward to an evening sitting in the audio booth watching the technicians from Global. But today, nobody gets to sit and watch.

"From the moment we got there, we were doing whatever anyone told us to do," recalls Mark. *"Someone would yell, 'Hey, are you busy? Go do this!' So we did a lot of different jobs."*

Dawn draws an interesting assignment: she's told she'll be taking care of some of the talent, bringing them to their interviews, taking them backstage for makeup, then leading them onstage. "Great," she says." Who will I be working with?" "Susan Aglukark and the host, Evie Mark."

Evie is beginning to feel the pre-show jitters. She and George are exploring their own little set, where they will introduce APTN to the world in less than two hours. It's a low-rise platform with a small awning and chairs for the hosts and guests, about 100 feet from the stage, behind the audience, in the middle of the field; cameras will be able to shoot their intros with the stage as a backdrop. Technicians are running cables and testing microphones; camera operators are trucking around the platform, looking for their angles and muttering into their headsets to Gil in the control room. The stage director is placing coffee cups and water on a small table.

For George this is old hat, just like the 1992 TVNC Launch. But this is a first for Evie—a live show, three hours long, and in English. She'd be more comfortable in Inuktitut, she tells George. Don't worry, he says. Just remember to breathe.

A runner arrives with their final scripts, still warm from Jordan's overworked printer. The area is now ready for the hosts. George glances at the sky. With all the bright lights he can't tell whether it's clearing or clouding over.

TVNC was now dealing with a clear and urgent new priority. The network needed to prepare a full application to the CRTC, a hard-nosed, detailed proposal for establishing a new national network, describing its structure, programming, distribution, finances, governance and staffing. And time was of the essence. While the CRTC hadn't specified a deadline, TVNC's existing licence was scheduled to expire in September 1998. A one-year extension of that license, just to keep the network on air, wouldn't be a problem; but everyone knew the Commission would be expecting a detailed submission as soon as possible.

The clock was running and so was the meter. Patricia Hutton, TVNC's financial coordinator, laid out the options to the Board in March. She estimated that it would cost roughly half a million dollars to prepare the CRTC application, including legal and consulting costs, meetings, promotion, and the simple expense of routine travel to some of Canada's most remote communities. The network had limited working capital, she warned, and this time TVNC really was rolling the dice. If the application failed, the network was cutting its own lifespan by several months.

"At that point," Abraham said, "There really wasn't much discussion. We had decided months before we were going to take the chance. I asked the Board and the Advisory Committee to start working on the application right away."

»———→ ○ ←———«

Just a week after the CRTC decision, the Board and Advisory Committee met face-to-face for the first time to begin the detailed planning. Of the original Advisory Committee members, Gary Farmer, Roman Bittman, and Alanis Obomsawin still remained; Jean LaRose represented AFN when Vice-Chief Ghislain Picard was unavailable. Jim Compton had also joined the group after the AFN Chiefs Assembly, at Abraham's request.

Discussion quickly returned to the long-simmering, familiar divergence of visions, given new urgency by the CRTC's invitation. Was this new network going to be an extension of TVNC into the South, or was it going to be reconceived as a new national service?

There were strong arguments and deep feelings supporting both positions. From the Board's perspective, TVNC stood for history, funding, network experience and an actual organisation; a federally funded, not-for-profit, northern-based, member-driven distribution system. As an informal alliance of northern broadcasters and educators, its members had worked together for years, creating a northern broadcast industry, and changing Canadian broadcasting policy. They had fought long and hard for their network, they were serving their northern audiences, and they were eager to bring their programming to a new national audience. They also needed new revenues to replace dwindling federal funding.

But the CRTC wasn't looking for an application to deliver TVNC in the South. They were expecting to license a service aimed at a national audience, both Aboriginal and non-Aboriginal—a network that would provide access to the emerging community of native broadcasters, film-makers, writers and performers in the North and South. Hopefully, it would be a network whose programming could eventually generate enough advertising revenue to support itself.

That national and southern Aboriginal perspective was represented by the Advisory Committee. These were seasoned, southern, mostly urban and for-profit producers, accustomed to working in English and producing for a mass, mixed audience. If this new network was going to succeed, the new group was going to have to find common ground with the old school.

"We were excited going into those meetings—but we were nervous," said Jean LaRose. "We wanted to participate, we wanted to influence decision-making. But there was an uneasy feeling that we would be tokens. Some were saying that this was just the North trying to get money from the South, and [the Advisory Committee] wouldn't have a say." Jim Compton likened the initial meeting to a bad first date. "They were sitting on that side of the room and we were sitting on this side. And no one wanted to dance."

Abraham, as always, poured oil on the troubled water. His own background in northern broadcasting meant he understood the fears of the TVNC group perfectly. But he also believed that a national service represented the only possible way forward. "There was a lot of tension in the room that day," he recalled. "I had to remind everyone that we were dealing with each other in good faith here. Yes, the APTN concept had begun in the North. But we weren't looking to create a northern network with southern participation. The goal was a network that would be owned equally and fairly by all. And I was trying to get that message across to both sides. Ultimately we were all working toward the same goal."

Somewhat reassured, the TVNC Board and Advisory Committee set aside their reservations—for the moment—and dug into the intimidating task of designing and building a new national network.

The first and most fundamental issue was the kind of distribution TVNC should seek. Having rejected the digital option, TVNC could request mandatory carriage, a license that would require that all cable systems carry the network's programming as part of any basic package of service. That would ensure that TVNC would be seen by the widest possible audience; but mandatory carriage had also traditionally meant that the channel couldn't expect to be paid subscriber fees. Or TVNC could seek subscriber fees: but that would mean the service wouldn't be carried on basic cable, but relegated to "specialty channel" status—just another voice in the increasing fragmented tangle of golf, lifestyle and special interest services. After nearly two years of debate, the lawyers and consultants still couldn't agree on which option to pursue, and neither the Board nor the advisors were confident enough to make a firm recommendation.

But as it happened, an old friend of TVNC was getting bored and looking for a new challenge; and he had some pretty strong ideas about how the network could proceed.

Patrick Tourigny had been a staunch advocate of Aboriginal broadcasting from his early days in cable to the CRTC's Third National Network hearing Decision in February 1998. He had never had much interest in politics, or the rise and fall of media empires; for Patrick, television was a medium that people should be able to use as well as watch. Aboriginal broadcasting represented one of the best real-world applications of the medium he had ever seen. Now approaching retirement, he decided that TVNC was where he wanted to end his career. After quiet discussions with Abraham, the announcement was made: Patrick would be leaving the Commission and joining TVNC for three years as Director of Regulatory Affairs.

"I started work at TVNC on April Fool's day, and that was sort of how I felt. I was jumping out of a window with no parachute," he recalled. "If the network hadn't got its licence, I would have been toast; that would have been it for both TVNC and my retirement."

It's not unusual for CRTC policy staff to move out into the industry, said Andrew Cardozo; but TVNC was particularly lucky in nabbing Pat.

"In most cases, there are many people within the Commission with the skills and experience a broadcaster is looking for, but not in TVNC's case. There was really only one person who could have been of use to the network, and that was Patrick."

One of Patrick's first tasks was to recommend the form of license TVNC should seek—mandatory carriage without subscriber fees, or specialty channel status, with fees but without a guaranteed audience.

After internal consultation and a careful weighing of the pros and cons, Patrick presented his recommendation to the Board. To everyone's surprise, he urged them to adopt George Henry's radical proposal: forget about precedent, don't give up anything, and apply for mandatory carriage with a subscriber fee.

His rationale was compelling. To achieve its social goals, TVNC needed to move beyond its primarily native audience and reach the majority of Canadians. The network and its members had argued for decades that Aboriginal voices were an essential part of the Canadian dialogue, and needed to be part of the public television system—not just as a discretionary specialty channel, but as a core service. In the absence of the kind of committed government funding that supports the CBC and the various provincial public television systems, subscriber revenues were the only conceivable way to keep the network afloat.

The approach was ambitious, unprecedented, and risky. There was support within the Commission for some kind of license, but no one knew how a request for mandatory carriage with a fee would be received. The only absolute certainty was strong resistance from the cable companies, who would fight any precedent imposing a new, untested service on them.

The Board was well aware of the risks. But this option felt right, in a way that none of the other, more "sensible" options had.

"Anything less would have felt like a compromise," said Abraham, "A betrayal of the last twenty years. We decided to go for broke."

>———→ o ←———«

With a distribution model now chosen, it was time to increase our promotional efforts. To most Canadians—even Aboriginal peoples—TVNC was still unknown. The high-profile Advisory Committee members prepared a hit list that included every major Aboriginal and broadcasting event scheduled for the next year, key politicians and bureaucrats, and any non- profit organisation or company that might be persuaded to support TVNC. Armed with pamphlets, promotional material and speaking notes, some of Canada's highest profile Aboriginal media-makers hit the lobby trail in the spring of 1998 to spread the word that a new network was coming; a new network that was still nameless.

We decided to generate interest and awareness by launching a national contest to name the network. Some of the entries were funny (everyone loved "TIPI-TV"), most were earnest (several people suggested the "National Native Network"). An early favourite was ABN, the Aboriginal Broadcasting Network—until a name search introduced us to the Asian Broadcasting Network, a Dutch Bank, and dozens of other Aboriginal organisations with the same acronym. The lucky winner was Paul Lutman from Fort Smith, who proposed the "Aboriginal Peoples Television Network," or APTN. "The name APTN is indicative of our commitment to showcase all Aboriginal talent and stories whether they are from a First Nations, Inuit or Métis perspective," said Abe in the network newsletter. "The name also includes the word 'peoples' to remind us of our audience, and the reason we exist."

The network got its name, Paul Lutman got a SONY VCR as a prize, and we got ready for our next contest—an invitation to submit logo ideas for the new network.

That didn't work out as well. Logo design is actually a highly sophisticated graphic art. Corporate logos must be distinctive and instantly recognisable, and suggest something essential about the company they represent; but they also have to be simple enough to reduce to a few elements. They have to look good in either black and white or colour, on materials ranging from business cards to coffee cups to trade show displays, and in sizes ranging from a website thumbnail to the side of a building.

The Contest Committee received dozens of designs, incorporating every conceivable artefact, animal, symbol or motif suggestive of "native" culture—sometimes all crammed into a single undecipherable image. We quietly abandoned the public contest, and invited submissions from professional graphic designers. There were dozens of bids: but when I received the design from Earthlore Communications, an Aboriginal communications company in Ottawa, I knew we had found the right image. The APTN logo is one of the most distinctive in Canadian broadcasting. With just a few strokes it conveys an unmistakeably Aboriginal sensibility. Without a single literal element, it suggests the sun, representing a new dawn in Aboriginal broadcasting; an eye, showing an Aboriginal view-point; a dancer in motion; and a stylised, modern petroglyph. The logo was an immediate hit, and to our delight began to surface on ball caps, t-shirts and fridge magnets across the country.

But ultimately, of course, a broadcast service is defined by its programming, not by its promotion.

Over the spring and summer of 1998, while Advisory Committee and Board members toured the country with a cheerful message of unity, discussions about programming and governance behind the scenes were getting even more heated. The impending reality of the new network forced a long, hard look at all the tough questions the members had never fully resolved. Broad statements of principle about "collaboration" and "full-service programming" had sufficed to date: now the organisation finally had to make tough decisions about how the new network would be governed and managed, and exactly what viewers would see on the air.

As part of its application, TVNC had to present a detailed schedule of proposed programming to the CRTC describing the range of program genres, including actual letters of interest from producers and existing series or documentaries that could be aired. The starting point for this exercise was the existing TVNC schedule, with its preponderance of prime-time, Aboriginal language programs, and broadcast slots designed to meet the needs of viewers in northern Canada. APTN's schedule would obviously incorporate TVNC member programming, but the existing template quickly brought several critical questions to the fore. How would the network balance programming for, and from, the North and the South? Who would decide what programs were played in prime time? Which independent producers out there had material that could be scheduled or re-packaged for APTN? How would the network accommodate new programs, not produced by the original TVNC members; like daily news, feature-length drama, or animation? Who could produce French-language programming? Would Aboriginal-language productions have to be versioned or subtitled? All these, and dozens of other questions would have to be addressed and resolved in the CRTC application.

Most of the initial planning was done by the Programming Working Group, an ad-hoc team comprised of Linda O'Shaughnessy, Peter Crass and Jim Compton, working with input from the Advisory Committee and Board members. The group began to seek out and solicit additional programming to complement the existing TVNC member programming, and Linda began slotting new shows and series into a draft broadcast schedule.

That first schedule was a work of speculative fiction as creative as any novel ever written. Linda was inserting titles of programs as if they were already produced and on the shelf; in reality, many were nothing more than one-page outlines from producers with a good idea who might, someday, with luck, move their concept into production—IF funding became available.

The fantasy schedule incorporated many interesting ideas. There was to be a talk show hosted by Tina Keeper called "The Absolute Truth... About Aboriginal Women", a travel/cooking show called "Native Feasts", and "Medicine Walker", a series about traditional knowledge. It also included daily news and current affairs programs, and an exciting range of arts, language, youth, and sports shows. The problem was, none of those programs actually existed, and most never would. "Hardly any of the new series we scheduled in the original application actually came to fruition," Pat Tourigny acknowledged."That didn't matter. They sounded good enough to get the license. What really mattered was to sound credible and look like we knew what we were doing."

One critical input to the schedule was an analysis of viewers' programming preferences for a hypothetical Aboriginal network, based on a series of APTN-commissioned research studies. These included an Angus Reid survey, a Pollara consumer study, and focus groups conducted by Coopers and Lybrand. The studies revealed an interesting split. Aboriginal viewers wanted to see more nature shows, educational programs and sports; the general population, on the other hand, preferred documentaries and movies.

After weeks of wrestling with all these options, needs and preferences, Linda and the Advisory Committee completed a draft schedule and submitted it the Board. It was the first opportunity members had to see what the new service would actually look like—and feathers, predictably, were ruffled. Northern members were angry about the volume of southern programming scheduled in prime time. Inuit members wondered how a non-Inuit programming working group could possibly judge the content or merits of Inuktitut programming. Some members were reluctant to subtitle their native-language programs, but felt they should still be aired in prime time. And nobody liked their timeslots.

The draft schedule committed APTN to broadcasting at least 70% Canadian content. That wasn't enough for some Board members; when informed that CBC carried 90% Cancon, they increased APTN's target to 90% as well. It was an impossible target; and two years later, in 2000, APTN quietly requested a reduction in Canadian content back down to the original 70%. But the Board felt that TVNC's extraordinary request for mandatory carriage with a fee would require a commitment beyond what other networks were offering.

Following a more-than-usually intense round of negotiation, compromise, histrionics and horse trading, a workable schedule was hammered out. No one was ecstatic about it, but no one was miserable; it was a work in

progress, it looked convincing, and it would do for the application.
A more challenging decision was the thorny question of board structure, or, more simply, actual control of the network.

The membership of Television Northern Canada was composed of all the organisations that produced programming for the network, most of which were non-profit, region-specific broadcasters funded by the NNBAP. Each year, every member organisation appointed a director to the TVNC Board. The system worked, although it made for an unusually large and slightly unwieldy governance body. But APTN was going to be a national network, not just a northern one: its Board and membership would have to represent all Aboriginal peoples in Canada. In the South there were no Indigenous, public broadcast organisations comparable to the NNBAP-funded groups; Aboriginal producers south of the Hamelin line worked as individuals, for established broadcasters, or for privately owned production companies. So in any new corporate structure, the North would be represented by organisations, while the South would be represented by individuals. To complicate things further, the TVNC members decided not to bring on any new members; southern interests would be represented on the Board alone.

At the heart of the matter was northern fear about loss of control. Their concern was understandable. The members of TVNC had taken decades to create a system that worked for them and their audience; now they were being challenged to share control of that system with untried partners in the South. But to members of the Advisory Committee, the distrust was disconcerting: after all, the new network was going to need southern support and production to get licensed. Jim Compton remembers thinking "Let's get the network first, before we start fighting over it."

Two TVNC members; the GNWT and Yukon College, agreed to step down from the Board in order to make room for southern Aboriginal directors. That left eight TVNC members and eight TVNC seats on the Board. Since none of the existing members were prepared to give up or share their seats, it would be necessary to add the same number of directors from the South.

The two-month discussion of the expanded Board structure exposed many of the divisions within the APTN team; north and south, private sector and non-profit, Inuit and First Nations, filmmakers and broadcasters. The tension was exacerbated by a difference in style. TVNC had always tried to operate in a spirit of real northern consensus. Major decisions often took months, or even years, and required long, careful consideration of all options, much deliberation, and informed consent by all parties. It was slow, and for outsiders it was frustrating; but it ensured long-term stability and harmony among the members. The Advisory Committee were all familiar with the dynamics of consensus decision-making. But they were also independent filmmakers, used to tight schedules and tough negotiation, and they were keenly aware of the approaching deadline for a proposal. They felt impatient, and pushed hard for quick decisions; the TVNC members felt rushed, and at times resented the Committee's proclivity for action without adequate Board consideration and Board approval. Tension grew to the point that the Board appointed a member to sit in on every Advisory Committee meeting.

But the looming application deadline did, in fact, force all parties to compromise. Everyone finally agreed on a structure that no one liked, but almost everyone could live with. The Board would be comprised of eight northern NNBAP directors, representing the existing TVNC members, and one northern independent producer, eight southern NNBAP directors appointed by NNBAP-funded groups who were not TVNC members (such as Wawatay and MBC), plus one independent producer; and three additional Directors-at-Large, one from the North, one from the East, and one from the West. It was a compromise; not a consensus, some TVNC directors served notice that they might reconsider the structure if and when APTN received a licence. Many staff and observers privately wondered how an organisation with more Board members than staff was going to be able to function.

An even bigger issue was the question of how producers could serve as Board members without conflict of interest. At TVNC, the programmers were the Board; they had always developed their own schedule, agreeing on which member organisations would get which timeslots for each season. But the new network would feature programming from a much wider range of sources and its schedule would have to be designed with a very different audience in mind. Programmers and producers would be needed on the

Board, but a more objective approach to programming and scheduling would be required. The solution was to create a standing Programming Committee, with a more rigorous process and formal mandate than the informal team drafting the schedule for the CRTC proposal.

In order to convince the CRTC, cable companies, and consumers that there really was an audience for APTN, TVNC commissioned several market research papers. An Angus Reid poll returned some encouraging findings. 79% of Canadians reported some interest in viewing the channel; 48% stated they would tune in at least once a week; and 66% supported national distribution of the service as a way to encourage understanding between Aboriginal and non-Aboriginal communities.

There were more positive results from a Pollara survey asking consumers about their television viewing patterns and their interest in an Aboriginal channel. More than 80% of Aboriginal people and 47% of the general population said they would watch the service. In a series of focus groups with Aboriginal people in Six Nations, Toronto and Winnipeg, participants responded enthusiastically to videotaped segments of programming. Comments from viewers included:

"It's about time...this channel will change perceptions ...it will help our children and ourselves ...it would be nothing but positive ...I would be interested in seeing more."

There was clearly an audience for APTN out there, an audience willing to pay. The Angus Reid survey found that 68% of the general population and 84% of the Aboriginal population would contribute an additional 15 cents per month to receive APTN. That finding was widely circulated, and referenced several times at the CRTC License hearing. I confess we were more circumspect when most respondents agreed with the statement "Canadian Aboriginal communities should compete for TV channels in the same way any network or TV station does."

Now TVNC had a draft schedule and governance structure to include in the CRTC application. But one major hurdle remained; TVNC would have to prove to the Commission that it could actually pay for the development and start up of APTN. The network's only collateral was its 96 low power transmitters scattered across the North. Until APTN started generating subscriber revenues, TVNC was going to need a line of credit. As a not-for-profit, charitable corporation whose only significant source of funding was government grants, TVNC was a risky investment. It took aggressive lobbying and weeks of negotiation by Brenda Chambers, Dave Tuccaro, and Patricia Hutton to extract a carefully crafted letter from the Royal Bank that just barely endorsed TVNC and provided a $2.2 million line of credit. The catch, of course, was that the line of credit was contingent on APTN being granted mandatory carriage with a fee; any other type of license, and the bank would withdraw its offer.

By early June, most of the pieces were in place. Staff, management, Board, advisors and a swarm of specialised consultants scrambled to assemble the final versions of the new network's management and board systems, technical infrastructure, capital and facilities budgets, financial operations, marketing strategy, programming plan, and, of course, the all-important justification for mandatory carriage with subscriber fees. To bolster that argument, Abraham brought in Sylvie Courtemanche, a lawyer and, like Patrick, a CRTC refugee well-versed in the regulatory process.

The only major gap, carefully fudged in the applications' discussion of proposed technical infrastructure, was the critical question of where the network's main production centre would actually be located. Three months simply hadn't allowed enough time to request and assess proposals from interested communities across Canada. TVNC already had a northern production centre in Yellowknife, but a headquarters in the NWT would be impractical, and prohibitively expensive, for a national organisation. As the final sections of the CRTC proposal came together, Ottawa, Winnipeg and Edmonton were all under consideration as potential host cities for the network headquarters.

The final application and its attachments were over 200 pages long. Shortly before APTN's hearings, a CRTC official complimented TVNC on having prepared such a detailed and eloquent application in just three months. While the compliment was certainly appreciated, it was slightly off-base: the application was the distillation of a vision that had been in development for more than twenty years.

The submission set out all the key elements of the proposed network in a supplementary brief, which provided a condensed description of APTN.

The new service would:

- Be a mandatory service
- Be a not-for-profit corporation
- Seek a monthly fee of 15 cents per subscriber
- Carry 90% Canadian content
- Provide 120 hours per week of programming in English, French and approximately 15 different Aboriginal languages
- Produce a daily, Aboriginal-themed newscast
- Commit $5.9 million to Canadian acquisitions in its first year
- Establish an independent program selection committee in order to ensure fair and equitable access to the network
- Be governed by a 21-member Aboriginal board of directors
- Launch in September 1999

The most controversial section of the proposal was the network's request for mandatory carriage with a fee. It was sure to draw fire from cable companies; so the application carefully laid out TVNC's rationale to build the strongest possible legal and social argument for this unprecedented arrangement.

At the heart of TVNC's legal argument was subsection 17(5) of the Broadcasting Distribution Regulations, part of the 1981 Broadcast Act, which includes this provision:

> *"If the Commission has determined that a programming service is of national public interest and has licensed the service as a mandatory service, the licensee shall distribute the service as part of the basic service."*

The Act further states that Canadian broadcast services must:

> *"…through its programming and the employment opportunities arising out of its operations, serve the needs and interests, and reflect the circumstances and aspirations of Canadian men, women and children, including equal rights, linguistic duality and the multicultural and multiracial nature of Canadian society and the special place of Aboriginal people within that society."*

Existing broadcasting services, including the CBC, had failed to serve or reflect Aboriginal Canada. The submission argued that only an Aboriginal network could do that, stating:

"It is vital that the Canadian broadcasting system adequately serve all elements of our population. We have no European homeland. No Asian homeland. No African homeland. Canada is the cradle of our languages and cultures. We can look nowhere else for the roots of our being."
APTN would represent the most distinctly Canadian broadcast service imaginable, giving voice to languages and perspectives found nowhere else in the world. It would introduce Canadians to the Aboriginal foundations of their own country, and provide a badly-needed mirror, reflecting Indigenous peoples to themselves through the eyes of their own writers, directors, journalists and performers.

The application concluded with a powerful commitment:

"This network is not simply for the empowerment of Aboriginal people in Canada. It will be for all Canadians. For as we tell our stories, you will begin to understand us better. And the better we understand each other, the easier it will be to respect each other and share in each other's lives. Lofty goals, perhaps. But ones worth striving for. And goals that, through APTN, we believe, are now within our reach."

A courier picked up the application documents at the end of day on June 5, 1998, and a small, exhausted group went out for pizza and beer. We toasted the network, the team, and the future, and went home early. The future of the network was once again in the hands of the CRTC. We knew it would be months before an eventual hearing and an opportunity to make our case in person. And we knew it was going to be a busy summer.

The communications team now had time to concentrate on raising awareness and support for APTN. While we had a striking logo and a few pamphlets, we needed a new promotional document. We needed a glossy, full-colour brochure, illustrated with photos of Aboriginal people busily engaged in all aspects of broadcasting. Those images were hard to find; very few of the TVNC members had the funds or the time to take production stills, and I needed the shots immediately. So we faked it. I called all my Aboriginal friends in Ottawa, contracted a photographer named Fred Cattroll, and bribed everyone with free pizza. We met at a local production company, where Fred arranged my friends in various dramatic, professional configurations, sitting behind desks, peering intently into studio cameras, gazing deeply into various digital scopes and gauges, posing with microphone booms and lights. None of our obliging models had a clue what they were supposed to be doing, but the photos looked great, and no one ever knew not one person in our new, glossy brochure was even remotely involved in broadcasting.

We rolled out the new brochure at the 1998 Banff Television Festival, where Abraham and several members of the Advisory Committee had arrived early to promote the APTN concept. It was only two years since TVNC had first appeared at the Banff Festival, handing out thermal coffee cups in a tiny rented hotel room and hoping for a little attention. Things were different this time around. Word had spread in the industry that APTN had applied for a national license, and suddenly interest was high. "Native" was clearly the flavour of the month.

The festival's highlight was an Aboriginal Luncheon sponsored by Cancom and held in a panoramic room overlooking the Banff Springs Hotel and the Rocky mountains. More than 100 politicians, broadcasters, journalists, Aboriginal leaders and artists dined and applauded as we unveiled our new logo and celebrated the CRTC application with music and dancing. Carole Geddes, Tina Keeper, Gil Cardinal and Drew Hayden Taylor, judges for the Telefilm/TVNC Aboriginal production award, were on hand to announce the winners; Journey Through Fear, a lovely claymation short by Dennis and Melanie Jackson, and a moving drama, Silent Tears, by Shirley Cheechoo.

Tina Keeper, star of "North of Sixty", capped the event with an impassioned speech about the need for APTN and the importance of listening to Aboriginal voices. "It is my belief that as we approach the 21st century, it is time to take our rightful place as the interpreters of our own reality," she said.

Also present were the winners of the Ross Charles Award, who had just spent several weeks at the Banff Centre for the Arts at a screenwriter's workshop. Created in 1995, the Ross Charles Award was originally an opportunity for northern broadcasters to learn more about Cancom and the CRTC through a three-month internship. By 1998, it had evolved into a demanding, week-long workshop where young northern Aboriginal broadcasters honed their screenwriting and production skills under pressure. The intensity of that experience inevitably created a sense of kinship among participants, and the team of young co-producers that bonded at Banff in 1998 included Gil Cardinal, Randall McKenzie, Tookie Mercredi, Jordan Wheeler and Evie Mark. Just one year later, that crew would be called on to stretch their new skills to the limit at the APTN launch.

The promotional team continued to tour the country, raising support and awareness. Their task was easier, now there was a definite buzz in the air and an announcement by Cancom added to the momentum. During their license renewal hearing at the CRTC, Cancom confirmed they would be contributing $400,000 to TVNC to offset the cost of the APTN application. The news couldn't have come at a better time. The network was increasingly in the public eye, and pressure was on to maintain the highest possible profile heading into the licence hearings. TVNC was proposing to operate a national network, essential to maintain the quality of its existing regional system. The Yellowknife centre was refurbished and redesigned as a full-service, centralised northern production and distribution centre. New master control operators were hired, technical infrastructure was upgraded, new edit suites were installed, and an updated schedule with high-gloss promotional materials and packaging was prepared for the fall.

The network attracted further attention in July of that summer for one of its first international co-productions. The Inuit Circumpolar Conference (ICC) is an influential northern policy organisation, with representation from Russia, the United States, Canada, and Greenland. In collaboration with KNR, the Greenlandic national TV service, TVNC broadcast up to two hours per day of the ICC General Assembly, an event held once every four years, from Nuuk, the capital of Greenland. The coverage included live proceedings of the General Assembly, analysis and commentary, and entertainment. It was a logistical nightmare, but a programming triumph, and offered Canadian and international audiences a rare glimpse of one of the world's least-known Inuit cultures.

Back in Ottawa, the legal and policy team began preparing responses to "deficiency questions"; requests from the CRTC for additional detail in areas like programming, distribution, closed captioning and the Southern production centre. They were also monitoring a potential strategic challenge. The TVA Group was a Québec-based, French language private television station. TVA had also appeared at the Third National Network hearings, and was also seeking national network status, with mandatory carriage. There were concerns that a favourable decision for TVA might weaken APTN's case. To avoid this, Patrick Tourigny wrote a letter to the CRTC and requested that the CRTC make a decision on TVA at the same time as APTN. Instead, the Commission went ahead and approved national distribution of TVA in October, 1998, and this precedent actually helped APTN.

On a Friday afternoon in late August, TVNC got the word, the CRTC hearing on the APTN application would be held on November 12, 1998 in Hull, Québec.

At this point in every licensing process, the CRTC publishes the original application and the proponents' response to deficiency questions, and invites the public to respond with further questions, comments, and letters of endorsement or concern. This was the opportunity for cable companies and political opponents to voice their opposition, Our job was to make sure that the voices supporting APTN were heard even more loudly and clearly.

The Advisory Committee and TVNC executive canvassed two dozen hand- picked individuals, requesting that they send letters of support and appear before the CRTC. It was a group of political leaders, celebrities, broadcasters, and educators, representing a good mix of north and south, Aboriginal and non-Aboriginal people, and potential viewers. Almost everyone agreed.

We knew it would also be necessary to prove there was broad-based support in the Aboriginal community for the network. Gary Farmer directed us to Cynthia Lickers, a Mohawk media maven working in Toronto at an independent video information clearinghouse. Cynthia's passion was linking Aboriginal media professionals together and she was in the process of creating just what we needed, a national Aboriginal media database. With Cynthia's help, TVNC was able to send out letters to more than 2,000 television producers, educators, First Nation communities, Friendship Centres, Aboriginal and non-profit organisations across Canada.

The requests for support went out, and every day we scanned the fax machine (the preferred medium in those pre-historic, pre-texting nineties) for responses. Feedback was critical. We had argued to the CRTC, this channel was both needed AND wanted; too many negative or too few positive letters would undermine the credibility of the whole application. The worst possible scenario would be no letters at all; a situation that seemed increasingly possible as the deadline for support drew closer and our visits to the fax machine grew more frequent and more anxious. But there was nothing at play more sinister than procrastination. By the October 19 deadline, we had received 286 letters of enthusiastic support. Fewer than a dozen was negative or conditional, and all but one of those was expected.

The wave of support was a welcome shot of encouragement, a much-needed confirmation to an exhausted team that we were on the right track. The letters were insightful and inspiring. A favourite at the office was a heart-warming collection of messages from an elementary school class in Alert Bay, B.C. (original spelling and grammar intact). Joseph Rufus wrote: "I feel that it would be pretty cool if we get a network for our people …I believe 100% that you can get are network for us. So have a good meeting."

DeAnna Twance looked forward to a career: "It would give us natives jobs and something to work toward. I think it would be cool to be on TV and see yourself and know what happened to our ancestors."

Tamara Scheck felt APTN would encourage accurate portrayals of Aboriginal people;

"I think they should let us northern Indian's have our own show. Because when I'm on the internet, chatting with someone from, let's say Europe, they think us Indian's live in igloos. But we don't…some people think we're prairie Indians, but we're not. We don't ride horses…we are the Kwa'kawakw Indians. And we have our own ways."

Letters poured in from all parts of the country and all types of people, from producers to academics to casual viewers fascinated by the prospect of a television bridge across an ancient cultural divide. Marilyn Jones of the University College of the Cariboo wrote,

"I feel the potential benefits of this project are boundless; benefits for native and non-native people will foster better community relations, sensitivity, and awareness."

Many non- Aboriginal people recognised the need to include Aboriginal people and stories as part of the Canadian media mosaic.

"We, as Canadians, all share the responsibility for the survival of Aboriginal cultures and languages, and of ensuring that Aboriginal children have the opportunity to grow up with pride in their culture and confident in the knowledge that their stories will be part of the continuum of Canada's rich heritage," wrote Terry Markus of Catalyst Entertainment.

Barbara Hagar's message summarised the view of most Aboriginal producers, educators and potential viewers: that Canada needed Aboriginal media to fight mainstream stereotyping.

"It's time for us to start taking control of the media messages that appear … on TV. We need to insist that the media starts balancing their stories about our problems and issues with coverage of all the positive, empowering things that are going on in our families and communities all across the country."

Most letters opposing the application—including those from the CBC, Rogers, Shaw, the Canadian Cable Television Association (CCTA), and CHUM—grudgingly supported the licensing of a national Aboriginal television network, but predictably balked at TVNC's request that the service be distributed on a mandatory basis.

Patrick Tourigny was in charge of responding to the negative letters. Most of the interventions were expected, although he was surprised by the lack of support from public networks like CBC and Vision. "I took it all personally," he said, "and I shouldn't have. They basically didn't want APTN to have any more rights than other networks."

Patrick was a recovering smoker, prone to furious gum-chewing under stress, and the entire APTN staff learned to evaluate the seriousness of an intervention by the vigor of his mastication each morning, after he disappeared into his office with the morning's faxes. One day the chewing stopped altogether.

APTN had expected opposition from the cable industry, from the private sector and perhaps, from disgruntled individuals. But it never expected opposition from one of its own members.

The letter came from Northern Native Broadcasting Yukon, and was signed by NNBY Chairperson Michelle Kola. It stated bluntly that NNBY refused to support the proposal unless changes were made.

"Documents prepared by TVNC suggest that some deep systematic changes will be forthcoming which could undermine the interest of the Aboriginal peoples of the North," said Ms. Kola.

The letter outlined the conditions under which NNBY would support the TVNC application. They included demands that every founding TVNC member would have to be guaranteed a Board seat, northerners would maintain ownership and control of the network, and that all founding TVNC members would be guaranteed the unrestricted right of continued distribution of their programs.

The letter may have been signed by Michelle Kola, but the tone was gratingly familiar to many at TVNC. NNBY's Executive Director, Barry Zellen, was a southerner who had moved north as an editor for ICS. He left Inuvik after attacking the regional Inuit leadership in print, and resurfaced at NCS in Yellowknife. Shortly afterward, he launched a letter campaign demanding fellow TVNC members NNBY and IBC voluntarily give up a portion of their funding to NCS, his new employer. His demand that NNBY relinquish its funding ceased when he left NCS and went to work for—of all people—NNBY. Now, it seemed, NNBY had found a new target.

TVNC staff and Board members were appalled. The network had just shot itself, very publicly, in the foot. The uneasy north-south coalition was fragile enough, now it seemed the northern members couldn't agree among themselves. Patrick addressed the next Board meeting bluntly.

"This intervention undermines TVNC's credibility," he warned. "It's very possible that the CRTC may deny the license if they think TVNC members are not united."

The network moved swiftly to control the damage. TVNC responded immediately and diplomatically to the CRTC regarding NNBY's intervention, assuring the Commission "All board members, including

NNBY, reviewed the APTN application and unanimously endorsed it during a board meeting in May, 1998, with the understanding that the proposed by-laws affecting the Board structure would be further addressed at the next AGM." Bernard Hervieux, the executive director of the Québec-based La Société de Communications Atikamekw-Montagnais, was firm but tactful in his message to NNBY at the next Board meeting.

"The NNBAP members also have some concerns with different aspects of the application," he said, speaking directly to the NNBY representatives in the room. "But we support the concept. We would like to work these details out. These are internal, Board questions and not something to send to the CRTC. This may be our last chance to put an application forward. This is not the time to jeopardize our effort."

Abraham made direct contact with Michelle Kola, and talked the Yukon's issues through. After much discussion NNBY agreed its concerns could all be addressed through normal governance and management channels. The application could proceed with their support. Neither northern nor southern media ever picked up the story of the brief schism. Barry Zellen left NNBY shortly afterwards.

In retrospect, the Yukon's position is easier to understand. Decision-making by consensus and lengthy consideration of long-term consequences, are more than just clichés; they're important values in Aboriginal culture. The Yukon was, in effect, serving notice that the pressure of time was forcing decisions from the TVNC Board without authentic consensus. Their concerns about loss of control were real and, some would argue, justified by subsequent events. What remains unknown is whether TVNC could ever have achieved real consensus, or whether APTN would exist today if the organisation hadn't moved as swiftly as it did.

While the most difficult intervention to respond to was no doubt NNBY's, the most comprehensive was the CCTA's, the organisation which represented 75 cable companies in Canada. The cable industry had deep pockets and lots of lawyers, and they were fiercely opposed to APTN's request for mandatory status. Their argument however, was at odds with their own practices, as Patrick Tourigny gleefully pointed out. Just months before, when the TVA Group had requested the same carriage as APTN, the CCTA had been silent.

"TVA is directly owned by the second largest cable operator in Canada," noted Patrick in the response. "TVNC cannot help but wonder whether this is the reason the CCTA chose to remain silent on the TVA request."

The CCTA's most substantive objection was to APTN's use of section 9(1)(h) of the Broadcasting Act, to justify special mandatory carriage. They pointed out that the Act identifies many specific groups, none of whom had ever requested special status. Instead, the CCTA recommended APTN be carried as a digital service. They framed their argument as a question of pure consumer choice, stating; "…in our view, customers must be able to decide what services they do and do not want to receive."

TVNC's response reasserted the unique position of Aboriginal people in Canada, and the important role APTN would play in strengthening a national, public television system that was failing to address the needs of all Canadians. It argued, "It is no longer acceptable to marginalise Aboriginal peoples or to obstruct their aspirations to fully participate in Canadian society through the 'publicly-owned' broadcasting system."

Aboriginal people were not simply another multicultural group or specialty audience: they were founders of the country, original inhabitants, and an important and neglected pillar of Canadian culture. APTN would simply not be viable as a discretionary service. If the CRTC agreed with the goals of the Broadcast Act, and if APTN represented a viable way to meet those goals, then the only practical solution was the service described in the APTN application. The bottom line was simple:

"TVNC believes that its application amply meets the criteria that justify mandatory carriage."

The preparation was over. In just 8 months, the application had been compiled, reviewed and submitted, the deficiency questions responded to, and the letters of intervention received and addressed. It was October, and time to prepare for the hearings themselves.

CHAPTER VI

THE PITCH

CONVINCING THE CRTC

6:30 pm, September 1, 1999

Backstage, in the dressing rooms and wings of the stage, performers are donning costumes, queuing for makeup, tuning instruments, reviewing set lists, or simply pacing. Duane Shuttleworth moves among them, nodding, smiling, scanning his extensive checklist for all the details to be confirmed before the lights go up and the show begins. All that planning appears to have paid off. Everything seems to be falling into place.

"Amazing," he thinks.

Abraham is first in line for makeup; He'll be one of the first people interviewed on air as part of the live show. He tucks a paper towel under his chin to protect his seal skin vest while a volunteer applies powder.

"Will the makeup hurt the sealskin?" she asks him. "I don't know," he says. "Most of the seals I knew didn't wear makeup." Across the makeshift hall, Alanis Obomsawin, looking serene, is in the women's dressing room, receiving a last-minute touch-up. She made her professional debut as a singer in New York City in 1960; she's been onstage too often to get nervous. She watches the younger performers anxiously pacing and adjusting their costumes and smiles. They'll do fine.

One of those performers is Lisa Meeches, who is literally jingling. Most of the APTN crowd know her as a broadcaster; but tonight, she'll be playing a different role. Lisa is a Jingle Dress Dancer; her regalia includes several rows of metal cones sewn on her brightly coloured dress. The cones create a rhythmic, bell-like sound as the dancers move. Lisa and the other dancers gather in the wings, the delicate tinkling of their dresses like laughter in the crowded backstage.

Laura Milliken wends her way through the performers, clipboard and stopwatch at the ready. She's still very worried that the entertainers are going to go over time. The whole show is clocked to the last second. Dozens of videotaped segments are cued up in Yellowknife, all relying on cues from the onstage and on-camera hosts. If one performer goes too long, the whole delicate balance between broadcast and stage show falls apart. She hugs a singer,

"Six minutes! Remember, you guys have six minutes!"

My official work is done for the moment, but I'm too keyed up to sit down, so I join a group of volunteers at our promotional table, selling T-shirts, baseball caps and commemorative buttons that say, "APTN Launch, September 1, 1999—I was there."

People are milling about in front of the stage area. Families, elders, dignitaries, APTN supporters and curious Winnipeggers out to see a free show. We'd hoped for a thousand people, but we're going to do way better than that—the chairs are already filling up. It looks like it's going to be a full house.

From the official perspective, a CRTC hearing sounds like a pretty dry affair. Its purpose is simply to clarify legal or regulatory issues arising from a written application.

However from the applicant's perspective, however, a license application hearing is a combination of trial, sales pitch, and symphony. Arguments have to be prepared, rehearsed, and carefully supported by unassailable (or at least well-spun) facts. Counter-arguments have to be anticipated and rebuttals developed. Beyond the legal and regulatory dimension of the hearing, proponents are also trying to sell a vision, convey their passion, and convince Commissioners their service is meeting a vital need. And of course, all the performers need to sing in harmony, ideally from the same score.

Like any orchestra, we rehearsed. On November 11, one day before our appearance, TVNC's legal counsel, Sylvie Courtemanche, set up a mock hearing. Playing the role of Commissioner, she grilled the TVNC presentation team with questions and drilled them on specifics of the application. She was a tough cross examiner—much tougher, in fact, than the Commissioners themselves would be. But at the end of a full day of rehearsal, everyone felt ready.

My job was to prepare the Board members and Advisory Committee for media inquiries. Broadcasters love stories about broadcasting, and they love conflict. We were expecting strong opposition from cable companies, from consumer groups, and possibly from other media outlets resentful of the competition. We anticipated a fair amount of media interest, and for days before the hearings, I worked with all our spokespersons to ensure everyone was conveying the same messages.

Although TVNC didn't know which CRTC Commissioners would be assigned to the APTN application, we knew they were preparing as well. There would be three Commissioners, and each would be reviewing a thick briefing book prepared by the Commission's legal and policy staff, analysing the application and setting out questions to be explored during the hearing. The Commission was a deliberately diverse body, and the Commissioners represented a wide range of social and political views. We had done everything we could to prepare for the hearings; In the end everything would depend on who was chosen to hear our application.

The morning of November 12 was overcast and the low clouds promised snow. The hearings were scheduled to be held at a cluster of nondescript government office towers in Hull, Québec ; Down the hall__past the food court, into a foyer outside what was simply called the Conference Centre. It looked like a large courtroom, stuffy and windowless.

The APTN license was number two on the Commission's agenda that day, preceded by a Bell Canada application for a pay-per-view license. APTN's hearing wasn't expected to start before noon, but we were there when the building opened, setting up displays, tables with network information and brochures, and monitors playing our promotional reel. The Bell Canada hearing began at nine and our presenters settled in for the wait, chatting up civil servants drawn by the display and drinking copious amounts of some of the National Capital Region's worst coffee. Nervous energy ebbed as the Bell proceedings dragged on past lunch and into the afternoon. By 3:00 pm we began to plan for a postponement to the next day—not an easy thing to do at the last minute, with more than a dozen out-of-town presenters lined up. But at 5:00 pm the summons came; the Commissioners would hear our opening arguments right away, and continue into the evening.

The TVNC team grabbed their files, briefcases and cell phones, filed into the hearing room, and arranged themselves in two rows facing the Commissioners. In the front row were Abraham Tagalik, Gary Farmer and Patrick Tourigny, joined by Joanne Macdonald from NNBY—a not-too-subtle message to the Commissioners that TVNC's unity was intact. Sitting in the second row were Roman Bittman, Glenn Stuart of Price Waterhouse Coopers, Alanis Obomsawin, Sylvie Courtemanche and Patricia Hutton. They were joined at the last minute by Linda O'Shaughnessy, who had been promised time and time again she wouldn't have to appear. But when the presentation team realised no one else could possibly explain APTN's complicated schedule, she was drafted.

"I was very nervous beforehand," she admitted. "But once I sat down on that panel, I was fine. The rehearsals with Sylvie were a lot tougher."

Sitting at a side table, armed with multiple volumes of technical information, were Jerry Giberson, Director of Network Operations, and Debra McLaughlin from Price Waterhouse Coopers. Behind the presenters was an audience of TVNC Board members, associate members, friends of the network, representatives of Aboriginal organisations, and a group of curious youth from a local Inuit training program.

As soon as we walked into the hearing room, Patrick scanned the three seated Commissioners like an experienced defense attorney evaluating a jury. He recognised them all, leaned over, and whispered to Abraham: "Dream Team."

With a background in law, Commissioner Andrée Wylie would Chair the proceedings. She was Vice-Chair of broadcasting at the Commission, a well- known advocate for consumers and a strong critic of cable companies. When she spoke, she didn't mince words.

Beside her was Andrew Cardozo. Relatively new to the Commission, when he joined, he knew very little about TVNC or Aboriginal broadcasters. Most of his work had been in the areas of employment equity, as an advocate for diversity and multiculturalism. But he had spent many hours in discussion with Patrick Tourigny, while Pat was still at the Commission, and he was fascinated by the work being done by TVNC and its members. He had actually met the TVNC Board and Advisory Committee for lunch months before in order to get acquainted with the network, and had been subjected to a pointed grilling from Alanis Obomsawin.

"She stood up, just looked at me with those piercing eyes, and said, 'Do you really think we can get through this or are we just wasting our time?' I said, 'I can't tell you, I have to see the application.'"

The third Commissioner was Joan Pennefather, a producer who had served as Chair of the National Film Board and was widely recognised for her tireless promotion of women in the film and television industries.

"They were all sympathetic, open-minded and forward-thinking," said Patrick. "We drew a flush."

Abraham began the hearing by greeting the Commissioners in Inuktitut; a short, friendly reminder of the language barrier Aboriginal audiences experience every day. He then switched to English for a powerful opening statement.

"Madam Chair and Commissioners, this is an historic opportunity. It is about breaking with the past and building for the future. It is about Canada, through the powers invested in the Commission, demonstrating a commitment to improving the quality of life of native Canadians. It is about providing a window on Aboriginal life and culture for all Canadians to see and share."

For the next hour, Abraham and the other TVNC presenters moved smoothly through the key points of APTN's proposal. Asked how he thought Canadians would respond to APTN's request for 15 cents per month subscriber fees, Abraham answered.

"Just think. For less than the cost of a Coke and a chocolate bar a year, our First Peoples will finally achieve their rightful position within the Canadian broadcasting system. We think Canadians will agree that this is a bargain."

The mood was positive and relaxed. After the presentation and a few preliminary questions from the Commissioners, the hearing was adjourned to the next day.

For the past two days I had been on the phone lining up our interveners and organising our support. CRTC hearings are usually pretty dull affairs, but we were determined to give ours a more human face. The plan was to fill the hearing room with Aboriginal people and let the Commissioners know their decision was going to have a real impact on First Nations, Inuit and Métis people across Canada. A few days before the hearing, we had put up posters at the Friendship Centre and all the Aboriginal organisations across the city, and we hired a bus and driver to collect interested people at specific collection points. I'm not sure whether it was the community's passion for Aboriginal programming, or the free tea, bannock, and goodies we were offering—but we got an excellent turnout.

The Commissioners were somewhat nonplussed at the surprising number of people wandering in and out of the hearings.

"We weren't really used to [all those people in the room]," recalled Andrew Cardozo. "I remember thinking, 'please don't clap'."

The Commissioners got the message: there was more to this network than suits and celebrities. This was about real people.

Questioning by the Commissioners was milder than anticipated and they seemed more curious than confrontational. After a couple of hours, Andree Wylie announced it was time to hear from the twenty-one scheduled interveners.

All but one of the interventions were completely supportive. Many were highly personal. George Swanson, the principal of an elementary school in North Bay, Ontario, talked about the need of children in communities for role models like Graham Greene and Chief Dan George, and the power of television to create them.

"These men became heroes worthy of imitation. They set standards for us to emulate and strive for. They personified realised dreams, signifying that it was okay for us to dream too. And they came to us via the big screen of television. APTN can begin to provide this kind of opportunity to the Aboriginal community and to society at large."

Tina Keeper spoke of the network's importance to aspiring media professionals.

"The major contribution to artists and producers and the like will be that they will be able to work," she said. "They'll have a forum that really has not been there before."

One surprising intervention came from Canwest Global, one of the only mainstream networks to support TVNC's application. Gary Maavara acknowledged the challenges facing APTN, but challenged everyone.

> *"… to ask himself or herself; when a visionary move has been easy?* APTN will succeed—but only if we all embrace their vision and look for solutions rather than obstacles."

Andrew Cardozo later acknowledged that the Canwest intervention had been very important. "It was unexpected, but it was good to have them on the record," he said.

As the interveners provided emotionally charged testimony on the need for APTN, I was in the foyer checking the names off the list. I was getting worried. One of our key presenters had not arrived and could not be located. It was Adam Beach, one of the most exciting young Aboriginal actors in the business.

Coincidentally, a resident of Ottawa. I had sent him messages over the previous weeks reminding him of the hearings, including the date, time and location. All the other interveners had confirmed their arrival time with me and shown up right on schedule—but not a word from Adam. I finally reached him at his home, and reminded him that today was the day of the CRTC hearings. Silence. Then,

"Right," he said. A pause. "Hmmmm."

It would be a problem, he said. He had to take care of his kids. He didn't have a vehicle at the moment. He wasn't sure he could make it. I immediately volunteered to babysit his kids and promised to send a cab to pick him up.

"Hmmmm," he said. "Yeah. I'll see what I can do."

"So much for that," I thought, and went back to the rest of my red-flagged to-do list. I was about to tell the clerk of the Commission that one intervener could be taken off the list, when Adam sauntered into the foyer.

"Hey," he said nonchalantly.

He explained that he really hadn't prepared very much, and what exactly did I want him to say?

"Oh great", I thought. As he walked into the hearing and moved to the presenter's table, I found myself wondering whether or not this had been a good idea. And then he sat down and began to speak.

"I will never forget the time I was on the set of the Disney movie Squanto," he began, leaning into the microphone and drawing everyone into his story. "The director asked me to 'run like an Indian, jump from a ledge and say something in Indian.' Of course, there were several difficulties with what I was told to do—the least of which was jumping from the ledge. First, how does one run like an Indian?"

A laugh rippled through the room, and I couldn't help but notice that the two female Commissioners were paying rapt attention.

"The second problem had to do with the language thing. 'Say something in Indian.' There is no one Aboriginal language. Plains Cree do not speak the same tongue as northern Québec Cree. Nisga'a peoples do not speak Innu, and I don't know Mi'kmaq. To be Indigenous does not mean to be the same as other native peoples. It means that we are the original peoples of the land."

Speaking off the cuff and directly to the Commissioners, he talked about his own life, both personal and professional, and about his belief in APTN's potential "to break down the stereotypes that the entertainment industry has built up about First Nations people."

He spoke movingly of APTN as a conduit through which First Nations could teach and learn from each other and from other nations. Without prompting or rehearsal, Adam Beach cut straight to the heart of the APTN vision.

"Was that okay?" he asked after he emerged from the hearing room. I assured him it had been perfect.

The only negative intervention at the hearing came from the CCTA. Their case was presented by Jay Thomson, VP of Legal and Regulatory Affairs, who recapitulated the issues raised in the CCTA's written intervention: The Association opposed mandatory carriage, there were no analog channels available to accommodate a new mandatory channel, in any case. The CCTA recommended digital carriage, framing their position as an argument for "consumer choice."

It was clear within moments that the Commission was unimpressed. Commissioner Pennefather asked when the "digital service" the CCTA proposed for APTN would actually be rolled out. Thomson was unable to provide an actual date. If there were no available analog channels for APTN, how had cable systems somehow found 'free' analog channels that could be converted to digital channels? Thomson said they found alphanumeric channels or reduced the number of pay-per-view channels, and acknowledged that there were various ways to make analog channels available. It was clear that if they had to, cable companies could find the space.

Commissioner Wylie bristled at the suggestion that APTN should only be offered to consumers willing to pay for the service, noting that she was being forced to pay for TSN, a sports specialty channel, as part of her basic cable package in Ottawa.

"Did I miss some survey or questionnaire sent to me in my home as to whether I would like more sports? Was there something sent out to establish why the cable company thinks I need more sports? I don't think so…so I have great difficulty in you coming and telling me, saying [APTN] goes against consumer choice."

»———→ o ←———«

It was the most heated discussion at the hearing. When Ian Morrison of the Friends of Canadian Broadcasting sat down at the presenter's table in the seat just vacated by Jay Thomson, he looked up and commented wryly,

"I am noting, Madam Chair, that the chair I am sitting on is very warm!"

Morrison himself added to the heat by shredding the CCTA's claim their systems lacked channel capacity.

"Stripped of its thin veneer of plausibility, he said, "What the CCTA is really advocating, is that you refrain from mandating carriage, thereby saving channel capacity for profitable and cheap foreign services, that you help cable with its price-elasticity modelling, and that you place APTN on the shelf, with its business plan in tatters, until the dawn of effective digital distribution."

There were many eloquent people who spoke that day—national organisations like AFN and ITK, other broadcasters, and founders of the movement like Gail Valaskakis and Rosemarie Kuptana. But the speaker I remember most clearly, twelve years later, was the last intervener of the day, a young Cree man named Greg Dreaver.

"A long time ago, a tree fell in the forest," he began. "And an Aboriginal person went and sat on that tree, on that log. And a non-Aboriginal person came up and he said, 'I notice you are sitting on a really beautiful tree there, do you mind if I sit down too?' And the Aboriginal person looked at this non-Aboriginal person and said, 'sure, have a seat.' And as time went by, the non-Aboriginal person invited his friends, he invited more friends, he even invited strangers and welcomed them to this tree until eventually the Aboriginal person stood up to make room until eventually that log was filled and the Aboriginal person was asking to sit back on that log. When I heard the CCTA present today, that is how I felt. Like we were asking to get a little part of that log again. That's what I would like to close with."

That was the message of the day: it is time to give Aboriginal people their rightful voice in the Canadian broadcasting system.

The hearings continued until 8:30 pm that night, but no one complained. Over the course of the day the mood in the hearing room had taken on a quietly celebratory tone. The combative, legalistic mood that characterizes most licence hearings was gone, and there was a strong, almost humbling sense that something very important was happening. As Patrick said in his closing remarks:

"This has been a historic two days."

Exhausted and elated, we returned to our homes and hotels. By any standards the hearing had been a huge success. The TVNC AGM and Board meeting was scheduled for the next day, and we were all looking forward to an exciting and positive meeting in the afterglow of a modest triumph.

The afterglow lasted for about twelve hours.

It was an unusually large group that gathered at the Capital Hill Hotel for the AGM next morning. In addition to all of the TVNC members and directors, four members of the Advisory Committee, in town for the hearings, were looking forward to participating in their first annual meeting. Since the meeting was taking place in Ottawa, several staff members dropped by to sit in.

The Annual General Meeting had barely begun when NNBY's representative, Joanne Macdonald, requested an in-camera meeting (a closed session for members only, with no minutes kept) regarding procedures and by-laws.

Gary Farmer was shocked. He had just spent two days at the Commission on APTN's behalf. He had a dozen projects on the go, and his time was limited; but he was here to be part of the discussions setting the path for the network following the hearing. There was nothing to do but wait with the other committee members and staff outside the closed session.

Inside, the tension between north and south, between dueling visions of what APTN should be, came to a head. The members had been through a year of incredible change, a grueling application process and an intense set of hearings. Everyone had shown a united front at the CRTC, and any internal differences had been papered over under pressure of deadlines. But now they needed to talk seriously about the implications of the decisions made over the past few months. The Yukon representatives were disturbed at the presence of so many non-members, they wanted to clarify who at the AGM would actually have voting rights. This was more than just a procedural issue: only APTN members could vote at the AGM, and only members had the power to elect people to the Board. Once on the Board, directors could then oversee the management of the organisation. After a couple of hours, the doors opened, the members emerged and Abraham reassured everyone that the procedural issues had been clarified, and all the members and directors were eager to work together. Yet the tension lingered.

"I'd watch the people around the table," recalled Alanis Obomsawin. "Some of them were protecting their own areas, and sometimes I felt it was difficult. How do you get everybody to listen to everybody else, and not only think of your own area? I think it was also upsetting for TVNC...and some people up north felt very worried about getting the South mixed in too, and in terms of control of what's going to go on television for all other First Nations people."

Jim Compton felt the tension even before the meeting began:

"One northern member arrived with her lawyer. That struck me as odd. Here we were, we had our hearts on our sleeve for this network, and we've pushed hard. And here they were with their lawyers, questioning if we are true to what we want to do." But he understood their sensitivity.

"In retrospect I can see how the Advisory Committee could be seen as 'those interlopers'. But we were all totally passionate."

Alanis agreed. "We were excited in terms of the possibilities and how it would include everybody. The Inuit were living in their language, but this was not the case for our people in most cases. We were witnessing languages dying, and it was very painful. So the idea that our languages would be included …was wonderful."

Abraham tried to lighten the atmosphere with an enthusiastic report on TVNC's many accomplishments in the past year.

"To say it has been a very exciting year for TVNC is an understatement," he said. "My time as Chairman of TVNC has brought me and this organisation to the edge of a dream."

The rest of the AGM unfolded smoothly enough through the presentation of annual activity reports, auditor's reports and the acclamation of Abraham as Chairman. Things became uncomfortable again, when one member proposed to open a Board of Directors meeting and immediately begin appointing new Directors at Large. Some members wanted the process to be held in-camera, some wanted it open, and some felt it should be deferred until the AGM was concluded. With the help of the lawyers' present, the issue was resolved and the appointment of Directors at Large was taken off the AGM agenda and added to the Board meeting agenda for the next day. But once again, an apparently minor procedural issue signaled a major division in the organisation over the question of control.

The Board of Directors convened the next morning and appointment of Directors-at-Large was the first item on the agenda. According to the TVNC by-laws, three Directors at Large could be elected to represent the Aboriginal community and since TVNC seemed poised to become a national network, those were three highly coveted spots.

Six names were brought forward for the three positions; Abraham Tagalik, Edward Mesher, Louise Profeit-Leblanc, Brenda Chambers, Wally Firth and Clayton Gordon.

"And then," said Abraham, "The shit REALLY hit the fan."

It seemed each nominee triggered someone's hot button. Abraham was already Chairman and had led TVNC through the successful hearings. However, some members felt the Chairman should not be a Director at Large, but a full TVNC member. Brenda Chambers had left NNBY and was now pursuing a career as a producer in Vancouver; but had initiated legal proceedings against NNBY when she left and there were three people from NNBY who were hostile to her nomination at the meeting. Clayton Gordon had recently resigned from the TVNC Board because he left ICS, a TVNC member organisation, and could no longer represent them. No one on that list could really be called a 'southern' representative.

Discussion of the nominees became heated, then vicious. Directors were accused by other directors of underhanded dealing. Staff was berated for keeping the Board in the dark. Personal attacks were erupting around the table. All the frustration of the last year and everyone's fears for the future spilled out in tears, anger, and shouting. Unable to bring the meeting under control, Abraham, visibly shaking, offered to resign on the spot.

Then Silpa Edmunds, an elder representing the OKâlaKatiget Society of Labrador, asked for the floor. She spoke simply and directly.

"There should not be internal fighting by the Board of Directors," she said slowly, quietly, looking around the table at every director. "Work together. Settle this."

Amazingly, a word from an elder was enough to bring the meeting into line.

The vote was held, and Abraham, Brenda and Clayton were elected as Directors at Large. The majority had spoken, but the minority was very unhappy. To further complicate matters, Brenda and Clayton were promptly appointed to the TVNC executive, as Board Secretary and Treasurer, respectively. For the first time the TVNC executive, with the authority to make decisions on behalf of the entire Board, would not include a single representative from the founding TVNC member organisations, nor anyone to represent the vast southern Aboriginal broadcast community.

Bernard Hervieux, the designated NNBAP representative, summed up the discussion.

"The founding members of TVNC are experiencing changes and evolution," he told the meeting. "It's difficult to go through these changes. We need to remember that there will always be opposition, but these changes are for the good of our country and our people. We must acknowledge some frustrations and understand that the ride will not be slow or smooth. Even though change is difficult, we have a common goal."

But the Board meeting wasn't over yet. NNBY asked for time to outline their concerns and they put their core issue bluntly on the table: the northern members did not want to give up control of the network to those in the South.

The discussion that followed was the frankest expression of the northern position to date. The pace with which TVNC had moved from the licence application to the hearing was extraordinary and the members were upset. Major decisions had been made on the fly and the TVNC Executive had failed to keep all members in the loop. TVNC staff, under pressure for time, had taken steps that, in hindsight, should have received more Board input and approval.

NNBY was bluntly saying what many Directors were feeling. TVNC members had supported national distribution to secure additional funds for northern broadcasting, but under the proposed APTN structure, no one could really see any financial benefit to the members. There was still no plan in place to open up the Board for southern participation. No one could see a way forward. On that note, the meeting ended.

It had been an exhausting week, and everyone was physically and emotionally drained. The Board agreed to convene a workshop in a month to resolve the critical issue of Board structure, and staff were instructed to draft a response to the concerns raised by NNBY. Abe adjourned the stormiest meeting in TVNC's history, and remarked somberly to Jim Compton as he left the room:

"It's going to be a hell of a network, if we don't all kill each other first."

»——————→ ○ ←——————«

Days passed and tempers cooled. But to no one's surprise, the much-anticipated Board structure workshop in December failed to resolve the issues dividing the network.

Harold Tarbell and Fred Weihs, two experienced organisational development consultants, hammered out a two-day process carefully designed to elicit everyone's views, identify the critical decisions required and walk the group through a decision-making process towards resolution. At least, that's what the workshop agenda said.

But when the Board, Advisory Committee and staff gathered once again in Ottawa two weeks before Christmas, it was clear from the opening exercise that the group was still deeply split on governance and on programming. Participants were asked to describe their goals for the workshop, and the divide was captured on the flipcharts.

"APTN must be a national network and avoid a North/South split," said one participant. "The voice of the North must still be heard in the new structure," said another.

Throughout the entire day participants argued, reasoned, discussed, analysed and reviewed multiple options for a new Board and membership structure. But they were at an impasse. The consultants' final report summarised the stalemate as diplomatically as possible.

"During the discussion it became clear to the participants that there were still too many uncertainties to establish both a new basis for membership in APTN and a new structure for the Board of Directors," they concluded. "While they recognised that a new structure of governance was needed for APTN, participants agreed that the process for carrying this out could not be rushed."

Put simply, some of the members wanted a national network with national representation, Others wanted to extend TVNC into the South, without losing control of the organisation or its programming. There was little common ground between the two camps.

The status quo, however, was no longer an option. TVNC had just made a very public commitment to change; something had to happen.

The tortuous solution, reached after two days of painful negotiation, was a transitional Board structure. If the CRTC granted the license application, the existing ten-member Board would be expanded to include eleven new Directors, creating a twenty-one-member Board. The new Director positions, "would be filled with an eleven persons recommended, (by majority vote) by the current TVNC Board of Directors, with the assistance of the Advisory Committee, and approved (by two-thirds vote) by the current full members of TVNC."

If that sounds convoluted, it was. Since only existing northern members could appoint directors, TVNC's original northern members retained control of the new network; but it opened and expanded the Board of Directors to include Aboriginal people from other regions of Canada.

The other bone of contention at the workshop was a discussion paper on programming, commissioned by TVNC and prepared by Roman Bittman and NextMedia. The paper highlighted the many issues that would have to be resolved if APTN received a broadcast license. Was there a way to allow northern member producers to broadcast their native-language programs in the North alone, while focusing on national programming in the South? How would the schedule be set? How would the network define an "Aboriginal" producer? How would APTN avoid conflicts of interest if producers participated in the Programming Selection Committee? How much of APTN's schedule would be dedicated to member programming, to independent production, to APTN in-house material? How would APTN set fees for acquiring programming?

Discussion of Roman's paper brought to light yet another division within the organisation. Advisory Committee members like Alanis Obomsawin and Roman Bittman were filmmakers, accustomed to spending months on a single production, with relatively generous production budgets, for national and international audiences. The TVNC members, on the other hand, were broadcasters, producing hours of programming every week for regional audiences, on a shoestring budget. It's the difference between a feature film and the morning show on a local news channel. The local talk show attracts its audience by being relevant and reflecting local people and issues; the feature film by its polish and quality. APTN would be programming to both local audiences in small Arctic settlements and urban, mainstream, non-native viewers in downtown Toronto. How would it strike a balance?

There were many questions and there were no answers. By the end of the workshop the most the group could agree to, was to eventually establish a Programming Committee; but only if APTN received a licence.

The workshop ended, members and directors returned to their communities after some Christmas shopping and for the next few weeks, the exhausted staff regrouped, trying to make sense of wildly divergent directions the network seemed to be heading. It was a strange Christmas; we all knew we had just been through something historic, but no one seemed very sure whether the path ahead was leading to a brave new network or a brick wall.

»———→ ∘ ←———«

The answer to the biggest question of all came fairly quickly.

On the morning of February 22, 1999, Abraham Tagalik was in his office at the Qikiqtaluk Corporation in Iqaluit, Nunavut. It was Monday morning, he was looking ahead to a full day of meetings, and it was Iqaluit in mid-February, which means pitch blackness until mid-morning.

"But for some reason," he remembered, "I was feeling really upbeat. I knew something big was going to happen that day."

And sure enough, after a particularly gruelling meeting, a colleague told him that someone named Patrick was desperately trying to reach him. With some trepidation, Abe went back to his office, closed the door, called Patrick Tourigny, and received the news. "We got it," said Patrick.

CHAPTER VII

PRE-PRODUCTION

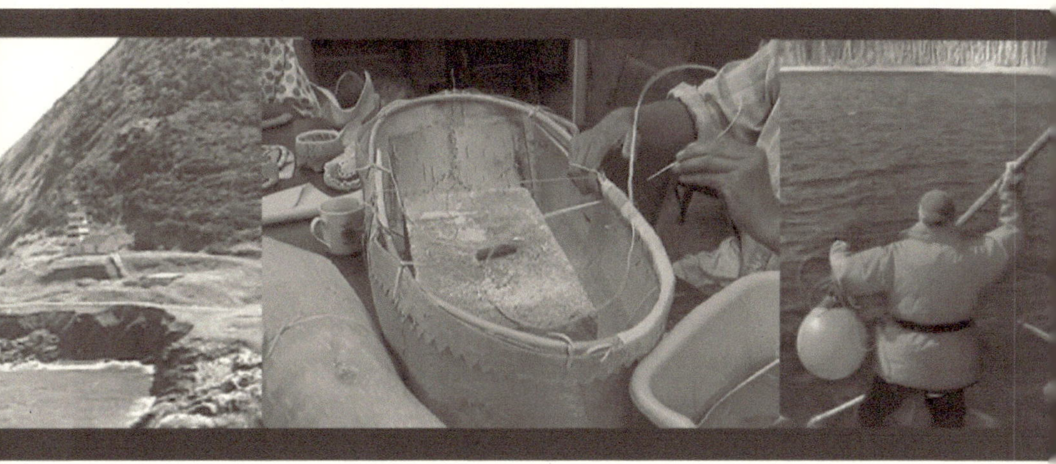

THE ARK OR THE TITANIC

Kevin Schofield is rocking the Bay Street Bistro in Ottawa.

The restaurant/bar at Laurier and Bay has been an APTN hangout among the younger set this summer—probably because of its proximity to the Glue Pot, everyone's favourite pool hall. Tonight the Bistro is Launch Central in Eastern Canada. The big screen over the bar, usually blasting either WWF or an NHL game, has a test pattern up with a discrete little countdown, ticking away the minutes to the broadcast. The place is packed.

Kevin is onstage, entertaining the crowd with a medley of country and blues tunes. He's one of several people who have spent long hours screening tapes, timing segments, and packaging shows in the Ottawa office for the past two months. The heroes of the evening are the APTN staff, the ones who couldn't fly out to Winnipeg for the big event. Office workers, the program packaging team, the receptionist—all survivors of six chaotic months of working flat out to get to tonight. But there are others here, friends, partners, staff of other Aboriginal organisations, a couple of musicians, an Inuit film-maker. Tonight's the night, and everybody wants to be part of—whatever. No one really knows how the show is actually going to look—the line-up seemed to change every day. It doesn't matter. It's history, and it's happening now.

Kevin kicks into a tune by Johnny Cash, one of his heroes. A friend picks up a guitar and joins him at the mic. Everyone is enjoying themselves but every so often, every person in the bar sneaks a surreptitious glance at that big screen with its little countdown clock.

The news that APTN had been granted a broadcast license hit Abe like the proverbial ton of bricks.

"I was speechless," he recalled. "Speechless, but very, very, very happy. I sat there with a big grin on my face, just thinking about all that work we did and all those people who supported us. You don't get that very often, that kind of an affirmation and recognition for something you work toward for years. I put on a pot of coffee, cancelled the rest of my meetings, and started making phone calls."

The CRTC decision was, quite simply, a bombshell. A small regional collective of Aboriginal broadcasters, operating on a shoestring, had just hit the jackpot ; a national channel with mandatory carriage. The decision was read, dissected and pored over by producers, lawyers, directors, and bureaucrats in studios, offices and boardrooms across Canada. No one could quite believe what had just happened, least of all the Board and staff at TVNC.

Back in Ottawa, staff read the decision a dozen times. But its first sentence said everything we needed to hear:

"The Commission approves the application by Television Northern Canada to operate a national Aboriginal programming network, to be known as the Aboriginal Peoples Television Network."

The rest was gravy, and the gravy was excellent. TVNC got everything it had asked for—mandatory carriage by Class 1 and Class 2 distribution undertakings, $0.15 per subscriber fee, 90% Cana- dian content, and a launch date of September 1, 1999.

In its rationale, the CRTC acknowledged "the substantial support for APTN expressed in the numerous interventions"15 and said that pursuant to section 9(1)(h) of the Broadcast Act, the Commission "considers it vitally important that APTN's new and unique service be available to all Canadians, consistent with the objectives of the Canadian broadcasting policy"16. The CRTC went on to counter the CCTA's arguments and outlined why and how distribution of APTN was warranted. There were no surprises in APTN's conditions of licence and nothing unexpected in the programming commitments.

The decision erased the rift between APTN's warring internal factions, at least for a brief truce. J.C. Catholique can still recall that moment.

"I remember thinking that it was an amazing feat. It felt really good. Our voices, our cultures, our languages were going to be out there. And all the people involved, it was just like a TV production; so many technicians, so many players, actors, everyone had a part. It was really incredible." Advisory Committee members were delighted too.

"I was so pleased," said Roman Bittman. "We had won a network equipped to survive and thrive—a place where Aboriginal producers and artistic talent could always come home to. We finally made it."

»———→ o ←———«

Word spread quickly. One of the most memorable responses came from Yellowknife, where a ten-year CBC veteran, production editor Wayne McKenzie (who had helped TVNC back at its launch), was pounding a freezing, early morning picket line outside the CBC Building with his colleagues. CBC technicians had been on strike for more than a month, and Wayne was bored, cold, and fed up. Originally from BC, he had moved to Yellowknife, and like most northerners began to watch TVNC, marvelling at what that small network could do while CBC, with more resources, was producing much less. He was friends with Linda O'Shaughnessy, and she informed him that morning that APTN had just gotten its license. That gave Wayne an idea.

"I took my sign, my placard that I was using while I was walking around, and I wrote on it, APTN HERE I COME. Let me tell you, it created quite a buzz on the picket line. My regional director came out, and she was not very happy."

But it was funny enough to make the local newspaper the next day, which was read by the TVNC staff in Ottawa.

Someone remarked, "We should hire that guy."

And in fact, we did: within a year Wayne was working for APTN, and at the time of writing this book in 2012, he was the Director of Network Operations.

Media picked up the news as well, and the backlash was swift. Most main- stream outlets spun the story as a tale of government interference in the market;precisely the line espoused by the CCTA and rejected by the Commission.

"Viewers to be force-fed by edict of CRTC," fumed the Calgary Herald.

"Why must viewers pay for new network?" the Edmonton Journal demanded.

"The CRTC is forcing a new Aboriginal TV channel—and its cost—on most Canadian cable viewers," growled the National Post.

The most virulent coverage came, predictably, from the conservative publications owned by Conrad Black's Hollinger International. "Any time the government forces the public to finance what it perceives as the common good," grumbled the Journal, "that is a tax. And as taxes go, this one is phoney, dishonest and disturbing." The Calgary Herald took exactly the same tack: "The CRTC has stepped over a line etched sharply in the sand in its unconscionable interference in the basic principles of an open marketplace where products flourish or fail on their own merits."

But even the free-market ideologues, though unanimous in their attack on the CRTC as a regulatory body, were careful not to condemn the APTN concept, or question the need for or value of an Aboriginal network. Some even expressed cautious optimism. The Calgary Herald editorial continued, "Now, this is no reflection on the APTN…which may well provide innovative, interesting and high-quality shows." APTN as a service was given a grudging 'wait and see' attitude, and private sector pique was reserved for the way in which the network would be distributed.

There was positive coverage as well. In an editorial published a few days after the decision, the Globe and Mail wrote:

"… we support the CRTC's decision to make this channel a part of the basic cable package. Not only will it provide a secure source of funding for the APTN's programs, but it will make the network something people will chance upon as they click their way along the TV dial. Aboriginal television will be inescapable. And that inescapability will express something that the isolation and marginality of many native peoples' lives often obscures."

Abraham, as Chairman, was front and centre in the coverage. His background in radio stood him in good stead, and the week of media interest yielded a number of quotable sound bites. "Some days, the little guy does come out on top," he told the Calgary Herald. "This is an outstretched arm for us to become full members of society." And in the right-wing National Post, he argued that "We have to be seen as basic service so that we don't get marginalised with the Space Channel or the Shopping Channel."

The media maelstrom subsided after a few days, but cable company executives continued to fume about having to find room for APTN as part of their basic service. Andrew Cardozo was accosted by a cable operator the day after the decision at a black tie affair hosted by Canadian Women in Communications.

"He took me on quite vehemently. He just about picked me up by the scruff of my collar. He was poking me in the shoulder telling me it was an outrageous decision and that they would appeal. It was highly inappropriate."

Cable companies were obliged to carry the network on their basic tier, and all eventually did. However, they had the option of burying it in the most obscure locations on the dial. Several operators placed APTN in the upper ranges, usually above channel 70 or 80. It was a bit of a slap in the face. But eventually the anger from industry subsided. Patrick Tourigny and Tony Greco, who had done affiliate relations for Vision TV, began to work out deals with cable companies to ensure they would be ready to carry the network on September 1.

Shortly after the CRTC announcement, I received an email from a friend with a tagline that summed up our situation that spring perfectly. I stuck it up on the office wall, and it became our mantra. It read,

"Professionals built the Titanic. Amateurs built the Ark."

That was a comforting thought. The problem was, Noah took roughly a hundred years to build the ark. We had six months.

Why the rush? There were several reasons. The CRTC had recently granted mandatory carriage to the French-language network TVA, and had also licensed several other specialty channels. All were scheduled to launch on September 1, and cable companies would be promoting the new services to their viewers, informing them of channel changes. We wanted to take advantage of that promotion; we also wanted to minimise potential negative subscriber reaction and cable company inconvenience. But perhaps the biggest reason was the simplest; we were going broke. TVNC's already-extended license was scheduled to expire on September 1st, 1999, and the network couldn't afford the time or cost of seeking further extension. APTN desperately needed to get on the air and begin collecting subscriber fees.

Once the elation subsided, panic began to set in. In a series of feverish planning meetings, staff and Board scrambled to identify everything required for a network launch. We had half a year to establish a new Board structure, locate and build a southern production centre, design an actual programming schedule, find and acquire productions to fill that schedule, ensure cable companies would be able to carry APTN, hire a CEO and programming staff, promote the network to Canadians, organise some kind of launch event; and of course keep TVNC on the air across the North until August, when the TVNC network would officially sign off for a month of transition prior to the September 1st launch of APTN. Those were just the most urgent tasks.

It quickly became clear the most critical gap was in leadership, at both the Board and the management levels. It was impossible to set priorities or coordinate everyone's activity; staff, Board members and the Advisory Committee were all working feverishly, everyone in their own direction.

The network needed to get its house in order and implement the transitional Board structure. However cumbersome, it would at least provide a final point of decision for all the urgent choices that had to be made immediately.

The first task was to revise the by-laws. A special members' meeting was held in April, 1999 to officially change the name of the corporation and adopt the new Board structure.

The next task was to elect six temporary Board members. A full new Board would be elected at the Annual General Meeting and Board meeting at the end of August; but in the meantime, interim appointments were required. The Advisory Committee recommended criteria for southern members, the executive solicited nominations, and in April the Board elected Advisory Committee members Alanis Obomsawin, Roman Bittman, and Gary Farmer, as well as David Tuccaro, Calvin Helin, and Cathy Martin, to serve for five transitional months. Cathy Martin was a respected Mi'kmaq filmmaker from the East Coast, David Tuccaro was a successful entrepreneur from Alberta who owned a number of companies in the oil and gas industry, and Calvin Helin was a lawyer and businessman from BC who had recently created the Native Investment and Trade Association. The new directors were professionals, business-oriented, and entrepreneurial; their approach marked a shift from TVNC's non-profit, community-service philosophy. But their advice in those formative months was invaluable as APTN sought to establish solid management and governance practices.

With the new governance system locked in, it was time to hire a manager. TVNC's management team had done a heroic job in getting the application through; but now there was a national network to plan, as well as a northern network to run. APTN needed a Chief Executive Officer.

In the best of all possible worlds, the CEO position would have been the subject of a three-month head hunt, a careful courtship, an extended negotiation, and a high profile announcement. With the clock at five months and counting and crises looming in every corner, that wasn't an option. What APTN urgently needed was an experienced manager who could hit the ground running, with a production, journalism and management background, a solid understanding of the APTN concept and history, and the tact to mediate between the various not-quite-warring north/south factions. George Henry had indicated his interest in the position, but no one was sure he could pull the organisation together as a team. There were several other interesting prospects. Then in April, Abraham Tagalik mentioned casually to J.C. Catholique that he was interested in the job.

J.C. Catholique raised Abraham's candidacy at the next Board meeting in April, and most of the Board enthusiastically endorsed the choice.

"Ideally, we would have sent it out to a competitive process," said Debbie Brisebois. "But there was just no time, and Abraham had done very good work for TVNC."

The position was redefined as Chief Operating Officer, which left final executive authority in the hands of the APTN Chairperson. Following the Board's approval, Abraham resigned as Chair, accepted the job of COO, and began looking for a house to rent in Ottawa.

"Of course I was nervous about it," said Abraham. "I was hopeful, and at the same time I was waking up in the middle of the night and wondering, are we actually going to be able to pull this off? And then I'd remember having exactly the same fears about getting TVNC off the ground. We had done it once. We were going to make this one work as well."

He was, in many ways, an ideal person—maybe the only person—for the job. As a northerner he understood the community roots of APTN, its importance to its audience, and the reservations of its members about this new wave of "southerners" moving into "their" network. But he also accepted that the network was going to have to change in order to compete for a national audience.

Perhaps most important was the fact that his quiet confidence and conciliatory approach created trust. As Jean LaRose remembered, "Abraham was always extremely honest, extremely respectful. He was true to his word. He was a visionary in a way that very few are, when it came to establishing a venture of this nature."

Abraham arrived to a desk waist deep in paper, an email-inbox already over its high water mark, and two dozen imminent crises. He began to sort, organise, and assign.

"I felt like an orchestra conductor," he recalled. "We had a great team, and my job was to coordinate them so they could all shine."

His biggest job in that first week was to return calls from media around the world. Journalists and broadcasters from New York to Japan were interested in what was happening at APTN. Ironically, there seemed to be much less interest from Canadian media. Working with marketing expert Nancy Smith of Next Media, we began to develop materials and a strategy to let 9 million Canadians know about the brand new channel they were about to receive.

Our task was to develop a "brand" for APTN—a consistent look and feel for all promotional items and network identification—followed by a full media and public relations campaign. This would include ads in all the major television industry publications, bus ads in larger cities, and a giant digital billboard in downtown Toronto—a radical new technology at the time.

A key element of the branding was APTN's new slogan: "Original People. Original Television." In just four words it summarised what was most unique about APTN and its strongest selling point; viewers would be tuning into programming unlike anything available on any other station in the world. It worked. The slogan achieved high levels of viewer recognition, and served APTN for its first three years of broadcasting.

We shipped 25,000 posters featuring the new logo and slogan to every First Nation, Inuit and Métis community and organisation in Canada. Earthlore designed brochures, business cards, stationery, pens, t-shirts, coffee cups and a programming guide. Armed with boxes of the new promotional material, APTN staff and Board distributed goodies that spring and summer at the Banff TV Festival, the Aboriginal Voices festival, the Dreamspeakers Film festival, the AFN Annual General Assembly, the CCTA convention, and at powwows, festivals, and conferences across the country.

Abraham and the Board quickly set up a series of staff/board subcommittees to move on the most critical issues. A Programming Committee was established to oversee the development of a real schedule, and to begin the acquisition of Aboriginal-themed, broadcast-quality material. A Membership Committee was mandated to work on the thorny issue of APTN corporate structure and governance. But the busiest group was the Management Committee, chaired by David Tuccaro and tasked with recruiting a Program Director and News Director, overseeing the procurement of equipment, and preparing recommendations on the best location for a southern production centre. The intent was originally that the Committee would meet monthly; but after reviewing the incredible volume of work, its members agreed to meet weekly for five months, giving up a good chunk of their summer for unpaid planning, meeting and writing.

Their most pressing issue was identifying the location of the network production centre. NNBY had proposed a second northern centre in Whitehorse; however, the Board felt that a national broadcaster had to be quickly accessible from all parts of the country, and that ruled out a headquarters in the North. The existing northern centre in Yellowknife would be maintained, but the network needed a new centre that would balance the northern operation with a prominent southern presence.

An initial technical survey of potential southern sites was conducted in April, and the new Board members had their first opportunity to review its findings in May. Director of Network Operations Jerry Giberson and engineering consultant Bob Linney tabled a review of potential locations in Edmonton, Winnipeg, and Ottawa. The discussion got off to a rocky start; NNBY was upset because their organisation had not been allowed to submit a bid. Other directors felt that specific cities had not been given enough time to assemble a stronger application, and that the process had been too rushed. They were right, of course, but once again the urgency of the need required a quick decision. After some heated discussion the Board agreed to move forward and review the findings of the report.

The CRTC application had proposed a site in Edmonton. The engineering survey, however, established that the suggested site was unacceptable. That left two cities in the running, Winnipeg and Ottawa.

Ottawa had advantages. It was the headquarters of most national Aboriginal organisations (as well as the southern offices of both TVNC and IBC), it offered easy access to newsmakers, policy wonks and funders, and it had a relatively large Aboriginal population, including Inuit. And of course, the existing TVNC staff was currently based in Ottawa. We were passionate about the network and would have loved to see the network remain in the city. But Ottawa's pool of Aboriginal broadcasters was very small and the city itself showed no active interest in APTN.

Winnipeg, on the other hand, had mounted an aggressive campaign, prompted in part by local Aboriginal producer Jeremie Torrie, to sell itself as APTN's new HQ. The City Council and Mayor Glenn Murray sent a warm letter of congratulations to APTN, urging the network to consider Winnipeg as its location. Several Aboriginal groups, including the Neeginan Development Corporation and the Tribal Council Investment Group, even proposed a specific site—the historic Starland Theatre Building, located in a growing hub of Aboriginal-owned buildings and businesses.

The Board chose Winnipeg. It was central, not identified with either eastern or western Canada, with good air connections to the Arctic. It had the highest urban Aboriginal population in the country, a strong production community to provide a pool of human resources, and a supportive local government and community. Ottawa staff were offered the option of relocating to Winnipeg; none did. No one quit in protest, or appealed the decision, it was clear that Winnipeg was the right choice. The next year saw a gradual passing of the torch as Ottawa staff hired, mentored and finally handed over their files to new staff members in Winnipeg.

As a city, Winnipeg was the best choice. Over the next few weeks, however, it became clear that the Starland Theatre would be a disaster. The neighbourhood was old, with high levels of crime; the "heritage building" (a realtor's euphemism for "collapsing") would require gutting and a complete interior rebuild; and the location was awash with other radio and microwave signals. APTN's uplink would have to be located blocks away and connected to the studio by underground, shielded fibre optic cable—at APTN's cost.

An alternative site on Portage Avenue was identified, and it seemed to have everything the Starland didn't: good visibility, connection to fibre optic cables, and easy access in a safe, downtown location. But finding, assessing and approving the Portage site took more than a month. It was mid-June before the Board gave Jerry Giberson the go-ahead to proceed with the extensive renovations and installations required. Workers moved in immediately and began to gut the first floor of the building and construct production, editing and studio space. No one knew whether or not it could be ready by September 1.

In June, the new Board met face-to-face for the first time. Instead of getting together in Banff, the Board decided to hold its meeting in Toronto to support the new Aboriginal Voices festival that Gary Farmer was organising.

Marty Ballentyne was one of the new transitional NNBAP members on the Board, representing MBC in Saskatchewan. Marty grew up in northern Saskatchewan and northern Manitoba. At the age of 12, he was bitten by the radio bug in Sandy Bay when he helped renovate an old building to establish a small community radio station.

"Radio was really cool," he said. "That was the first time I realised you could make radio, not just listen to it."

At 19, he was working at the community radio station in La Ronge, Saskatchewan, then moved up to the region's largest Aboriginal radio station, the Missinipi Broadcasting Corporation. MBC's studios walls were plastered with photos from NNBAP and TVNC meetings, shots of people like Clayton Gordon, Brenda Chambers, Debbie Brisebois, and Abraham Tagalik; and those photos surrounded Marty during the hundreds of hours of his DJ and announcer-operator work. When he walked into the meeting room at the Carlton Hotel in Toronto for that first Board meeting in June, he was awestruck.

"All these people were like celebrities," he recalled. "I was thinking, there's Brenda! That's Debbie! For years they had been like mentors, like teachers. These were the people who had taken up the challenge, the people that had done all this good work. I felt honoured to be among them."

During a break in the meeting Marty wandered out into the lobby for a stretch, and spotted a familiar face.

Jennifer Podemski was an actor living in Toronto, best known for her roles in Dance Me Outside and The Rez. In the summer of 1999 she was playing a small part in Riverdale, a CBC soap opera, and rethinking her choice of acting as a career. Just two months earlier, while hosting the National Aboriginal Achievement Awards, she had talked with awards show producer Laura Milliken about an idea for a television show about Aboriginal youth. After the Achievement Awards show, they got together and chatted further about their mutual interest in becoming producers, and their experience growing up as Aboriginal girls in the city. Mostly, though, they talked about the complete absence of anything on television to engage urban Aboriginal kids. "We really wanted to create television that appealed to that demographic, that young, disgruntled person with no identity. We wanted to encourage young Aboriginal people to break the cycle of abuse and not give up on life."

They worked up a concept for a series to be called Seventh Generation, a 'feel good' look at exceptional Aboriginal youth and their achievements, with some practical advice and resources for youth. The world, however, is full of would-be producers with shows to pitch, and most buyers won't talk to anyone who's not already well established. Jennifer was living in her dad's basement, Laura was working full-time, and they had no actual office or productions to sell; so creating a power buzz was a bit problematic. Nevertheless, they did their best to build the perception that they were big players in the industry, doing business exclusively by cell phone, incorporating the grandly-named Big Soul Productions, distributing Big Soul postcards and business cards. "We created a myth that we had this big company," Jennifer laughs, "And everybody treated us like we were big time."

Even so, corporate sponsorships weren't easy to come by.

"We asked Ford to sponsor our first season and they said 'No,'" said Jennifer. "The woman I met with told me that Ford wasn't interested because native people don't have enough money to buy their products."

However, they impressed enough private sector investors and government program officers to cobble together funding for a pilot episode of Seventh

Generation, and began shopping it around to the networks. They had received some encouragement from Jim Compton months earlier when he was on the Advisory Committee, but APTN didn't exist at that point, and Jim could not make any commitments or promises. That's where the dream got stuck. No one wanted to buy a 13-part series profiling Aboriginal youth. "Literally every door was shut in our faces."

And then, in June 1999, walking through the Carlton hotel, she saw Marty Ballentyne.

Jennifer had met Marty at a conference years ago in Sandy Bay. They exchanged greetings, then gossiped over coffee. Jennifer described her new series, and the frustration of trying to find an interested broadcaster. Marty explained that he was attending his first meeting with the APTN Board. APTN was going to need a lot of programming, and quickly. Seventh Generation sounded like exactly the kind of series APTN needed, and he was sure the network would be willing to take a chance on some up-and-coming producers. Encouraged, Jennifer agreed to submit her show, and Marty raced back to the meeting.

"It was synchronicity," said Jennifer. "If APTN hadn't launched when it launched, and if we didn't have the show ready to go into production at that time, [Big Soul] would never have succeeded."

Seventh Generation became one of APTN's first hit series, ran for several seasons, and marked the beginning of a string of innovative and edgy series and movies by Big Soul, including the award-winning *Moccasin Flats*.

»———→ o ←———«

Marty's chance encounter with Jennifer wasn't the only meeting that would yield programming gold for APTN that day. When the Board returned to the meeting room after lunch, their first order of business was an introduction to the woman everyone was hoping would answer the terrifying question— what exactly are we going to be putting on air in just two months?
What the network had to offer was old and new programming by its TVNC members; important cultural material, to be sure, but not nearly enough

material, and not quite the full-service, 18-hour per day feast of northern and southern Aboriginal production the network had promised the Commission. Recruitment had started for a Director of Programming to buy new and existing series, but that was a long-term solution. Meanwhile the shelves were bare and the clock was ticking.

Senior staff polled their industry contacts for someone willing to step into the breach, and Gary Maavara from CanWest Global suggested Gail Morrell. Gail was a consultant who had recently retired from CTV, where she had served as both Vice-President of Communications and Director of Programming. She had worked for decades in network programming, promotion and scheduling, in an era when women at the executive level in broadcasting were rare and often unwelcome. Years of stubborn refusal to fail would prove a good preparation for one of the most difficult assignments of her career.

"I knew it wasn't going to be easy," Gail recalled. "Patrick Tourigny called me, and the first thing he said was 'APTN is going to air on September 1, and we don't have a program schedule'."

A big city TV executive from Toronto, Gail knew nothing about Aboriginal programming, Aboriginal culture or Aboriginal sensibilities. Pat suggested that she drop by the upcoming Toronto Board session. Accustomed to high-speed power meetings, Gail left her family in the car outside the hotel, planning to quickly duck in, introduce herself and leave. Instead, to her shock, she was invited by Chairperson JC Catholique to formally address the Board, members of the Advisory Committee, senior management, and a handful of curious onlookers. She got as far as her first sentence, introducing herself as a native Montréaler, when one of the Board members interrupted her with a terse:

"You're not native."

"Of course, I went beet red, realised what I had said, and apologised. I didn't know that they were kidding me until someone pulled me aside during a coffee break and said they did it as a bit of a joke. They kept laughing and ribbing me about that native comment."

That was Gail's introduction to the first law of cross-cultural communication in Indigenous circles—if we tease you, it means we like you.

Gail would have plenty of time to get used to Aboriginal humour. Over the next few weeks she began the daunting task of researching, locating, screening, acquiring and scheduling almost every Aboriginal-themed program available in Canada. It was a bigger challenge than any other start-up network had faced; APTN had been licensed with some strict conditions.

"We couldn't just go out and buy any old movie or cop series," Gail said. "We had to find Canadian programming, because you had that 90% Canadian content rule. CBC became my best friend because they had some programming we could use, and my next best friend was the National Film Board."

Old NFB films and long-gone CBC series like Rainbow Country and Forest Rangers were resurrected from the vaults. Many of the programs hadn't been seen in years, but they had Aboriginal characters, even if the storylines and characterisations were stereotypical, and often downright politically incorrect.

There were newer, more culturally appropriate shows out there—programs like CBC's popular *North of 60*, or the American series *Northern Exposure*. But most were unavailable or too expensive. For its first season, the network needed volume; it would be several years before APTN would be able to afford the kinds of shows its viewers had been hoping to see. There was admittedly a certain irony to the fact APTN's first season would rely heavily on the kind of programming that network had criticised so strongly for so long. But Gail had no choice, timeslots had to be filled.

Gail wasn't alone. Linda O'Shaughnessy was shuttling between Yellowknife and Ottawa, working with Gail to stitch together a coherent schedule out of TVNC member programming, old movies, CBC reruns and NFB docu- mentaries. Screenwriter and musician Clarence Michon was enlisted to screen and log tapes and winkle out hidden caches of Indigenous programming in the vaults of various freelancers and smaller production houses.

With just eight weeks to go, some Aboriginal broadcasters miraculously pushed new series into production. Cynthia Lickers, about to launch the first ever ImagineNative film festival, somehow managed to design and host ImagineNative, a program showcasing independent and short films by Aboriginal filmmakers. The most intriguing new title was Cooking with the Wolfman, one of the few original shows pitched to the CRTC that actually made it into production. A traditional cooking show hosted by professional chef David Wolfman, it showcased Aboriginal and European recipes, from bannock to Daubed Agneau Provencale; as well as Loma Mathias, the mandatory attractive co-host. The show became APTN's first original hit, and, as of this writing, is still producing original episodes.

Gail and her team were putting in sixty-hour weeks screening, digging through archives and negotiating licensing agreements and acquisition deals. IBC's commercial production division, Inuit Communications Systems Ltd., began to produce a series of slick network and program promos. Built on the backbone of the TVNC member programming, and fleshed out by a motley collection of reruns, old films, new packaging and quirky originals, a broadcast schedule was taking shape. It finally began to look as though Canada's newest television network might, in fact, have some television programming to show AFTER its launch.

The launch itself, however, was a different story.

CHAPTER IIX

DRESS REHEARSAL

THE SLEEPLESS SUMMER

6:45 pm, September 1, 1999

Gil Cardinal is sitting in the director's chair, in the mobile unit, facing a bank of six monitors. He checks the time. The butterflies he was feeling earlier in the day have now put on weight and started doing calisthenics.

"It's interesting, these special butterflies you get just before doing a live show," he thinks. "Something very few people get to experience."

Camera operators are checking in on headphones, confirming their opening shots. He checks the time. Yellowknife is standing by, monitoring the uplink feed. He checks the time.

Standing behind him in the control room is Tookie Mercredi. "There's nothing left to do," he thinks, "Anything we could think of is taken care of. In ten minutes we're going to find out what we didn't think of."

There's no room in the truck for Randall, but he doesn't want to be there anyway. He's in the audience, with his family. As the minutes tick down, he wonders briefly what crises he's missing backstage and in the control room. He remembers an assignment from the training session at Banff—was it really only a year ago? He had had to role-play the part of producer, overseeing a crew in a mock production. He remembers the exhilaration of completing that assignment. He looks around at the thousands gathered at the Forks, at the lights playing across the stage, at the cameramen taking up their positions. That's what he trained for. It's been a long day. A long two months. Please let it work.

Abraham Tagalik is sitting with the APTN Board and some friends and family. He stands to look across the crowd. The Forks is now jammed; the crowd numbers in the thousands. All the seats are full, and crowds are forming at the back. An old friend approaches Abraham, Mrs. Tootoo, an Inuit elder, now living in Winnipeg. She knew Abraham as a child. She hugs him and speaks quietly to him in Inuktitut.

"These are your people," she says with a smile. Abe smiles back.

"Imma," he says, "Yes, they are."

George Tuccaro is backstage, cool as a cucumber. Actually, cooler than a cucumber. He's freezing. The temperature is dropping, and a few drops of rain are hitting the stage. He's wearing his blue ribbon shirt, and as the wind picks up, he wonders whether people are going to hear his teeth chattering on the air. He hides a jacket just off camera to slip into during the breaks.

Just before 7 pm, the crowd stands for the playing of O Canada. They settle back into their seats expectantly.

Dawn Olivence is putting the finishing touches on Evie Mark's makeup and George Tuccaro is reviewing the script, when they hear the countdown from Gil.

"5…4….3…2…cue the hosts…"

At the June board meeting, with only three months to go, the Board had decided that nothing less than a three-hour, live broadcast and gala event in Winnipeg, would do for the network's inaugural show. In retrospect, even Abraham admits it might have been a bit too ambitious.

"We just couldn't leave well enough alone. We were looking ahead at three impossible months of work already, we were wrestling with every technical challenge you can imagine and we're brand new at this whole thing. But nobody could resist the idea of a live broadcast and a real celebration. I think we just knew we had to get people's attention and we really wanted to showcase our network." He laughs. "That all sounds familiar. Didn't I say the same thing about the TVNC launch?"

The first order of business was to find a producer willing to create a three-hour live spectacle for an untested network, from scratch, with no budget, in eight weeks. As it happened, we found two. After screening several proposals, the Board chose Randall McKenzie and Tookie Mercredi. They were both seasoned producers. Randall, originally from Manitoba, was working for NNBY in the Yukon in a range of technical and production positions. Tookie was a first-rate camera operator and award-winning film-maker from the Yukon. Neither had ever produced anything approaching this scale before. But their production concept was a strong one—a live concert, a big community party, and a showcase of Aboriginal talent from north and south, from BC to Nunavut to the Maritimes. Randall knew the Winnipeg production scene and could pull together a crew quickly. Most importantly, it was clear both were willing to throw everything they had into the project. They'd have to.

"We only had about seven weeks to pull it all together," Randall remembers.

He was going to have to use up all of his holidays and take an unpaid leave of absence to take the assignment but he couldn't resist an opportunity to be part of Aboriginal broadcasting history.

With Randall and Tookie chosen to produce the show, the next task was to set up a team to fundraise, organise, and coordinate the entire event in Winnipeg. Working with my new communications assistant, Racelle Kooy, a trilingual native of B.C. and the Launch Committee, we went looking for local organisers willing to do the impossible in the seven remaining weeks. Duane Shuttleworth and Barbara Bruce, two Winnipeg-based Aboriginal consultants and event planners, took up the challenge.

"People thought we were absolutely nuts because we only had seven weeks to get ready," Duane recalled. "But we knew we could do it. We knew enough people to pull it together. And we saw it as an historical event. This was going to be the first network across the globe that was directed by Aboriginal people, and we wanted to be part of that."

Another reason people may have thought Duane and Barbara "absolutely nuts" was that their assignment came with no money. Their task was to organise an outdoor concert and public event, with live national broadcast coverage, AND to raise the approximately $300,000 it would cost—including their own fees—in seven weeks. But Duane remained confident. His plan:

"no sleeping, no breaks, no time off. Just go, go, and go, seven days a week."

Raising a quarter-million dollars in sponsorships in just over a month would have been a full-time job for most people; but Duane and Barbara were also designing the entire stage show, which meant locating and negotiating with performers from BC to Nunavut to Cape Breton.

"We tried to make sure that we had a good mix of First Nations, Métis and Inuit," says Duane. "And then we had to organise the performances so that the show would flow smoothly."

The headliner was easy to choose. Susan Aglukark, the young Inuit singer whose debut had launched the TVNC network, had become one of Canada's best-known and top-selling Aboriginal artists. As it happens, she was also Abraham Tagalik's niece and after a quick phone call from her favourite uncle, she agreed to participate, at a greatly reduced rate.

The line-up quickly filled out. It wasn't a hard sell; if you were an Aboriginal musician in Canada, there was clearly only one place to be on September 1st, 1999. AFN Grand Chief Phil Fontaine put in a special request to APTN Board member Cathy Martin for Champion Mi'kmaq fiddler and composer Lee Cremo, one of Cape Breton's favourite musicians. As soon as he was asked to perform, he agreed immediately. So did the Inuvik Drummers and Dancers, co-founded by the many-pocketed ICS manager Debbie Gordon- Ruben. Fifth Generation, five brothers and sisters with a unique blend of soul, R&B and pow-wow beats, would represent the new face of Aboriginal popular music. There were Métis jiggers, a children's choir, pow-wow dancers, and the Yukon comedy duo Sarah and Suzie—a kaleidoscopic mix of young and old, modern and traditional, music and dance. It was an exciting cross-section of talent, and a tantalising hint of APTN's potential.

While the production team scrambled to build a broadcast, the Board continued to wrestle with an even trickier construction project; the task of restructuring APTN's membership and Board. The CRTC application had addressed the question of Board structure, but it hadn't defined who the "members" of the non-profit APTN would be. TVNC's members had been the NNBAP-funded broadcasters who used the network, the government of the Northwest Territories, and Yukon College; officially, that remained the membership of APTN. A Membership Committee comprised of Ron Nadeau from NCI, Bernard Hervieux from SOCAM and Abraham was mandated by the Board to determine whether and how the new national network could expand its membership, to include broader national representation, especially from southern Canada. After all, the South was where the overwhelming majority of APTN's audience would be living, where most of APTN's new producers would be working, and where APTN's new political support from groups like the AFN was based. A national broadcaster needed national membership.

But the Committee promptly ran into a very familiar brick wall. Once again, the original members felt they were being pressured into a decision they weren't prepared to take; others were simply unwilling to see the North lose any control over the network. The Committee and the Board grappled for weeks with the question of membership and its implications. How could a handful of northerners represent the whole of Aboriginal Canada? Would the original members give up their right to appoint a Director? Could non- Aboriginal people be members? After nearly a dozen meetings, page after page of legal advice, and hours of heated debate, the Committee was no closer to a decision. They decided further discussion before the launch would serve no purpose; a decision on membership would be deferred until September 17.

But the appointment of a new Board of Directors couldn't be deferred. That was part of the CRTC Licensing Decision, and it had to be done before September 1st. The Management Committee recommended criteria, and Board members began frantically to solicit candidates. All nominations had to be reviewed and confirmed in time for the first APTN Annual General Meeting, to be held in Winnipeg one day before the launch.

To some, the interminable process of rebuilding the organisation from the inside was becoming exhausting.

"There was a lot of tension," said Debbie Brisebois. "We were already feeling a bit of detachment from the network. There were people moving out, new people moving in—there was a sense of separation, as if APTN was already becoming this big entity 'over there.'" Other directors were feeling the tension as well.

"It was a lot of work to try and get representation from as many areas as possible," said Alanis Obomsawin. "It is very hard for a Board to be together and be fair to everybody. Different people want different things, and that creates tension. What's good for the South might not be good for the North. But that is why everybody needs to have a say."

But Roman Bittman found the process energising.

"I actually remember a real sense of camaraderie at the Board meetings. We knew we were building something important, something with a long-term life. We were building something we could be proud of."

»——— › ∘ ‹ ———«

In Winnipeg, the APTN office on Portage was being gutted, with drywall and wiring being slapped into place even before a studio design had been finalised. Meanwhile videotapes were piling up in the hallways of the APTN office in Ottawa as Gail and Linda scrambled to create a schedule. Terry Rudden was hired to help pull together the various planning threads and organise a plan for the recruitment and hiring that would be needed. He recalled his first morning on the job.

"I showed up at this typical downtown Ottawa office building on Albert Street. APTN was in a suite of offices at the end of a nondescript hallway, on a floor with a few small, quiet lawyers' offices and NGOs. Nothing very grand about it. Then you walked into this space that looked like an outtake of "Hoarders". Paper and tapes and magazines and coffee cups everywhere. Down one hall, Abe was being interviewed by some reporter in a little boardroom that doubled as a storage area and backdrop for interviews. Gail and Linda were in a tiny space with flipcharted schedule notes plastering the wall and stacks of tapes up to the ceiling. Patty was in one cubbyhole arguing with the banks, Jennifer was in another talking to some graphics people, Jerry was on the phone all day with Winnipeg and the techs, Patrick was yelling at the cable companies, and then there were a bunch of guys sitting in the dark cutting promos. Every hour or so they'd all burst out laughing hysterically. Nobody knew why—too much coffee, I think."

It was a TV studio, network HQ, conference centre, library and command post, all in the space of a four-bedroom apartment. At one point someone suggested that the senior staff should try to hold a daily staff meeting to keep up on what was happening. But we dropped the idea when Abe pointed out that since everybody's office door was open all the time, we heard everything anyway.

There was no office space for Terry, so he was installed at the end of a dark, windowless hall at a battered metal desk facing the wall, below a huge oil painting of a desolate, abandoned DEW Line site in Iqaluit.

"All this hysteria behind me, and this weird northern landscape hanging on the wall. It was like working inside a Dali," said Terry.
From his surreal cubbyhole he began the task of staffing the network in a month.

On the day APTN received its licence, the network had a staff of six. By the end of July, that had mushroomed to nearly 20. Most were on contract, hired in the rush to get APTN on the air for September 1; there was no plan, no corporate structure, no job descriptions, no hiring policy, and no salary scale. Within a month, a new TV network was going to kick off from shiny new studios on Portage Avenue in Winnipeg—but who was going to be pointing the cameras, and who were they going to be pointing them at?

The challenge of staffing a network already in preproduction was akin to that of designing, building and driving a car—all at the same time. Three cars, actually—Yellowknife, Winnipeg AND Ottawa, all housed key elements of APTN, and all three required a staffing plan.

The process of hiring that summer consisted principally of wooing every available Aboriginal media person who might be interested. Abraham hired his unflappable Executive Assistant, Susan Heavens. When he arrived early at the office, found her waiting outside the door, and discovered that he had forgotten his keys. They conducted the job interview sipping coffee in the hallway outside the elevator and Abraham hired her on the spot.

"Anyone who could roll with that," he told us that morning," is exactly the person I want for the next month."

There was one critical job, however, that couldn't be hired on the fly. The network needed a Director of Programming to turn APTN's lofty vision into an actual broadcast service. The man to fill the job, as it turned out, was right under our nose, Jim Compton.

With the creation of the new Board of Directors, there was no longer a need for an Advisory Committee. Alanis Obomsawin and others joined the new Board, others resigned. Jim Compton, for one, had no intention of missing the excitement ahead.

"I knew they were going to need a Program Director," he recalled.

"I had told Abe to be sure and send me the Program Director job description when it came up, because I was interested."
The call came sooner than Jim expected, and it was urgent: the position was opened in mid-June and APTN needed someone to start immediately. Jim was on contract as a producer for the Pan American Games (being held, coincidentally, at The Forks in Winnipeg). He would not be available to start until the end of July. But no other applicant came close to his experience or his knowledge of the network, and APTN agreed to delay the start.

Jim arrived in Ottawa at the end of July, and discovered that he had become the most popular guy in town.

"From the moment I walked in the door I was getting a hundred calls a day. People were pitching me their programs all the time," said Jim.

That was literally true: over the course of a one-hour lunch break at a neighbouring food court, Jim was stopped by three different people with program ideas, and after two days on the job his desk was shoulder deep in proposals. Fortunately for Jim, the evaluation of these proposals was the task of the Programming Committee.

Jim spent his first week with Gail, breaking down and scheduling the impossible volume of work required before the September 1st launch. APTN had to establish its own distinct on-air personality, its brand, right from day one. Hundreds of hours of existing programming would have be timed, re-packaged and promoted with the new network look. That meant hiring packaging producers to screen, edit and prepare master tapes: on-air presentation producers to develop promos, public service announcements, and fillers; and voice-over announcers for promos, credits and other announcements. Above all, it meant organising all these new people to carry out this work.

The shelves were slowly filling with programming, real and potential. But by the end of July, APTN still needed to find an additional 13.5 hours of programming per week.

"We needed to coordinate what we were doing," Jim recalled. "Gail was acquiring programming like crazy, but no one was organising it."

Jim drafted Frank Coyle, a short, plainspoken technical producer from the Weather Network. Frank immediately quit his job, moved from Toronto to Ottawa, found an apartment and with boundless energy dove into the mountain of tapes; packaging new shows and logging the tapes for broadcast. But Frank was hamstrung; APTN's Ottawa office had only one video machine for screening. Jim went begging for a second video player to Don Young, Jim's former boss in Winnipeg and a well-known Canadian producer with a production company in Ottawa.

"I was in our glass-walled conference room in my office in downtown Ottawa, talking to my lawyer," Don recalled. "We looked up, and there was Jim in his buckskin jacket, wearing a big black cowboy hat, braids hanging down, casually strolling out of my front door with a $25,000 machine under his arm. My lawyer turned to me and said, 'friend of yours?' To which I replied, 'But of course.'"

While Jim and Frank began to edit boxes of old NNBAP and NFB material into slick new packages, the Program Selection Committee dug into the stacks of proposals for new series. The Committee met frequently through-out the spring and into the summer. Their task was difficult. Most start-up broadcast services have one target audience, and one simple goal—make a profit. That would have been relatively easy. APTN's roster of new programming, however, had to meet a whole series of contradictory goals.

New programs would have to compete with big-budget, slick mainstream productions for a national audience, but still attract viewers in rural and remote communities and on reserve. The schedule needed to offer the wide variety promised in the CRTC license application, meet the mandatory requirements of the licence, and still address the network's social priorities.

The Committee quickly established a formal process for evaluating proposals. The most controversial criteria were those which awarded points based on the level of Aboriginal participation in a project—the more Aboriginal people involved, the more points, with a strong advantage to production companies that were 100% Aboriginal-owned. It sparked a bit of muttering about "reverse racism" and "hiring quotas" in the independent production community; as one cynical non-Aboriginal producer commented, "APTN was trying to make Red the new Black."

But APTN was adamant. The network had been created, in part, to give Aboriginal people access to the airwaves, to jobs, and to training in the industry. APTN wasn't going to be producing much of its own programming and would rely on acquisitions: if you wanted to pitch a program to APTN, you were going to have show how you were going to employ or train Aboriginal talent. For the first time, being a native actor, technician or director wasn't a stigma, but an advantage.

It worked. In the summer of 1999, it seemed every small production company in Canada was beating the bushes for Aboriginal technical, production and onscreen talent. That intake laid the groundwork for the creation of an entirely new production community and provided entry opportunities for hundreds of Aboriginal people working in the television industry today.

One of the network's biggest gaps was in the critical area of news. Jeff Bear, a Maliseet filmmaker and producer, had been commissioned earlier in the year to come up with a concept for an APTN news program. Jeff's discussion paper pointed out that providing coverage of news and current events from an Aboriginal perspective would be one of the network's most important tasks. Indigenous audiences needed reliable, objective coverage of events and issues from "Indian Country"; non-native audiences needed to hear Aboriginal stories from an Aboriginal perspective.

The network hired Dan David, a Mohawk from Kanesatake, to develop the network's news service. Dan was a seasoned journalist and award-winning writer who had worked in both radio and television at CBC, as well as for Vision TV and TVOntario. He had a strong reputation for thoughtfulness and integrity and the network knew he'd lend credibility to the news department. His thoughtfulness, however, turned out to be a double-edged sword: one of the first things he did upon arrival was tell Gail to scratch the projected daily newscast from the schedule. There was simply no way to create a brand new news program in the five weeks remaining to the launch.

"Journalism" isn't a universal standard, Dan pointed out. In its form and in its content, journalism reflects the culture in which it occurs. Reporters in Beijing, Toronto and Riyadh interpret their roles in very different ways; for that matter, so do the reporters who work for CBC and Fox News. There was no point to an Aboriginal news service that would simply mimic the content and form of mainstream media. APTN would have to define the meaning of "Aboriginal journalism" from scratch, design its own news service, then hire and train staff with the right approach; and that would take months.

Dan was right and his decision to delay the launch of APTN news was justified over the next few years, when the network began to win awards for its unique coverage. But at the time, all we could see was the yawning one-hour daily void in the schedule that had once been labelled "News". Dan and Don Young (who had followed his video recorder to APTN) began to set up their news team and design a news format for a new show to launch in February 2000. Anywhere else in the world, a five-month schedule to create a national news service with multiple bureaus would have seemed an impossible challenge; to the rest of us, labouring in the looming shadow of September 1st, it seemed like luxury.

The delay of the news service wasn't the only casualty of our impossible timelines. In the first week of August, Jerry Giberson was forced to report to the Board that the Winnipeg production centre on Portage would not be ready in time for the September launch. The lease had been finalised, and APTN staff were in the building, dodging painters and drywall workers, and working from folding bingo tables. But the main floor—where the studio, control room and edit suites were to be installed—was a wide open, dusty tangle of cables, wiring, sawhorses and unopened crates of equipment. That meant that Yellowknife would have to handle the launch and function as the network's only master control centre for the first few weeks of the network's operation. In today's digital and wireless world, television programs are transferred instantly to any point on the planet at the push of a button. In 1999, however, Winnipeg's delay meant that every second of programming would have to be physically shipped, on videotape, from its source—often a remote location like Nain, Labrador, or from the growing mountain of tapes in Ottawa—to the Yellowknife uplink, to be logged and played on air.

For Jim Compton, what had been a programming challenge became a logistical nightmare. Hundreds of hours of scheduled programming were at various stages of completion across Canada; some still being packaged in Ottawa, some still in production across the Arctic, and some in transit, entrusted to the dubious mercy of tiny northern airlines. Everything had to be redirected to Yellowknife. These were master tapes, not copies. In most cases, there were no backups.

"When the network launched," Jim recalled, "we had programming onsite for just a couple of days of the schedule. That's all. If anything had happened to a plane, or if someone at TVNC didn't answer that door and get those tapes, the network wouldn't have launched."

But Linda O'Shaughnessy in Yellowknife wasn't worried. It was no big deal: she had been dealing with crises like this for years. TVNC knew how to uplink, how to package and how to track errant videotapes stuck in Churchill or Rankin Inlet. She and Jerry quickly worked out a contingency plan to hire and train additional master control operators, and find a broadcast-savvy technical producer to get the station ready for its expanded role.

The man for the job, as it turned out, had already advertised his availability with an "APTN Here I Come" placard during the 1998 CBC strike. Wayne McKenzie was immediately hired as an editor, promoted quickly to Master Control Operator, then assigned to work with Linda and Jerry on the technical aspects of getting APTN on air. Yellowknife would be ready.

While Jim agonised over the hundreds of hours needed to fill the APTN schedule, there were at least three hours he didn't have to worry about; the September 1st launch broadcast. Those 180 minutes were Randall and Tookie's headache; Randall and Tookie were already doing what producers do best, calling in favours.

Their first call was to Gil Cardinal, whom they had met at the Banff production workshop a year earlier. Gil had been part of the first wave of Aboriginal film directors, winning attention and critical acclaim for *Foster Child*; an award-winning cinema-verité documentary in 1987, about his search for his family roots. He had become one of Canada's most respected writers and directors and in the summer of 1999 had just finished directing the big-budget CBC drama, *Big Bear*. Directing a film and directing a live three-hour broadcast have about as much in common as sculpting and juggling.

"If you're looking for an Aboriginal director," thought Tookie, "why not start with the best?"

"I think Tookie remembered that I had spoken about being a live television director many years ago," Gil said. "So they invited me to be the director. I hadn't done live television in about 23 years. But I said it would be a very interesting challenge, and I was quite happy to say yes."

The show also needed a writer, so Randall and Tookie drafted Jordan Wheeler, another instructor from the Banff workshop and an award-winning Aboriginal author, story editor and screenwriter. Jordan would later win a Gemini award for his writing on an APTN series called *renegadepress.com*. The prospect of scripting a three-hour show in less than a month was both terrifying.
"It was the first time I had ever had to write a script for a live show like that!" and irresistible. He agreed.

Backing up Jordan was Bruce Spence, an Aboriginal writer freelancing to various newspapers. Bruce was assigned to write the script for the on-stage hosts.

With Gil and Jordan filling key positions behind the cameras, the last big question was who'd be standing in front of them. Randall and Tookie wanted to present every facet of APTN—new and established, First Nation and Inuit, male and female—and they came up with what seemed to be the ideal duet. Evie Mark, yet another alumnus of the Ross Charles workshop at Banff, was a young Inuk from northern Québec. An accomplished performer and throat singer, she had worked with Taqramiut Nipingat Inc., though she had never done live TV. To co-host the televised portion of the show, Randall and Tookie recruited seasoned broadcast veteran George Tuccaro, who had hosted the Yellowknife segments of the TVNC launch in 1992.

Alanis Obomsawin and Marty Ballentyne would round out the hosting team, handling the onstage portion of the show for the live audience. When Bruce learned who he'd be writing for, he blanched.

"Writing for Alanis Obomsawin? Who does that? I mean, she doesn't need me, she writes her own stuff! I knew her reputation, which was a little bit intimidating, and I thought to myself, I hope I can do this," But Marty Ballentyne was reassured.

"I know Bruce. He's a really good writer, and I knew he'd give us great stuff to work with."

With those key positions filled, Randall and Tookie sent out a call to the northern communications societies and other producers across Canada for short segments to illustrate the extraordinary diversity of Aboriginal cultures and landscapes, and to introduce the history and context of Canada's newest national network. The show would combine the excitement of a live concert with a fast-paced, panoramic tour of Indigenous Canada.

Assuming, of course, APTN could afford it. With just three weeks to go, Duane and Barbara had only been able to raise $50,000 of the $300,000 needed for the launch. There was a contingency plan prepared for a more modest event, and some of the staff and Board planners were quietly suggesting that it was time to scale back. But Duane said no. He was convinced that sponsors would come through.

"Usually we have about six months to do this kind of work, but it just had to be done, so we did it, " he remembered."We just kept calling people."

Counting on that No-Sleep program.

Between fundraising calls, he and Barbara were also recruiting and organising more than 200 volunteers—parking attendants, stage wranglers, makeup artists, setup and teardown crews, promotional volunteers, and dozens of other tasks involved in staging a reception, a concert, a live television broadcast and a public party at the same time. Fortunately both Duane and Barbara were from Winnipeg; they knew a lot of people and they could call in a lot of favours.

Laura Milliken was one of their first volunteers. She had just finished a gig as stage manager for the National Aboriginal Achievement Awards, and she was interested in what was going on in Winnipeg.

"I called the Winnipeg organisers out of the blue and offered my services. They said, 'OK, we'll pay your flight, but we can't really pay you.' That was fine with me."

She was quickly assigned the role of stage manager for the live show.

»————→ ∘ ←————«

With just two weeks to go to the launch, the atmosphere in the Ottawa office had escalated from mere hysteria to full-scale frenzy. Stacks of paper, piles of videotape and boxes of equipment were rising in every corner and walls had disappeared under layers of checklists, press clippings and flipchart sheets. Bell Canada technicians were in the office every other day to install additional phone and fax lines. Small groups huddled in every available corner, discussing the network sign-on, or the uplink from The Forks, or the list of new Board members, or the travel schedule to Winnipeg, or a program concept from an eager new would-be producer. No one really knew what anyone else was working on. No one was really sure that we were going to pull this thing off. In fact, no one was exactly sure what this 'thing' really was. Everyone simply worked sixty-hour weeks on their own section of the jigsaw, assumed everyone else was doing the same, and trusted that somehow, at the end of the month, it was all going to come together into a glorious big picture.

None of this showed to the outside world, of course. Reporters love stories about media, and they love a good train wreck. So we were careful to project an aura of calm, competence and professionalism to the journalists who began to line up stories for September 1st.

Typical of those stories was an article by Tony Atherton, a seasoned journalist who wrote extensively on television issues and had a syndicated column in Southam newspapers across Canada. His opinion mattered and a positive column would bring APTN to the attention of mainstream viewers who might otherwise never have heard of it. He arrived at our office to interview Abraham, graciously pretended to ignore the chaos as I ushered him to Abraham's office and talked for an hour to Abe about the network's history and aspirations. His article, when published, was generally positive, with just a faint hint of amused condescension—he was particularly taken with a small plaque on Abraham's wall that read, "I'd rather be hunting." To Tony Atherton, it was a charming cultural joke; to Abraham and the rest of us, it was a heartfelt wish.

With less than two weeks to go, Randall and Tookie had officially given up on real life, and were holed up in a Winnipeg hotel, working round the clock. A typical day would include a review of rough-cut bridge and documentary segments, multiple consultations with CKND—the local Global station contracted to provide technical support, cameras, camera operators and the mobile equipment necessary to uplink the launch—a site visit to The Forks, a check-in with the writers, innumerable phone calls to Jerry in Ottawa and Linda in Yellowknife on technical details of the broadcast, an update for the hosts, a status report from Duane and Barb, bad food gulped down in the front seat of Randall's Pontiac Firefly and, on the good nights, maybe even a couple of hours of sleep. Randall remembers racing from site to site muttering the phrase that became his launch mantra,

"you gotta do what you gotta do."

A few days before the launch, Randall and Tookie moved into the Fort Garry Hotel, where the Board was about to meet and where a small production and launch show office had been set up.

"We grabbed our computer, our printer, our files, our editing machine—everything—and we packed it into this crazy little car, this little Firefly. The first person we see on the steps of the hotel is Gil Cardinal. He looks at our little car and says, 'Hey, you must be the executive producers!'"

Moving into the Fort Garry was going to haunt Randall, literally.

"I had worked all day; it was the end of the day and I lay down on the bed. I was thinking about being in this sweat lodge that I had been in just a few days before—it was nice and warm and comfortable. I was feeling good about the work that was coming together. Then all of a sudden, right in my ear, I heard someone say 'boo', like a real whisper. I could feel my hair standing up on end. I jumped up. 'What the hell?' I said. I looked around and there was no one there."

Shortly afterwards, the lights began flickering on and off, and the television changed channels on its own. It was time to take action. When Tookie returned, they both burned sweetgrass in the room, in defiance of hotel regulations.

"We opened the door and just said, 'Hey spirits—hit the road, you know?'"

It's not clear to this day whether the spirit was one of the ghosts reputed to haunt the venerable Fort Garry, a symptom of Randall's exhaustion, or supernatural saboteurs from a rival TV network. Whatever the case, the impromptu exorcism did the trick.

Randall's prayers were not the only ones offered up that week. We were all praying, everyone in their own way. Jim Compton remembers spending time with his friend, elder Tobasonakwat Kinew, seeking spiritual guidance about how best to honour the ancestors through the launch. Others prayed that all the pieces would fall into place, the weather would hold, the tapes would arrive, the uplink would work. Just before boarding the plane to Winnipeg, I issued a tongue-in-cheek directive to my staff: anyone whose spiritual practices did not include prayer was respectfully asked to spend launch day with their fingers crossed.

Even in a city with the largest Aboriginal population in Canada, the number of brown faces converging on Winnipeg in the last week of August 1999 was remarkable. TVNC members and Board directors, politicians, funders, reporters and long-time supporters of TVNC were flying in from all corners of the country. Performers, dancers, and musicians were arriving with instruments, regalia, props and equipment. For the first time, the solid organisation underlying the apparent chaos began to show. Thanks to Duane and Barbara, there were volunteers at the airport to meet and assist the arriving travellers, to provide initial orientation to the city and the launch event, and to gently ensure that everyone knew when and where they were expected to be.

For the arriving board members, first stop on the Winnipeg tour was the new production centre on Portage Avenue. It wasn't a very inspiring sight: an office building beside a mall, plaster dust and plywood, a studio full of dangling wires and equipment boxes, and a suite of second-floor offices with no furniture or equipment. But to TVNC members, those two floors of rented space represented everything they had worked towards for twenty years. This would become the hub of Aboriginal broadcasting in Canada. It was real.

After the whirlwind tours, introductions and settling in, the various work teams scattered, each to their task. I met Bruce Spence for a greasy spoon breakfast, then headed over to The Forks to set up our media room at the site. We'd be working from a cold, dilapidated, bright red trailer set up behind the stage. We had press conferences scheduled, interviews lined up, media releases to write, phones and fax machines to install, and Board members to brief. As I plugged in the old-fashioned walkie-talkies the crew would be using to communicate, I remember thinking how glad I was to be onsite and working. At least I didn't have to attend the entire marathon three-day Board meeting beginning that morning back at the Fort Garry.

The final, pre-launch meeting of the Board may not have been haunted by the same spirit that visited Randall. But there were definitely ghosts in the air. An era was ending, a new one beginning and that was simultaneously exciting, unnerving, and a bit sad.

The meeting began with reports from the various committees. Dave Tuccaro thanked his management committee, which had met every week over the last five months. With their help, the network had hired a News Director and Program Director, negotiated a lease for the new Winnipeg production centre, launched a business-planning process and established a policy- based management framework.

Jerry Giberson reported that studio construction was well underway, Yellowknife was ready to manage the launch and network master control functions, and the Winnipeg Centre would be up and running by November.

Clayton Gordon, APTN's treasurer, presented the most positive financial report the Board had ever received. With a projected increase in the annual budget from $2 million to more than $18 million, APTN was solvent. For the first time the network would be free to concentrate on building its service and focus on programming and production.

And there was even more good news. Brenda Chambers, as chair of the Launch Committee, reported to everyone's astonishment that Duane and Barbara had managed to raise nearly the entire budget for the launch event.

In just seven weeks, they had lined up 96 performers, 200 volunteers and a quarter million dollars in sponsorships. There was a spontaneous round of applause at the announcement, which Duane and Barbara weren't there to hear; they were, of course, working.

My report summarised the media coverage the new network was attracting. We were definitely the story of the day; I was fielding calls from as far away as Australia and we had received good pre-launch opinion pieces in several newspapers. CBC was covering the launch as local, regional and national news, and every major Canadian daily had a story ready to file for the day after the launch. Word was getting out. I expected a large audience and unless the stage caught fire, positive coverage.

In the midst of all these reports, Marty Ballentyne was whisked off on a compulsory shopping spree. While we all had the utmost confidence in his ability to host the launch, we had somewhat less faith in his wardrobe.

Brenda Chambers and Racelle Kooy marched him over lunch to the nearest mall for a quick makeover.

"It was frantic," he reported. "I was being referred to in the third person while they discussed whether or not my frame worked with this kind of shirt,and whether or not a different shirt would be better, that kind of thing. They picked out a shirt and a nice leather vest and some shoes for me and we all rushed back to the meeting."

With wardrobe issues and routine reports out the way, the Board turned to the real business at hand, the selection of the new Directors. But first, the network officially bid farewell to two of its veterans, Peter Crass and Dudley Morgan, the acerbic, iron-livered GNWT representative, had been part of the original TVNC consortium, and a passionate advocate for Aboriginal programming.

Dudley, the Yukon College member, was a calm consensus builder, and had helped to find compromise in several difficult meetings. Both would be missed. But Peter felt no regrets about leaving.

"It wasn't so much the passing of an era," he thought, "but the passing of a torch."

It was time to make room for new people and new ideas.

In seeking those new people, the interim Board had searched across the country for weeks for nominees. The list of candidates now represented most regions in the country, with a heavy preponderance of people connected to the old TVNC network and NNBAP membership. Many of the Advisory Committee members also agreed to let their names stand.

The Board adjourned its last meeting mid-afternoon on August 30th and small groups scattered to the various bars and restaurants in the neighbourhood to lobby for their preferred candidates at the AGM election next day. The preferred gathering place was the huge, domed bar at the Fort Garry; beside the grand piano and under the giant crystal chandelier, at least three candidates huddled with supporters in their respective corners, scarfing down spiced cocktail sausages till closing time and locking down votes.

Next morning, after the formalities of an AGM were concluded, the election of Directors was held. The new Board, to no one's surprise, was a cautious mixture of old and fresh faces; but most were familiar players with a long history in the TVNC movement.

New directors included:

- Jeff Bear, a seasoned producer and former manager of NACS, who had done APTN's initial discussion paper on a news service;
- Rauri Ellsworth, a young Inuk from Iqaluit associated with the National Inuit Youth Committee;
- Garnet Angeconeb, a journalist and leader of Wawatay, northern Ontario's NNBAP-funded broadcaster;
- Clayton Gordon, formerly of the Inuvialuit Communications Society; and
- Edward Mesher, an Inuit community worker from northern Quebec who had been nominated by TNI.

They joined current directors and advisors Calvin Helin, Clarence Martin, Alanis Obomsawin, Dave Tuccaro, Gil Cardinal, and Brenda Chambers. The Board then re-elected J.C. Catholique as Chairman.

It wasn't quite the great leap forward some had sought, nor the revolutionary transformation some had feared. The southern and independent production communities were still under-represented; most of the "southern" board member slots had gone to former employees or associates of NNBAP groups. But after two years of turmoil, a bit of continuity was, perhaps, not a bad thing.

With that, the work was over for the Board. Their next official assignment would be to show up at the sunrise ceremony next morning, and, of course, pray. That gave J.C. Catholique an idea.

As the meeting room slowly emptied, J.C. approached Tobasonakwat Kinew, the Winnipeg elder, and broached the subject of a ceremonial pipe for APTN. What would that involve? Tobasonakwat said he would be happy to make such a pipe himself. While everyone went back to their rooms to relax as best they could before the next day, Tobasonakwat Kinew went home and began to carve a 20-inch long pipe from wood.

Upstairs in the Fort Garry Hotel, Jordan Wheeler worked late into the evening in the tiny production office amid piles of crumpled paper, screening the final edits of each pre-recorded video segment and cranking out page after page of "improvised" banter for Evie Mark and George Tuccaro.

Duane Shuttleworth was tracking down the last of the performers. The Inuvialuit Drummers and Dancers had arrived safely, with their drums and regalia intact, spare strings had been located for Lee Cremo's fiddle. Did anyone brief Abe about the boat trip? Had anyone talked to Susan Aglukark's people about the set list? Do the kids know where to stand on stage? What about…?

Jim Compton was arriving on the last flight from Ottawa. He had just confirmed shipment of the first week's programming to Yellowknife. Now he could start to think about tomorrow's meetings, the press conference in the afternoon, the radio interview at 9, and the sunrise ceremony.

I was still onsite at the Forks, putting the final touches on tomorrow morning's media releases, proofreading speaking notes for Abe and Jim, and trying to track down the fax machine I had been promised.

In Yellowknife, Wayne McKenzie and the technical crew were painstakingly reviewing dozens of tapes—segments, intros, extros, transitions, bridges—verifying timing, in and out cues and doing a final technical tune-up of the Master Control room. If anything is going to go wrong during the show, they both agreed, it's not going to go wrong in Yellowknife.

It was long after midnight when Tobasonakwat Kinew put down the newly-decorated pipe, lovingly carved and carefully fitted with its ceremonial red stone bowl. Like so much of APTN, it had been completed at the last minute.

The sky was still dark outside, but in just a couple of hours it would be time for the sunrise ceremony.

It was Launch Day.

CHAPTER IX

CUE TALENT

APTN LIVE

6:58 pm, September 1, 1999

APTN was born prematurely.

The very first shot that 9 million Canadians were supposed to see was an image of a sunrise, with the sonorous voice of Gordon Tootoosis, one of Canada's best known Aboriginal actors, welcoming and introducing the new network. But either technology or human error gave the world an unexpected preview. The uplink suddenly went "live" at 6:58 pm, two minutes before the scheduled start time of 7 pm. Viewers saw a wide shot of the stage at The Forks, with Alika Lafontaine, a member of the musical group Fifth Generation, warming up the crowd and chanting, "Aboriginal Peoples Television Network!" Alika, laughing, then introduced the stage host as, "MISTER Alanis Obomsawin," and the sound cut out. The camera quickly zoomed into a medium shot of Alanis and Marty, and then the screen went black.

No one at the Bay Street Bistro in Ottawa remembers that glitch. The music in the room stopped the moment colour bars and tone on the big barroom monitor gave way to black. The room hushed as the APTN logo appeared on the screen at exactly 7 pm central time. The voice of Gordon Tootoosis boomed into the room, and across the nation. "Our stories have been passed down for generations," he intoned, and viewers saw soaring panoramas of Canada and images of Aboriginal people across the country. "APTN is our new oral tradition", said Gordon. And the birth of APTN is a "new creation story." For all the people in the bar who had put their heart and soul and sweat and tears in the anxious months leading up to the launch, the feeling of relief and pride was palpable from the very first shot.

"It was almost like New Year's Eve," said John Cooke, an APTN cameraman/ editor. "There was hugging and kissing, and congratulating people you didn't even know. That was the moment. That first shot, when the network came on the air—APTN became real. It finally hit me. Things had changed."

The shot dissolved to an introduction by on-air hosts George Tuccaro and Evie Mark. "Welcome to the inaugural live broadcast and celebration of the Aboriginal Peoples Television Network!" said George, beaming at the crowd and the cameras. For the old-timers, it was a warm echo of George's greeting from Yellowknife at the TVNC launch seven years before.

»——————→ ○ ←—————«

In downtown Toronto, Dan David, just out of a series of meetings with potential media trainers, raced from bar to bar, looking desperately for a bartender who'd let him watch the show on a decent monitor. No luck. Even Duke Redbird's café, the Coloured Stone, was playing hockey instead.

"To hell with it," he thought. He grabbed a six pack and drove back to a friend's place to watch the rest of the show on a tiny home TV screen.

»——————→ ○ ←—————«

While TV audiences across the country watched an introductory video, the live show opened with a prayer and drum song by a foursome called "Linda McEvoy and Friends". One of the "Friends", now running purely on adrenaline, was Duane Shuttleworth. Having raised a quarter-million dollars, organised a huge concert and supervised a massive crew of volunteers, he couldn't resist the opportunity to contribute one more ounce of energy as a performer. He swears to this day there was no irony intended in their choice of opening song—a traditional Dakota piece called "I'm Tired, Take me Home."

»——————→ ○ ←—————«

Catherine MacQuarrie watched the show from her home in Ottawa, glowing with pride. "The whole TVNC launch came back to me. I remembered it all. I knew what an achievement this was and all I could think of was how hard everyone must have worked to get there."

»——————→ ○ ←—————«

Bursting with excitement, the children from Ma Mawi Wi Ichita came tumbling onto the stage, wearing brand new APTN T-shirts and freshly painted APTN logos on their faces. Laughing, they brandished red, blue and yellow placards and yelled,

"We celebrate APTN!", as a cloud of matching balloons floated upwards, you had to be pretty cynical not to smile.

»———→ o ←———«

David MacLeod, sitting in the Winnipeg audience, was feeling anything but cynical.

"You could just feel the pride in the Aboriginal people who were there. All the talent on that stage that night, First Nations, Inuit and Métis. APTN launched on exactly the right foot."

»———→ o ←———«

Lee Cremo from Eskasoni took to the stage and the crowd cheered in recognition. A fiddler since the age of seven, Lee had performed for Queen Elizabeth, released albums, composed dozens of tunes, and won more than 80 Canadian and international competitions; including, "Best Bow Arm In the World", in Nashville. The "Mic' Maw Goodwill Ambassador" was in fine form tonight, clearly enjoying the crowd, his performance glowing with energy, humour and his distinctive, jaunty Cape Breton fiddling technique. George Tuccaro beamed as his old friend Lee won the audience over.

None of us knew this would be his last major performance; Lee Cremo died a month later.

»———→ o ←———«

It was all coming back to Gil Cardinal in the control room—the art of keeping your eyes on multiple monitors lining up the next three shots in your head and talking the cameras into position. Of simultaneously tracking what's happening onstage, backstage, in the control room, in your headset, and at the uplink. When you get it right, it's like conducting music. Gil, and the show, were finding their groove. It was working. It was really working.

The Inuvialuit singers and dancers took to the stage. A troupe of performers from Inuvik, they had revived the tradition of Inuvialuit drum dancing in recent years—an art which had all but disappeared during the twentieth century. Under the bright stage lights, with the fading sunset behind them, their performance was spellbinding, a sensory feast of traditional dance, caribou-skin hand drums, chanted legends and beautifully handcrafted mukluks and caribou fur. The ancient rhythms roared across The Forks. The audience was entranced.

Gil sent a camera crew prowling behind the scenes, punctuating the broadcast with live, backstage interviews. The performers backstage were flustered, excited, nervous, thrilled at the audience response and above all, proud. Said one young dancer, grinning from ear to ear,

"It's a wonderful night to be Anishnaabe in Winnipeg, Manitoba."

Go for Baroque, an Aboriginal Ensemble performing classical music. *Sarah and Susie*, a hilariously bawdy comedy duet improvising a side-splitting dialogue about men, trapping, and bingo. *The Nikumoon Top Hat Choir*, with a medley of jazz and show tunes. The show went on and on, each act unveiling a surprising new facet of Aboriginal culture, a fusion of centuries-old tradition and cutting-edge, urban native cool.

Wayne and his Yellowknife crew were the most relaxed APTN team in the network. The broadcast signal was strong and clear, beaming all the way from Winnipeg, through the Yellowknife uplink and across Canada. Until the launch show was over and his crew had to start inserting tapes for the rest of the schedule, Wayne could sit back and marvel at what h was seeing.

"It was surreal for me," he recalled. "I was transfixed by the images that came from the Forks. I had butterflies in my stomach right up until the show began. But then I settled in and kicked back. I looked around the control room. Everyone was beaming."

There were a few visible glitches as the evening rolled on and the show approached its climax—the inevitable result of trying to run a complex three hour concert in parallel with a live three-hour broadcast dipping into and out of the concert. Jim Compton stumbled when the teleprompter failed to provide the cues he needed to bring on *Sarah and Susie*, the Yukon comedians; Evie Mark froze on her intro to Susan Aglukark. Watching from the wings, Jordan Wheeler, the writer, flinched at each glitch. 'Those were my lines', he thought.

This must be why people don't do live TV anymore.

But in the end, experience trumped technology. The unflappable George Tuccaro took it all in stride, covering each glitch smoothly with a joke and filling each gap with improvised chat.

"I remember one time when the teleprompter went off. We had no script, so I just filled in, talking about what was happening, talking about Winnipeg, talking about the people milling about. The floor director kept stretching his arms, telling me to keep going. No problem. That's live television."

"Ladies and Gentlemen, Susan Aglukark."

The shy Inuit teenager had grown up in the seven years since her TV debut on the TVNC launch. She now had a major label record contract, three hits, a host of awards and a tight, polished four-piece band. She hit the stage like a rock star, smiling; the audience roared and the band kicked into *"O Siem"*, her trademark hit from her album *"This Child"*.

Backstage, hosts and performers were hugging.

"There was a huge sense of relief," said Marty Ballentyne. "Susan was on the stage, and I thought 'OK, there's the show.' It went well. The crowd was great. Everyone was happy."

Abraham was smiling more broadly than anyone in the audience, watching his sister-in-law, Canada's most prominent Aboriginal musician, dazzle the crowd. Realisation was beginning to sink in. We had done it.

Stepping up to the footlights, Susan introduced her last number with a nod to the importance of APTN.

"It's an exciting time to be here this evening, she told the crowd. "It's about time that we had this kind of representation." As the band launched into an irresistible beat, she invited all the performers to join her on stage for the finale, *Hina Na Ho*, an anthem of celebration. The crowd surged to its feet, clapping, cheering, singing along.

As group after group emerged from the wings and joined the performance, cheering, drumming, singing and dancing, an overwhelmed Gil Cardinal momentarily lost it in the control room.

"I just couldn't keep up with all the camera shots that needed to happen. So the switcher, who was very nice, just took over for a bit."

The song swelled as each new performer joined Susan onstage. Powwow dancers and the Inuvialuit drummers added a pulse of ancient, rhythmic power to the chorus. Jazz harmonies, fiddles and classical violins joined the hypnotic, chant-like chorus. The audience swayed and sang. The Forks rocked.

At the climactic final chorus a young woman danced ecstatically onstage with a huge Nunavut flag and Abraham's eyes filled with tears. A new territory. A new network. All in six months. All culminating here, in this moment.

Then, as the song reached its climax, with the audience on their feet, someone gave the cue:

"Start the fireworks."

》———→ ○ ←———《

Two banks of launchers had been installed on a raised bunker of earth behind the stage, one on either side. The fireworks were mounted on wooden 2x4s, secured by stakes driven into the ground; but the ground, moistened by the light rain of the last two days, was softer than usual. No one knows if the launcher holding the fireworks began tilting forward during the day, or if it was jolted out of alignment by the force of the first firework. Whatever the cause, the fireworks on the right side of the stage fired into the sky, as intended; the ones on the left side arced above the stage, then straight out into the crowd.

At first Abraham thought he was seeing sparklers tossed in the air by people in the audience. But then the barrage got worse.

"The audience was backing up toward the exit. They were holding up chairs to protect themselves from these missiles. It was absolutely crazy."

Duane Shuttleworth's six year old cousin, weeping and terrified, asked his mom:

"Are they trying to kill us because we're Indians?"

From the stage, with performers facing into the glare of TV lights, it was impossible to tell what was happening. Susan finished her song, and peered into the audience to make sense of the sudden activity. Viewers at home watching the show saw only a dozen or so dim red sparks flying across the dark sky in front of the stage; then Gil in the control room had the presence of mind to cut to a series of close-ups onstage. Duane Shuttleworth could be seen pointing into the crowd with his drum stick, and then quickly moving back and off the stage. George Tuccaro and Evie Mark delivered their wrap up speeches and as the audio faded and the video dimmed to black, Evie can be heard in the background asking,

"Is everyone okay?"

I was on my way back to my trailer when I heard the commotion. I turned and rushed back to the stage, visions of screaming headlines and lawsuits running through my head. As I ran into the crowds, Ron Nadeau, a lawyer and the President of Native Communications Inc., with great presence of mind, had grabbed a live microphone and was inviting anyone who had been injured to come up to the stage. Amazingly, no one had been. One audience member lost a pair of shoes in the scramble. Joanne Awa, a reporter with CBC North, had her hair singed by a near-miss from one of the fireworks. She laughed it off.

"It just made the evening that much more exciting," she said. J.C. Catholique recalls one of the Inuvialuit dancers getting hit in the head with flying cinders.

"I remember apologising to her and telling her I was so sorry this had to happen. And she said, 'that's OK, now I have a souvenir.'"

What a souvenir!

Once the adrenaline drained away and it became clear that no one had been hurt, we were able to take deep breaths and start making the first shaky jokes about what had almost happened. The fireworks catastrophe became just the last entry in the long list of disasters narrowly averted on the road to our network.

Once again, as it had for the last twenty years, things had miraculously come together at the last minute. Somehow, the funding had always come through. Somehow the Commission had always come onside. Somehow the equipment system had always worked. Somehow the Board had never quite blown up. Somehow, the ceremonial pipe was completed in time.

Somehow.

»——————→ ○ ←——————«

The drizzle had held off all evening, but it was beginning to fall now. The last stragglers were leaving The Forks and the teardown crews were moving in, packing up the stage for its next event.

Tomorrow would mark the beginning of the real work—picking up on the thousands of loose ends we had put aside in our race to the launch. Putting together a TV show would turn out to be a lot easier than putting together a network. But tonight we had put on a hell of a show and today, had been a day for the history books.

EPILOGUE

EPILOGUE 2012

It's been more than ten years since APTN first went on the air. In some ways, that's no time at all. The title of Laura Milliken and Jennifer Podemski's first series, *The Seventh Generation*, reminds us that within Aboriginal cultures change is measured in lifetimes and centuries, not decades. But even its critics will acknowledge that over the last decade, APTN has changed broadcasting in Canada.

I left APTN in 2000. I loved the network and its people and I believed completely in what it was trying to do. But I wanted to start a family in Ottawa and all my relatives were in Ontario. I wasn't prepared to move to Winnipeg. Instead, I started a consulting company. I was lucky; my work kept me in touch with many of the people you've been reading about and with many more Aboriginal people across the country. So I've had the opportunity to watch this improbable little network become a household word and an integral part of the Canadian broadcasting scene. Just about every Aboriginal household in Canada has had a relative or friend on the network in the last decade and will tell you about their appearance in great detail. Even the Aboriginal families that don't watch the network regularly, know someone involved with it, and have an opinion about it. In just ten years, APTN has become a national institution. That's impressive.

The network launched in 1999 with a patchwork schedule of NNBAP programs, old NFB films, and ancient reruns and movies featuring any Aboriginal actor, in any role. It's a mark of APTN's progress; that a schedule like that would be inconceivable today.

As promised, APTN opened the door to Aboriginal talent across the country. Producers and directors suddenly had a network where they could pitch their ideas, actors and writers had a market for their material. The result was the explosive expansion and success of the Aboriginal production sector.

Producers like Laura Milliken and Jennifer Podemski got to produce that first series they described to Marty in Toronto. It was raw and low budget, but they learned. Just a few years later they were winning awards for their gritty, cutting-edge drama, *Moccasin Flats*. Andrea Menard, now an established playwright, actor and jazz singer, got her big break on television through APTN in shows like *The Velvet Devil* and *Rabbit Fall*. Rick Harp made his journalistic reputation as the sometimes provocative host of APTN's early current affairs show, *Contact*. Melanie and Dennis Jackson created the award-winning children's show *Wapos Bay*, loved by millions of children across Canada and around the world. Without APTN, it's unlikely these talented people would be working in television today; but thanks to APTN, a career in television is a real option for Aboriginal youth.

As Dave McLeod from NCI said, "APTN…has given Aboriginal people a voice. It's allowing youth to dream even bigger dreams than the original dream that George Henry had at that momentous meeting in Banff. And it's really opened up the gates for a new generation of broadcasters."

One of the skeptics' biggest fears—that APTN could produce "television good for you, but not good television"—has been emphatically laid to rest. Over the last decade APTN, its members and its contributors have garnered Junos, Geminis, awards and praise at festivals around the world and many APTN-sponsored programs have been snapped up for distribution in other markets. APTN surprised many with its ground-breaking, multilingual coverage of the 2010 Olympics, as part of the media consortium that gave audiences around the world the unique experience of hearing, "He shoots… HE SCORES!",in Inuktitut.

With guaranteed subscriber fees, APTN no longer has to scrape by on dwindling Government funding and charity from industry. APTN is self-sustaining and through cable revenues, sales, and shrewd management, has built an entire production community and a huge, diverse inventory of programming.

Ten years ago, Aboriginal producers had to give up their creative autonomy and partner with larger production houses and broadcasters in order to tell their stories. Today, the situation is reversed. Mainstream production companies are clamouring to partner with APTN and to work with the Aboriginal producers who have access to the network. This has created dynamic partnerships and expanded the reach of Aboriginal programming onto other networks like Vision TV, Discovery and CTV.

Some things haven't changed over the years. The unwieldy 21-member board structure is still in place. It remains one of the largest Boards in Canadian broadcasting. Most of the people I spoke to in preparing this book agreed that the system is expensive, awkward and inefficient; but there is little political will internally to restructure.

More troubling are the North/south tensions at the governance level that continue to divide the organisation. Many northerners still feel that their network was taken away from them. In a disturbing echo of the unhappiness that first led to the creation of TVNC, some northern members and viewers believe APTN no longer reflects Inuit lives and reality. They point to the loss of prime-time programming in Aboriginal languages, the loss of territorial news and legislative assembly coverage, and a growing reliance on high-budget, southern-based material and second-run movies. There are even discussions of creating a new Inuit television network, reviving the original vision of TVNC.

The frustration is understandable. Despite attempts at compromise, it has become clear that APTN cannot simultaneously woo and hold sophisticated, urban southern audiences while providing prime-time native language, community-based programming. The concerns voiced by the Yukon a decade ago were, in some ways, prescient.

But many northern viewers love the new programming and enjoy the dramas, series, and animation based in southern Canada. The success of APTN—its growing national and international profile, its strong financial position, and the increase in the quality and diversity of its programming—has provided opportunities, audiences and exposure to northern filmmakers and producers that would never have existed in the old days of TVNC.

Like any success story, the evolution of APTN away from its northern and community roots, has meant losses as well as gains. APTN owes its existence to TVNC and the North is an ineradicable element of the network's DNA. It's a safe bet that the same arguments will be raging within and around APTN when the network celebrates its twentieth anniversary.

Even more disturbing are recent signs that the federal government is slowly withdrawing its support from the fundamental policies that provided the foundation of the NNBAP, of TVNC and ultimately of APTN. Funding for public broadcasting, from the CBC to the NFB on down to NNBAP-funded groups, has been chopped for several successive years. Many of the institutions that provided training or training support for film and video producers have been closed. Other cuts have crippled the Canadian Independent Film and Video Fund, the New Media Fund, and a wide range of programs supporting arts, culture and broadcasting in Canada. These cuts, of course, are especially damaging to organisations and communities outside the mainstream, those without access to other funding or support. APTN is also facing all the same issues confronting public broadcasters around the world—the convergence of media, the fragmentation of audiences, advances in production technology and changes in viewership and distribution, challenge the traditional network models that have informed broadcasting for almost a century.

But APTN has shown the resilience to cope with those challenges. The network can trigger production funds, leverage other funding, broker partnerships, provide digital service and sponsor live events. More importantly, APTN still retains at lot of George Henry's indifference to what other people think it could, or should, do.

Aboriginal broadcasters are no longer 'a voice crying in the wilderness'; APTN has put them at the table as legitimate, established and equal players on the Canadian broadcasting scene. Marty Ballentyne described it well in a comment on the success of producer Dennis Jackson, from his early student production award to his National Aboriginal Achievement award and successful series, *Wapos Bay*:

"Just to see a success story like that, to see a person who had a vision, was dedicated to it and was able to take an opportunity from APTN and turn it into such a great success story. I think that is a really good microcosm of what has happened at APTN."

≫——→ ∘ ←——≪

And so I end as I began. APTN's mission is built on four powerful words: share, celebrate, inspire and honour. It has been my honour to share stories of how the network came to be and to celebrate what it has come to mean to so many people. Perhaps I can close by telling you what it meant to me.

APTN taught me the power of a vision. The network came into existence because for thirty years, a succession of thoughtful and talented people— artists, politicians, performers, leaders, lobbyists, elders, business leaders— glimpsed the possibility of creating something important and decided it was worth committing to. Some put in time, or money, or prayers, or their entire career. Some were Aboriginal, some not. But what they all shared was an idea that meant more than ego or profit, an idea worth striving, fighting, and, occasionally, failing for. Even the differences that still divide the network, speak to the passion and commitment inspired, by everyone lucky enough to participate in the weaving of this incredible web.

Finally, from APTN, I learned something about Canada. I can think of no other country whose government—however slowly—would take a long, critical look at its own broadcasting system, would rewrite its own laws, and finally would support the creation of an Aboriginal network; simply because it was the right thing to do. In this book I've touched on some of the political and economic pressures brought to bear on decision makers. That's how the world works. But in the end, APTN remains a rare example of what can be achieved between Aboriginal people and Canada with good faith, goodwill, and mutual respect. Sure, we had a lot of internal strife, violent disagreements, and sleepless nights.
Sure, there were many naysayers who said APTN could never happen. But it did, and it's still here.

That is a story worth telling.

Jennifer David

231

AFTERWORD 2024

As we celebrate the 25th anniversary of the launch of APTN, here are some thoughts from APTN's longest running CEO, and APTN's current CEO, to reflect on how far the network has come, and what the future holds.

The book you've just read chronicles the origin and launch of a historic and truly unique institution. The long-time dream of creating the world's first Indigenous television network attracted our best artists, writers, performers and planners, who worked for non-stop brainstorming ways to achieve the impossible - defining our mission, mandate and programming goals and preparing our CRTC submission within a year, without models, templates, or precedents.

But a voyage that begins without a roadmap can lead to amazing places. From the day of the launch, the APTN story is filled with firsts.

The phenomenal achievements of our producers and the expansion of our scope and scale of service are well known, and we are proud of our record as the first network to provide funding for truly Indigenous-led productions from across Turtle Island. APTN began broadcasting in 1999 with productions from a small number of Member Societies and six independent producers. By 2019 that roster had grown to include nearly 100 independent Indigenous producers. We were the first Indigenous network to launch its own fully HD channel; the first to air over 15 hours a day of live Olympic programming in 8 Indigenous languages as well as English and French; and the first to broadcast NHL games in an Indigenous language, to the great delight of our Cree audiences.

But beyond the growth and expansion of our programming, APTN has proven itself a leader in many other areas as well. More that 66% of our contributors were women-led production companies, and APTN is the first to be recognized for having a Board of Directors made up of 90% Indigenous women. We have consistently been awarded one of Canada's and Manitoba's top employers. And the list of journalists, performers, artists, writers and producers whose careers began with APTN is a virtual Who's Who of contemporary Indigenous culture.

We can all be proud of the team of dedicated professionals who proved to the world that we could provide entertaining, insightful and award-winning programming for, by and about Indigenous Peoples in Canada; and we can all look forward with excitement to what the next decades will bring.

Jean LaRose, APTN CEO 2002 to 2019

I am delighted to be part of this reflection on the quarter-century legacy of APTN, and to bridge its past achievements with what promises to be a very exciting new era for this special organization.

APTN was born of the belief that our Indigenous languages are the heart of our cultures and identities, and that the broadcasting industry plays a direct role in preserving and revitalizing those languages. Since our launch in 1999, APTN has broadcast our stories and experiences in 54 of our own languages. It is one of the strongest tools we have for reinforcing, proclaiming and embracing our identities.

One of our most exciting plans is a bold restructuring to further promote the reclamation of Indigenous languages. APTN applied in June 2023 to the CRTC to amend our current broadcasting licence, seeking to consolidate our four distinct feeds into two channels. APTN will feature a broadcast schedule featuring award-winning programming of national interest in both English and French. We also applied to create a brand-new channel, APTN Languages, showcasing the rich diversity of Indigenous-language programming from across the country.

In May 2024, APTN received the green light to launch this new service. Both are available to all cable subscribers in Canada, bringing the depth, diversity and richness of our Indigenous languages to new audiences across the country, and providing an invaluable resource for all who study, teach, and speak in the many voices of our peoples.

This marks another proud milestone in the history of Indigenous broadcasting, and an exciting introduction to APTN's next quarter century. And this is just one of the exciting changes our audience can look forward to in the years ahead.

Keep watching!

Monika Ille, APTN CEO 2019 to current (2024)

APTN MILESTONES
September 1999 to September 2024

January 1992:	Television Northern Canada (TVNC) makes its debut with a live three-hour show from Whitehorse, Yellowknife and Iqaluit.
February 1998:	The Canadian Radio-television and Telecommunications Commission (CRTC) releases a public notice stating that TVNC is "a unique and significant undertaking" and that a national Indigenous channel should be made available to Canadian audiences.
June 1998:	TVNC submits an application to the CRTC to grant a broadcast licence for APTN.
Sept 1999:	APTN launches nationally in more than nine million homes via cable television, direct-to-home satellite and wireless service providers.
March 2000:	APTN introduces *Contact*, the first live national call-in current affairs program about Indigenous issues in Canada.
April 2000:	APTN's first national television news program, *InVision News,* begins broadcasting twice weekly.
May 2000:	APTN opens a news bureau in Ottawa, Ont.

July 2000: *InVision News* provides live coverage of the Assembly of First Nations elections from Ottawa, Ont.

November 2000: *InVision News* covers Canada's national elections live from bureaus in Halifax, Ottawa, Vancouver, Toronto and Winnipeg, with a strong focus on Indigenous perspectives.

July – Aug 2002: APTN serves as national host broadcaster for the North American Indigenous Games, the largest gathering of Indigenous youth athletes on the continent, marking the network's first major event coverage.

Oct 2002: *APTN National News*, a daily news program, launches with the first Indigenous television journalism team in Canada and the world.

January 2003: An APTN news bureau opens in Yellowknife, N.W.T.

September 2003: An APTN news bureau opens in Montréal, Que.

July - October 2003: *APTN National News* covers national elections for the Assembly of First Nations, Métis National Council and Inuit Tapiriit Kanatami.

June 2004: *APTN National News* hosts two historic all-party debates and launches an interactive news component on its website in conjunction with federal election coverage.

August 2004:	An APTN news bureau opens in Edmonton, Alta.
September 2004:	APTN news bureaus open in Saskatoon, Sask., and Iqaluit, Nunavut.
Aug. 31, 2005:	The CRTC grants a seven-year licence renewal to APTN.
May 2006:	APTN opens a news bureau in Vancouver, B.C.
Oct 2006:	The network's third channel, aptn w, launches, featuring programming specially focused on Western Canada.
June 2007:	APTN hosts the inaugural APTN Indigenous Day Live (IDL) and broadcasts the event nationally from network headquarters in Winnipeg, Man.
September 2007:	The network launches Digital Drum, an online music media platform that showcases Indigenous talent, culture and history through user-generated videos, audio, text and image content.
2008:	APTN joins the World Indigenous Television Broadcasters Network (WITBN), a global alliance of Indigenous broadcasters worldwide. This sets the stage for multiplatform deliveries of Indigenous content to national and international audiences.

April 2008:	APTN programming gets a visual upgrade with the launch of its new channel, aptn hd, with 17 hours of distinctive HD programming weekly.
July 2009:	*APTN National News* airs special coverage of the Assembly of First Nations Annual General Assembly and election in Calgary, Alta.
September 2009:	APTN launches *APTN InFocus* and *APTN Investigates*, two original current affairs programs.
Feb 2010:	As the world's first Indigenous Official Olympic Broadcaster at the 2010 Vancouver Winter Olympics, the network broadcasts up to 14 hours of daily coverage in eight Indigenous languages as well as English and French.
January 2012:	*APTN National News* provides special coverage of the historic Crown-First Nations Gathering in Ottawa, Ont.
March 2012:	APTN becomes the only Canadian television broadcaster to provide extensive coverage of the 2012 Arctic Winter Games in Whitehorse, Yukon.
Aug 2013:	The network's broadcasting licence is renewed for a five-year term. The CRTC recognizes APTN's unique role and exceptional contributions to Canada through its award-winning news and programming.

| **January 2014:** | News bureaus open in North West River, N.L., and Toronto, Ont. |

| **March 2014:** | *APTN National News* covers the Truth and Reconciliation National Event in Edmonton, Alta. |

| **June 2014:** | APTN hosts the World Indigenous Broadcasting Conference, a biennial international Indigenous media event established by WITBN. APTN holds chairmanship of the organization for two years. |

| **July 2014:** | *APTN National News* broadcasts the opening ceremonies of the North American Indigenous Games and provides daily event updates. |

| **Aug 2014:** | APTN enters into a Terms of Trade Agreement with the Alliance of Aboriginal Media Professionals. This establishes a baseline of commercial terms for development and broadcast licence agreements. |

| **September 2014:** | Home-based bureau opens in Thunder Bay, Ont. *APTN National News* welcomes four new specialty half-hour newscasts: *Nation to Nation*, *Face to Face*, *InFocus* and *The Laughing Drum*. |

<table>
<tr><td>June 2015:</td><td>Digital Drum relaunches as a content-driven music media platform that showcases innovative Indigenous talent.</td></tr>
<tr><td>October 2015:</td><td>APTN National News provides special coverage of the 2015 federal election, including virtual town halls with party leaders, French candidates panel discussion and live election night coverage.</td></tr>
<tr><td>December 2015:</td><td>The Final Report of the Truth and Reconciliation Commission of Canada calls on APTN to support reconciliation by continuing to provide programming that reflects the cultures, languages and perspectives of Indigenous Peoples, and expanding media initiatives that inform, educate and connect all Canadians.</td></tr>
<tr><td>January 2016:</td><td>APTN presents a formal application to the CRTC for five urban radio licences, creating a new, national Indigenous radio network.</td></tr>
<tr><td>June 2016:</td><td>APTN National News makes history by securing the first live, in-depth interview between a sitting prime minister and Indigenous-owned media. This special broadcast event featured call-in and social media interaction between the Prime Minister and viewers.</td></tr>
<tr><td>August 2016 – June 2017:</td><td>APTN provides continuous coverage of the Dakota Access Pipeline protests and (#NoDAPL) camp at Standing Rock, N.D., where thousands of Indigenous Peoples from all over world gathered to oppose a controversial oil pipeline. APTN National News hit the three-month mark of sustained daily coverage on July 19, 2017.</td></tr>
</table>

Oct. 5, 2016:	*APTN InFocus* becomes a one-hour live, interactive and live-streamed show on social media.
May 28, 2017:	APTN and the Canadian Association of Journalists announce a new Indigenous Investigative Fellowship, which provides the recipient with a 12-week paid placement with the *APTN Investigates* team.
June 2017:	ELMNT Radio – First Peoples Radio Inc., a non-profit corporation established by APTN, is awarded two radio licences from the CRTC to operate English and Indigenous-language Type B Indigenous FM radio stations.
June 12, 2017	APTN joins Canadian Heritage, the CBC, the Canada Media Fund, Telefilm Canada, the Canadian Media Producers, the National Film Board and other associated partners to create an Indigenous Screen Office.
June 21, 2017:	APTN Indigenous Day Live (IDL) is hosted in eight cities across Canada, making it the largest celebration of National Indigenous Peoples Day to date. APTN also broadcasts live coverage of the largest round dance in Canada.
July 24, 2017:	APTN intervenes in the press freedom case regarding coverage of Muskrat Falls.

July 26, 2017:   Stingray Music partners with APTN, NCI FM and ELMNT Radio – First Peoples Radio Inc. and launches two channels to promote Indigenous music from Canada.

April 2018:   APTN partners with the Canadian Association of Journalists to create a new award, the CAJ/APTN Truth and Reconciliation Award recognizing exemplary journalism that educates and informs Canadians about Indigenous experiences.

Aug. 31, 2018:   The CRTC renews APTN's mandatory carriage broadcasting licence for a five-year term.

Oct. 10, 2018:   *APTN Investigates* celebrates 10 years of Indigenous investigative news programming in Canada, having aired more than 150 episodes since its inception.

Oct. 24, 2018:   Launch of ELMNT FM, an urban Indigenous radio station, in Ottawa and Toronto.

January 2019:   APTN conducts a National Indigenous Music Impact Study (NIMS), the first of its kind in Canada.

March 24, 2019:   Scoring a milestone for Canadian television history, APTN teams up with Sportsnet to broadcast the first NHL game in Plains Cree.

Aug. 26, 2019:	APTN launches _Nouvelles Nationales d'APTN_, Canada's first national Indigenous news program in French.
Sept. 1, 2019:	APTN celebrates its 20th anniversary and launches APTNl lumi, the networks' first Indigenous-focused streaming platform.
November 2019:	APTN releases the results of the first-ever National Indigenous Music Impact Study (NIMIS), initiated in January 2019, providing the first in-depth profile of and insights into the community of Indigenous musicians across Canada.
May 2020:	APTN and The Discourse launch _IndigiNews_ with the goal of developing a new business model for independent Indigenous news.
December 2020:	APTN lumi becomes available on Apple TV channels, increasing the number of viewers who can check out APTN's unique Indigenous content.
Dec. 21-25, 2020:	In light of the COVID-19 pandemic, APTN broadcast the first _APTN Indigenous Day Live Winter Solstice_ event, bringing the celebration coast to coast to coast with pre-recorded performances from Indigenous and non-Indigenous talent.
June 2021:	Launch of all-new podcast _APTN News Brief_ with Rick Harp, offering audiences a daily 10-minute wrap up of news highlights from previous day.

June 2021:	APTN premieres its very first APTN lumi original series, *Querencia*. This new 2SLGBTQ+ series follows the story of two Indigiqueer women who fall in love and help show one another the ropes in their opposing and often colliding worlds.
September 2021:	An APTN News anchor becomes the first-ever Indigenous journalist to represent a national Indigenous broadcaster at the federal leaders' debate.
Jan. 15, 2022:	APTN and Sportsnet team up once again to bring Canadian audiences NHL games in Cree, with the debut of *Hockey Night in Canada in Cree*.
March 3, 2022:	APTN and CBC/Radio-Canada sign a Memorandum of Understanding to enhance creation of First Nations, Inuit and Métis programming, increase access to and awareness of this new content, and connect Indigenous and non-Indigenous people across Canada.
June 18, 2022:	For the first time since 2019, APTN Indigenous Day Live (IDL) returns to an in-person, live event hosted at The Forks in Winnipeg, Man.
Sept. 30, 2022:	In honour of the second annual National Day for Truth and Reconciliation (NDTR), APTN partners with the National Centre for Truth and Reconciliation to host a one-hour commemorative special entitled *Remembering the Children*.

Dec. 7, 2022:	APTN and Whakaata Māori—New Zealand's national Indigenous broadcaster—sign a Memorandum of Understanding to facilitate the sharing of Indigenous stories.
May 6, 2024:	APTN relaunches a 30-minute daytime edition of APTN National News.
May 14, 2024:	The CRTC approves APTN's request to amend its broadcasting licence (Decision 2024-106), paving the way for the new APTN Languages channel.
September 1, 2024:	APTN consolidates its four programming feeds to two feeds: APTN and APTN Languages

PRIMARY SOURCES

Thank you again to everyone who took the time to sit down with me and reminisce about TVNC and APTN. You all had great stories to tell and I enjoyed hearing them. I would personally like to acknowledge:

Marty Ballentyne

Roman Bittman

Debbie Brisebois

Gil Cardinal

Andrew Cardozo

J.C. Catholique

Brenda Chambers

Jim Compton

Lyndsay Green

Patricia Hutton

Tobasonakwat Kinew

Rosemarie Kuptana

Jean LaRose

Jules Lavallee

Cynthia Lickers-Sage

Catherine MacQuarrie

Randall McKenzie

Wayne McKenzie

Laura Milliken

Gail Morrell

Dave McLeod

Mark Nabess

Alanis Obomsawin

Dawn Olivence

Linda O'Shaughnessy

Jennifer Podemski

Terry Rudden

Duane Shuttleworth

Greg Smith

Bruce Spence

Abraham Tagalik

Patrick Tourigny

Jordan Wheeler

SECONDARY SOURCES

Newspapers

 "Aboriginal network a welcome addition; APTN goes to air tonight with a party from Winnipeg," Toronto Star, Sept. 1, 1999.

"Aboriginal Pride swells as TV Network turns on," Winnipeg Free Press, Sept. 2, 1999.

"Televisionquest," National Post, Sept. 1, 1999. "TVNC to launch," Ottawa Citizen, Oct. 30, 1991.
"Winnipeg beats out Ottawa as base for native broadcaster," Ottawa Citizen, May 6, 1999.

Atherton, Tony. Northern exposure: the Aboriginal Peoples Television Network begins its 18-hours-a-day service on cable systems across the country today. One of four new channels to begin operation today, it's the only one that cable companies have to carry on basic cable," Ottawa Citizen, Sept. 1, 1999.

Boettcher, Shelley. "New channel stirs controversy and excitement," Calgary Herald. Feb. 24, 1999.

Brown, Barry. "Northern Comfort," Toronto Star. Jan. 11, 1992.

Chwialkowska, Luiza, "Coming soon to your living room: the CRTC is forcing a new aboriginal TV channel-and its cost-on most Canadian cable viewers," National Post, Feb. 23, 1999.

Editorial, "Aboriginal network coming to TV dials," Saskatoon Star Phoenix, Feb. 23, 1999.

Editorial, "APTN a tax," Edmonton Journal, Mar. 1, 1999. Editorial, "The native media," Globe and Mail, Feb. 24, 1999.

Editorial, "Weather warning," Winnipeg Free Press, Sept. 2, 1999.

Editorial, "Why must TV viewers pay for new network?" Edmonton Journal, Mar. 1, 1999.

Edwards, Ian. "A people find their voice: Chief Dan George worked tirelessly for native Indians to be seen and heard on TV and in film. Years later, aboriginal people finally have their own network," National Post, Mar. 29, 1999.

Haggarty, Dolores. "APTN's long road to the air. With a budget of $15-million, the Aboriginal Peoples Television Network finally goes on air tonight after clearing many hurdles," Globe and Mail, Sept. 1, 1999.

Lakritz, Naomi. "Viewers to be force-fed by edict of CRTC," Calgary Herald. Feb. 28, 1999.

Oswald, Brad. "Will good-for-you TV become good TV?" Winnipeg Free Press, Sept. 2, 1999.

Platiel, Rudy. "North channels its resources Native groups ready to launch TV network next week," Globe and Mail, Jan. 18, 1992.

Pritchett, Jennifer. "Aboriginal network a surprising alternative: cable channel's diverse programming provocative viewing for natives, non-natives," Ottawa Citizen, Sept. 3, 1999.

Winnipeg Free Press, "Fireworks Awry," September 3, 1999.

Whyatt, Sabrina. "Filmmaker wins big in Banff (Dennis Jackson's Journey Through Fear)". Windspeaker, July, 1998.

http://www.nunatsiaqonline.ca/archives/nunavut010831/nvt10803_09.html

Reports

Arctic Institute of North America, Man in the North Project report: MIN Conference on Community Development, 1972.

Austin Curley & Associates. Evaluation Report Northern Native Broadcast – Access Program. Ottawa: Secretary of State, 1993.

Caplan, Gerald and Florian Sauvageau. Task Force on Broadcasting Policy. Canada: Minister of Supply and Services, 1986.

Consilium, "Northern Native Broadcasting A Policy Survey," prepared for Department of Canadian Heritage, January, 1995.

Gailforce Communications, Program Consulting Report and Recommen- dations for the Aboriginal Peoples Television Network.

Gailforce Communications, Program Consulting Report and Recommendations for Aboriginal Peoples Television Network, Sept. 29, 1999.

Gaspe Tarbell and Associates, Study on the Needs and Interests of Broadcasters Final Report. Ottawa: Department of Canadian Heritage, 2000.

Government of Canada, A Broadcasting Policy for Canada: Report from the Standing Committee on Communications and Culture, 1988.

Government of Canada, Broadcasting Act, 1991 section 3 (d)(iii)

Greg Smith & Associates, Television Northern Canada: A Proposal for a Shared Television Distribution Service in Northern Canada, 1987.

Kerr, Terry. Communications Project Management for Socio-Economic Development: A Description of two projects by the Department of Communications. Ottawa: Secretary of State, 1973.

Kooy, Racelle. APTN Inaugural Live Broadcast and Celebration, Board Members Report, Aug. 30, 1999.

Lougheed and Associates. Report on the Native Communications Program and the Northern Native Broadcast Access Program. Ottawa: Secretary of State, 1986.

Royal Commission on Aboriginal Peoples, Final Report, Canada: Department of Indian and Northern Affairs, 1993.

Therrien, Real. The 1980's—A decade of diversity: Broadcasting Satellites and Pay-TV. Report of the Committee on Extension of Service to Northern and Remote Communities. Ottawa: Canadian Government Publishing House, 1980.

CRTC Documents

CRTC letter of deficiency, July 17, 1998.

CRTC, "Additional National Television Networks-A Report to the Government of Canada Pursuant to Order in Council P.S. 1997-592", 1998.

Decision CRTC 81-25 (Cancom) Decision CRTC 81-252

Decision CRTC 91-826

Decision CRTC 99-42 Distribution Order CRTC 1999-2

Public Hearing CRTC 1998-6 Transcript of Proceedings, November 13-14, 1998.

Public Notice 1997-48 Call for Comments concerning Order in Council 1997-592

Public Notice CRTC 1985-274

Public Notice CRTC 1989-53 « Review of Northern Native Broadcasting: Call for Comments »

Public Notice CRTC 1990-12 « Review of Native Broadcasting-A Proposed Policy »

Public Notice CRTC 1990-89 Native Broadcasting Policy Public Notice CRTC 1992-13

Public Notice CRTC 1993-77

Public Notice CRTC 1998-8

Public Notice CRTC 1999-70 Order respecting the distribution of the Aboriginal Peoples Television Network.

TVNC, "License Application for Aboriginal Peoples Television Network," submitted June 5, 1998.

Books

Alia, Valerie. Un/covering the North: News, Media and Aboriginal people. Vancouver: UBC Press, 1999.

Francis, Daniel. The Imaginary Indian: The Image of the Indian in Canadian Culture. Vancouver: Arsenal Pulp Press, 1992.

Nordicity Group Ltd., Cancom Discussion Paper regarding proposed funding for the development of a First Nations channel, Sept. 3, 1996.

Roth, Lorna. Something New in the Air: First Peoples Television Broad- casting in Canada. Montreal: McGill-Queen's University Press, 2005.

Rutherford, Paul. When Television was Young: Primetime Canada 1952-1967. Toronto: University of Toronto Press, 1990.

Valaskakis, Gail. Indian Country: Essays on Contemporary Native Culture. Waterloo: Wilfred Laurier University Press, 2005.

Other Sources

Aboriginal Peoples Television Network, "Towards a Truer Mirror," Submission to the House of Commons Committee on Canadian Heritage, 2001.

APTN Launch broadcast, Sept.1, 1999.

APTN management committee meeting minutes, June-August, 1999. APTN staff meeting minutes, June-August, 1999.

APTN, "Original People Original Television", promotional brochure 1999.

APTN, "The Roles and Responsibilities of the APTN Board of Directors," June 19, 1999.
APTN, Program Guide, September 1999.

Assembly of First Nations, Resolution #17/97 Nov. 4, 1997: Development of a national Aboriginal broadcasting network.

Coopers & Lybrand, Advertising Study Aboriginal Peoples Television Network, June 5, 1998.

Coopers & Lybrand, Consumer Interest in the Aboriginal Peoples Television Network. June 5, 1998.

Coopers & Lybrand, Focus Group Research Consumer Interest in Aboriginal Peoples Television Network, June 5, 1998.

CueTwo Communications, Winnipeg Site Location operational consider- ations (and status reports, 1999.

David, Jennifer. Communications Report to APTN Board of Directors, Aug. 28, 1999.

Gordon, Larry "Managing Expectations" APTN Media strategy document, Sept. 8, 1998.

Inuit Broadcasting Corporation, Ten Years of Inuktitut Television 1982-1992.

Letters of support for TVNC from AFN, ITK, NAFC, MNC. January to April 1998.

Morrell, Gail. Memo re: Getting the Schedule to Air, July 27, 1999.

Morrell, Gail. Programming Report to APTN Board of Directors, July 30, 1999.

Rudden, Terry, Report on Staffing and Human Resources to the APTN Board of Directors, July 27, 1999.

Television Northern Canada, Update submitted to the National Aboriginal Communications Society, June 1989.

TVNC "Replies to interventions submitted with respect to an application by TVNC for a national aboriginal television network Application # 199804068.

TVNC Advisory Committee meeting minutes, 1998-1999 TVNC Board of Director meeting minutes, 1988-1999 TVNC brochure, "The Dawn of a new Era", 1992.

TVNC Chairperson's Report, 1994-1998. TVNC Executive meeting minutes, 1990-1999 TVNC Launch broadcast, Jan. 21, 1992.

TVNC Scheduling Committee reports and meeting minutes, 1990-1998.

TVNC, "TVNC elects new executive for 1997-98," press release, June 10, 1997.

TVNC, Application To Obtain A Licence To Carry On A Programming Undertaking: Television Network, June 5, 1998.

TVNC, Letter requesting letter of support for APTN. Sept. 23, 1998.

TVNC, Letter to CRTC regarding Public Notice CRTC 1997-48, June 4, 1997.

TVNC, North Link: TVNC's newsletter, June 1998

TVNC, second stage submission letter to CRTC regarding Public Notice CRTC 1997-48, Sept. 26, 1997.

Various letters of support, conditional support and intervention in response to Notice of Public Hearing CRTC 1998-6.

Notes

[1] Lorna Roth, Something New in the Air, (Montreal: McGill-Queen's University Press, 2005) 57.

[2] Daniel Francis, The Imaginary Indian: The Image of the Indian in Canadian Culture, Vancouver: Arsenal Pulp Press, Vancouver, 1992): 221.

[3] Paul Rutherford, When television was young: Primetime Canada 1952-1967 (Toronto: University of Toronto Press, 1990) 49.

[4] Lorna Roth 78.

[5] Arctic Institute of North America, Man in the North Project report: MIN Conference on Community Development. 1972: 22..

[6] Terry Kerr, Communications Project Management for Socio-Economic Development: A description of two Canadian projects by the Department of Communications, Ottawa, Canada, 1973) 4.

[7] Réal Therrien, The 1980s: A Decade of Diversity-Broadcasting, Satellites and Pay-TV (Ottawa: Canadian Government Publishing House, 1980) 12-15.

[8] Lougheed and Associates, Report on the Native Communications Program and the Northern Native Broadcast Access Program,(Department of Canadian Heritage, 1986) section 2-14..

[9] Elaine Bomberry, Association for Native Development in the Performing and Visual Arts. Royal Commission on Aboriginal Peoples report(Toronto, Ontario, 2 June 1993) Vol 3, Ch. 6, 3.2.

[10] Gerald Caplan and Florian Sauvageau. Task Force on Broadcasting Policy, 1986.

[11] Presentation to the CRTC on Cable Tiering and Universal Pay TV, by Inuit Broadcasting Corporation, 1982.

[12] Caplan 25.

[13] Austin Curley and Associates, Evaluation Report of the Northern Native Broadcast Access Program, (Secretary of State, 1993): H-1, H-2, H-12

[14] "TVNC to launch," Ottawa Citizen, Oct. 30, 1991.

[15] Decision CRTC 99-42: 4.

[16] bid: 8.

[17] Twelve years later, nothing has changed: the official membership of the network is still comprised of the original seven northern communications societies.

[18] Ten years later, in the course of conducting interviews for this book, I asked Gil Cardinal what happened. He was first confused, then horrified: in the decade since the launch, he had never watched a tape of the broadcast, and had no idea that was what viewers had seen.

Photo credit: Canadian Institute of Planners

ABOUT THE AUTHOR

I was born and raised in Chapleau, a small community in north eastern Ontario and I'm a member of Chapleau Cree First Nation. My family, like many people in northern Ontario, love to go hunting and fishing. But not me. I did spend a lot of time in my canoe and on our beautiful lakes when I was growing up but I was also drawn to Chapleau's tiny library. I loved reading fiction, history and dreaming about the wider world. My first taste of that world came when I was selected as an exchange student, and traveled to Australia. I returned to the big city lights of Ottawa, where I did a Bachelor's Degree in Journalism at Carleton University. A course on Aboriginal literature first sparked my interest in First Nation politics, writing and history; and when I graduated, I jumped at the chance to work for a new northern broadcaster called Television Northern Canada. Heard of them? If not – have I got a book for you! TVNC at the time was a group of northern, mostly Aboriginal and Inuit broadcasters that distributed community-based programming across the North. I was hired just as the movement to establish a national network was catching fire, and was privileged to work with the TVNC staff, board and member organizations through the crazy, energizing, historic period chronicled in Original People, Original Television, leading to the establishment of the Aboriginal Peoples Television Network in 1999. When APTN launched, I was the network's first Director of Communications, based in Ottawa. When the network moved its headquarters to Winnipeg, I decided to stay in Ottawa and establish my own Aboriginal communications consulting company, Debwe Communications, providing public and media relations, writing, video production, research, publishing and creating communications strategies. In 2008 I joined a group of friends and associates to create a new First Nation management consulting company, Stonecircle Consulting, where I'm currently Vice President and Manager. Writing has always been an important part of both my life and my work. I've written several non-fiction books; I've also contributed to several magazines and journals, and am currently a regular columnist for a new magazine in Ottawa called Capital Woman. I live in Ottawa with my husband and two children.

Jennifer David